WOMAN OF TODAY

WOMAN OF TODAY

Sue MacGregor

headline

First published in 2002
by HEADLINE BOOK PUBLISHING

10 9 8 7 6 5 4 3 2 1

Cataloguing in Publication Data is available
from the British Library

ISBN 0 7472 4989 X

Typeset by Palimpsest Book Production Limited,
Polmont, Stirlingshire

Printed and bound in Great Britain by
Mackays of Chatham PLC, Chatham, Kent

HEADLINE BOOK PUBLISHING
A division of Hodder Headline
338 Euston Road
London NW1 3BH

www.headline.co.uk
www.hodderheadline.com

For Emily, Susanna and Isabel

CONTENTS

Foreword

Not long ago a journalist from a glossy magazine, rather to my surprise, asked me some questions for an article she was writing on 'powerful women'. She wanted to know about my career path, how I'd managed to stay the course, and my thoughts on working with men. I acknowledged that the *Today* programme was an important contributor to the national political debate, and that therefore interviews on it could be considered influential, but I said I certainly didn't consider myself powerful. I must have convinced her. In the end the journalist used only one tiny quote from our conversation – in which I appeared to attribute any success I'd had to not having had children.

That same day I found myself standing next to a man at a publication party in a book shop in Covent Garden. We swopped names, and he asked me about myself. I told him I worked on Radio Four's *Today* programme. 'Oh,' he said 'splendid programme. I listen to it every morning. Have done for years.' I must have looked pleased. 'Now tell me,' he said, 'what do *you* do on *Today?*'

This book attempts to answer that question, and also give an account of how I got there.

Over the years I have kept no detailed diaries, but working on the book has meant an enjoyable trawl through my own collection of letters, press cuttings, photographs and tapes. There is a greater emphasis here on my professional than my private life, though I have tried to indicate important moments in that too. One or two names have been changed. I have used 'Peking' for the Chinese capital in chapter six, as that is what we called it before it became Beijing. A large number of friends and colleagues, past and present, have been generous with their time in helping me recall events. Among them Jenny Abramsky, Tony Bilbow, Dr Ian Campbell, John Cary, Sandra Chalmers, Roger Cook, Gertrude and Wilfred Cooper, Dr Chalmers Davidson, Pamela Diamond, Frances Donnelly, Andrew Duncan, Anna Ford, Liz Forgan, Doreen Forsyth, Tess Gill, Nick Guthrie, Francis Halewood, Phil Harding, Sandra Harris, David Hatch, Julian Holland, Gillian Hush, Nizaam Hussein, Anne Karpf, Rod Liddle, Tim Luckhurst, Gerard Mansell, Liz Mardall, Iain Milne of the Royal College of Physicians of Edinburgh, Roger Mosey, Nigel Murphy, Eleanor Ransome, Mary Redcliffe, Garry Richardson, Clare Selerie, Julia Somerville, Pat Taylor, Nick Utechin, Stanley Uys, Arnott Wilson, archivist of Edinburgh University and Nancy Wise. I am grateful to Najwa Hendrickse at the South African National Library in Cape Town for her help; to the BBC's Sound and Written Archives, especially Christine Marsh and Fiona Brazil, and to Chris Mobbs of the National Sound Archive at the British Library. I also acknowledge with thanks Helen Boaden's permission to use the BBC's archive facilities, and Imke de Gier's additional research. I found Paul Donovan's book *All Our Todays* very useful, as has been Sally Thompson's as yet unpublished history of *Woman's Hour*. Gilliam Bromley kept an immaculate professional eye on the text, and my editor at Headline Heather Holden-Brown and my agent Felicity Bryan have been unfailingly encouraging. Without them this book would not have happened.

CHAPTER ONE

Today

So let us begin at the beginning – of a *Today* day, that is. What follows is a fairly accurate, if entirely subjective, account of a morning's work on a relatively normal news day. It takes no account of the events of 11 September 2001 and their aftermath. As I write we are still, as I make clear in my last chapter, trying to come to terms with that terrible and tragic day.

0250: The alarm goes off. I keep two next to my bed, just in case one fails, and they're battery-powered. One morning John Humphrys had to be woken by his taxi driver throwing stones against his bedroom window; his clock was electric, the power had gone off in the night, and he'd switched off the phone. As I am one of nature's slow starters, I do not wish to be catapulted into the pre-dawn ritual by strange knockings. I stagger over to the coffee machine, which starts to gurgle itself, and me, into life. Strong black coffee will begin the process of ungluing my brain. I have a quick shower listening to the three o'clock news. My clothes I have laid out the night before; I am incapable of making a thoughtful sartorial choice at this hour. Thirty minutes later I leave, clutching my bag and a banana.

0325: The BBC car has a new driver, so instead of reading the papers on the back seat (they come with the car) I have to direct him most of the way to White City. Usually it's Colin, who is inhumanly cheerful at such a dreadful hour, and absolutely reliable. He used to be in the antiques business, he once told me. London's roads are hardly less busy in the middle of the night than in daytime.

0340: I persuade security guards to let me in; since the Real IRA car bomb there are more of them on duty, though never the same two days running. I lug the papers up to the office, which I enter with a magnetic fob, collect the post from my pigeon-hole and greet a weary night team, who try to look pleased to see me despite having been on duty since eight o'clock the night before. Didn't someone say that between three and four in the morning is when people die? I examine the programme's running order to see who's doing what. John, who's not yet in, is my on-air partner and I see he has the main political story of the morning after eight o'clock. I start writing the script on the computer just to get a bit ahead of myself as I have to record a discussion in twenty minutes' time with Charles Powell and the Chinese dissident Harry Wu, both of whom are in the United States. After a couple of false starts because of poor lines it turns out rather well, though Lord Powell evidently wasn't expecting to be challenged by Mr Wu on China's human rights record, which Mr Wu has good reason to know is abysmal; he was imprisoned for nineteen years in a *laogai* – a labour camp. Charles Powell is of the opinion that China's gaining the 2008 Olympics will be beneficial to human rights, as the country will have to allow in more foreign journalists.

0410: Back to writing the script – John and I will each have a dozen or so 'live' interviews in the course of the programme – while at the same time consulting the papers, which Jim always impressively seems to have read by the time he comes in. I have a quick look at the office gossip on 'Ed Notes' in the computer system. Someone has lost a pen and found it again. Someone else is running what looks like a car boot sale. A former cabinet minister is furious at having been stood down the day before, and there's a warning about being extra polite with him next time. The minute Humphrys arrives he starts ferreting in the office fridge with loud exclamations of disgust. He throws out the smelly milk and demands to know where the skimmed is for his cereal. Perhaps *The World At One* have pinched it. The office fridge is a disgusting sight indeed: our regular experts on nasty diseases would have a field day. John, squirrel-like, keeps little bags of muesli in a small drawer near his computer, and slices a banana into the breakfast bowl. He also keeps bits of cold toast in his pigeon-hole – strange. I eat my banana later, and some cereal during the break just after ten past six. There's time for a quick gossip with John before we both settle down to our writing. He has definitely mellowed since the birth of young Owen, who's now over a year old. He talks proudly of Owen not just walking, but running. Like father, like son. Mostly the briefings are helpful, but some are a bit ropey and have been overtaken by events during the night: we have our usual moan. Kind overnight producers wrest more useful stuff from the system. Brian Redhead, I remember, used to shout: 'Which illiterate wrote this?' – to which, unsurprisingly, there came no reply. Poor researchers: working for hours on projects which we deal with so cruelly.

0500: There's been more trouble in Belfast. The running order is changed so that we can carry accounts of the violence soon after 0630. It's hard not to feel that we've done all this so many times before. How *do* the politicians find the energy – and the optimism – to think a solution can be reached? *Are* there any new questions to be asked?

0530: Someone does a hot drinks round – elsewhere in the building surprisingly decent coffee can be found. A short straw is drawn for the producer who has to ring those whom the overnight editor has decided must be dropped from the programme, for reasons of time or topicality. Not nice for interviewees who've been awake all night practising their answers, I think. The script is nearly finished now, or at least it ought to be. Some of what we do is unscripted and spontaneous, but we write little introductions to everything, to give listeners – and technical staff – just enough information ahead of the interview. The trick is not to sound as if you're reading the script on air. Short sentences work best. It's always tempting to write too much.

0555: Quick march into the studio clutching papers, script, water supply. I greet the newsreader and turn off the overhead TV monitors – too distracting. The top headlines and 'menu' are rushed in with one minute to go. There's just time to do a quick rewrite of one phrase.

0600: Moment of calm – deep breath – off we go. After all the intensity of the preparation, the moment of going on air feels curiously relaxing, and the anticipation of the three hours ahead more enjoyable.

0610: Nigel Cassidy bursts in with his business slot guests: he'll pop back at regular intervals during the programme. Once the business news is 'on' we can sneak out for a break. I attack a bowl of cornflakes and go back to my desk computer to check the latest wires on Northern Ireland – and China, in case there have been developments – while still keeping an ear on the business news. This is our longest break in three hours.

0624: Garry Richardson is here with his sports news. He grins. He's still mustard keen after twenty years. We first met covering Charles and Di's wedding, walking the route for the next day's commentary. When we go on the road and do part of the programme in front of an audience, he's a terrific warm-up man. His Frank Bruno story always goes down a storm.

0630: We hit the half-hour pretty much on the dot, after a dreadful

Radio Four trail for something miles ahead on the network – at the weekend. Faces pulled all round.

0631: Suddenly I remember the Web Cam surveying us from the studio ceiling. When it was first installed I was highly suspicious: where's the precious mystery and imagination in radio, I wanted to know, if people listening to us can also *see* us? Now we've got used to it we pay it no attention. I wonder if it, and therefore millions out there, can clearly observe live on the internet our grimaces and wild hand signals to the production team. John is a neat partner in the studio, keeping his papers tidy. Jim, who also chews the rim of his Styrofoam coffee cup into a little brown-stained frill, spreads his all over the place, and under the pile he sometimes loses the weather.

0632: Quick change of running order – the line to one of our correspondents in the north of England has gone down. We start with Belfast instead. We take it in turns to do a smooth canter through the top morning stories – plus a bit of 'Yesterday in Parliament'.

0700: Only a nine-minute break here for the news bulletin. I go back to my PC in the main office to check the wires once again – and rewrite a cue, as the prerecorded discussion on Chinese human rights has had to be cut slightly. Sometimes quite intensive rewriting has to be done against the clock. This is when you can feel a real tightness in the chest. I put aside any thoughts of heart attacks: I've been at this for long enough not to panic. Rod Liddle, the editor, is now in, on what's called the 'interfering' shift. He's been listening at home and in the car, and now he's listening on the spot. He'll have gone to bed the night before fairly sure of what the programme will be like next morning, but often the overnight editor will have made changes because of what the papers are saying: added items or dropped them, or simply decided to change tack over a political story. Rod often strongly suggests following up something the night team hasn't thought of, especially if it's in the tabloids. This means presenters can get told about a live interview only thirty seconds before they actually do it. Well, I tell myself, that's what we're paid for.

0708: I'm back in the studio a bit early – just as well, as the bulletin finishes fifteen seconds light. We launch into the first story of the middle hour – domestic politics, which this time I do. It's all bouncing along quite nicely now. Most of the contributors so far, bar the business guests, have been 'down the line': on the phone or from a remote studio. The technical glitches have been minimal – but it's still a pity: naturally we all prefer it if people come in and talk to us face to face. This isn't always possible, even with London interviewees, especially now that we're out at White City, a long way from Broadcasting House; contributors are wary of getting stuck in the traffic on the way back. But I think it makes a difference to quite a lot of interviews if you can engage with someone directly.

0725: Garry is back with a second tranche of sport. I have just finished an interview about an escaped iguana which jumps at women and could grow big enough to eat a baby. Garry gets the giggles, which continue, only slightly modified, throughout his slot. It's not as bad as the day Charlotte Green ended the news bulletin with a story about a Vietnamese colonel called Tuat. That day Jim – the worst studio 'corpser' – had to follow Charlotte with a tale about a trapped sperm whale. We all cracked up. It's a bit like giggling in prayers at school: a release of tension.

0745: 'Thought for the Day', almost always impressively topical. It's Angela Tilby, down the line from Cambridge, with judicious comments on our multicultural, multiracial society after a new bout of racial tension in a northern town. Rabbi Lionel Blue is a favourite 'Thought' man, with us and with the listeners. He loves his food.

He once brought me in a packet mixture for making matzo balls, which is still in my kitchen cupboard.

0753: This is quite often a political slot. Some cabinet ministers are adept at 'talking up to the weather': fending off questions to ensure their last answer goes right up to the forecast at 0757. Jim once quite openly accused Alan Milburn of doing this, and was backed by listeners who reacted crossly about Milburn in emails to the programme. Today it's Ken Clarke, who plays it straight.

0800: In the break for the news Rod and John commune on the form of attack to be used in the 0810 interview with a government minister. The *World At One* team is now largely in place. We walk past them into the studio which will be theirs in two hours' time. Nobody much looks up.

0815: I chair a discussion on the 'Men Are From Mars, Women Are From Venus' theory as it applies to Westminster politicians. The former Tory minister Angela Browning subscribes to it and can now say so openly. Coincidentally, I have just read a story in the *Guardian* about most women being 'too nice', and wanting too much to be liked, to get to the top. I mean to ask John whether he thinks this applies to me, but the moment has passed.

0830: We're running late, and Garry with sport is beginning to look a bit agitated.

0840: The home stretch, and I wonder if it shows in our voices. Preparing this book, I have been listening to the *Today* voices going back over more than fifteen years. Jim's has barely changed in the seven years he's been with us, although I can tell if he's tired. You can with all of us. I don't think I sound terribly different from the way I did when I first started doing *Today*, but listening to older tapes from South Africa – going back to the sixties – I've been appalled by my careful vowels. When John first joined the programme – I'd forgotten this – he used to pronounce words like 'laughter' with a long *a*, in the best Received Pronunciation style. Now, with a shorter *a*, he sounds a bit more Welsh.

0900: Phew! Another one under our belts, and nobody crashed the pips. We troop into Rod Liddle's office for a ten-minute post-mortem. Rod is sharp as a pin despite his lethargic pose. He has an eclectic mix of posters on his (glass) office walls: a Taliban calendar proudly showing the destruction of the giant Buddhas, a pouting picture of Angelina Jolie, and a graphic photograph of a bleeding thumb cut from a medical magazine. We discuss what worked and what didn't, and what went wrong technically. Dozens of emails from listeners have come in since we went on the air at six o'clock. One of them complains about my 'arrogance and bad manners', sitting at a 'command console, barking orders' to interviewees. 'An absolute disgrace to the BBC . . .'

0920: Time to go. The day team is already in place thinking of tomorrow, and I slope off to the gym. If it's been a hectic programme with lots of last-minute things to do, I feel physically tired even if everything's gone well, and I need to unwind. By lunchtime my body clock will be nudging me to say the day is over. After all these years it's still a bit confused.

CHAPTER TWO

Yesterday

SM: Hella Pick, you came to Britain just before the war began, as a child, as a refugee, aged ten and quite on your own. Can you remember what you made of us when you got here then?

HP: The one distinct memory I have is being put on to a train in Vienna to come to England and arriving at Victoria Station and being taken into some large waiting room and waiting to be picked up by the family who had volunteered to take care of me and my first words, my only words in English, which were to say 'goodbye'.

Interview with *Guardian* journalist Hella Pick, broadcast on
Conversation Piece, 29 November 1993

I was a war baby, born at the end of August in 1941 in Oxford, and with a very large head. My poor mother had a difficult time. My condition – hydrocephalus, or water on the brain – made my birth painful for her and must have made my appearance rather odd. At one point a doctor, peering down at me doubtfully, told her that I had perhaps three days to live. But the medical staff at the Radcliffe Infirmary did a good job at draining away the excess fluid, and for all that initial pessimism my large head diminished and I was pronounced viable – which was just as well, as my mother was to spend a great deal of uninterrupted time with me for the next few years.

My father Jim was a serving soldier at the time of my birth – as a neurologist, he was a captain in the Royal Army Medical Corps

– and soon after my arrival was sent off to India and Burma, which meant that he was not to see my mother or me again until after the end of the war. I have a copy of one of his letters to her, dated 3 August 1942, from the Number 2 Mobile Neurosurgical Unit, British General Hospital, Poona, India. It is carefully typed and stamped as passed by the military censor. 'My darling Biddy, Yesterday I got two post cards – one from Susan [as I was less than a year old at the time I must have had some help] and the one about tax and pay written to Pa's dictation – I must say I don't understand it but then I don't suppose he understood it either.' Understanding tax and money was never my father's strongest point.

My parents were both entirely Scottish; indeed, my mother, Margaret – who was always called Biddy because a nurse when she was a baby had called her a 'dear little Chick-a-Biddy' – was a MacGregor before they met, although they were not related. She was orphaned early. Her father died of tuberculosis at the age of thirty-eight when she was only a few months old. The Reverend John Charles MacGregor, a Presbyterian minister, possessed, according to his obituary in the *Inverness Courier* of 23 December 1913, 'an exceptionally winning and loveable personality'. He was from Gairloch in Wester Ross, and from a very poor family. Until he was ten he spoke only Gaelic; from the age of twelve he earned money to help pay for his education by working in the fields and doing other forms of manual labour. Fortunately he was bright, and won scholarships to school and a bursary to Aberdeen University. There he completed a divinity course. I have a faded photograph of him in his dog collar, young and clean-shaven, squinting at the camera with a faint smile.

My mother was the last of his five children. She was born in the manse in the village of Fordyce, which is between Banff and Buckie on the Banffshire coast. By the time she was three TB had also claimed her mother and her eldest sister Anne; the remaining four children were farmed out to different 'guardians' who brought them up strictly and without much love. One of my mother's earliest memories was of kneeling against a sofa with her elder brother Iain for daily prayers in a large drawing-room. They amused themselves and infuriated the grown-ups by squeezing the dogs until they growled loudly; despite her pedigree, serious religious devotion never caught on with my mother. Iain, whom my mother adored, eventually died in the war serving in the RAF in the far east. He is buried in the Commonwealth Cemetery on the Indonesian island of Ambon. Of the three remaining MacGregor children – Biddy, Sheila and Mona – it was only my mother who as an adult found it easy to show any real affection towards others.

My father's background was much more secure. He was born in 1911 into an expatriate Scottish community in Malaya: it gave him, he said, a lifelong preference for living in a warm climate. His father, Tom MacGregor, was the manager of a tin mine and later went on to work for the colonial government. This meant a generous house in Kuala Lumpur with plenty of servants, including an 'ayah' (nursemaid) each for him and his elder sister Betty. There are sepia photographs of him aged six, wearing a miniature solar topee and standing with one foot on a stuffed alligator. There was a cook who made ice-cream for special occasions, but when he was dismissed by my grandmother Eliza for incompetence he took a terrible revenge: on the day he left, he put salt in the ice-cream which had been specially prepared for my father's fifth birthday party. Having eagerly anticipated this treat for weeks, none of the children could eat it. Years later, this was one of my favourite bedtime stories. Such domestic crises apart, Jim's early childhood was a contented one. His father was a kind man and indulged him, though his mother, who had once trained as a Presbyterian missionary, was a rather stern woman who favoured Betty. These MacGregors lived a highly sociable life; my grandmother claimed later that she knew almost all the original characters in Somerset Maugham's colonial short stories, including the woman who shot her lover in 'The Letter'.

My father ended up having part of his education in Australia. During the First World War it was virtually impossible for colonial civil servants to get permission for a passage home, and when peace was eventually declared the ship's cabins were so fully booked that the family ended up instead in Melbourne, and Jim at Scotch College, a Presbyterian academy. The headmaster was an Aberdonian who recommended he should go on to Aberdeen Grammar School 'back home'; so he was despatched there, and his parents went back to Malaya.

In Scotland my father had an extended family to look after him. He spent his holidays with cousins who lived on a lowlands farm called Garbity. There were long walks and summer picnics; he enjoyed himself. In his late teens he was an attractive young man: slim and athletic, with wavy brown hair, he was a popular companion, and clever. Accepted by Edinburgh University to study medicine, here he found a talent for boxing and represented the university as a flyweight.

Not long after beginning his course he was introduced to my mother at a students' dance: 'You two MacGregors must meet each other!' somebody cried. She was on a catering course at Atholl Crescent in Edinburgh and planned to work in the hotel world; she was small and pretty, with dark brown hair and large blue eyes. The attraction was instant, and they fell in love. Marriage, however, was to prove more difficult than they had anticipated. My father's mother, who had by now returned to Britain, disapproved strongly of her son joining a family with such a strong history of TB, and she would not hear of a permanent relationship. She was also suspicious of his leftish political leanings: my father had briefly joined the Communist Party to show solidarity with the anti-fascist forces during the Spanish Civil War. Jim and Biddy decided to ignore the disapproval and marry once he had graduated. But he had his doubts about becoming a doctor, and in 1933 left the university at his own request. He was a talented watercolour artist, and thought he might instead take up painting full-time.

After a period of some months travelling around Scotland with my mother, she put her foot down and told him he must complete his degree. As the conventional university route was no longer open to him, he returned to his medical studies, through what was called the Triple Qualification course, run by the Edinburgh and Glasgow Royal Medical Colleges. He graduated in 1937 and married my mother the same year.

The year before he had taken part in a student prank which almost ended his medical studies altogether. He and a number of other students – several dozen of them, according to the account in the *Scotsman* the following day, 30 April 1936 – decided to 'kidnap' the actress Renée Houston, who was then heading the bill at the Empire Theatre, and hold her to 'ransom' to raise money for their annual charities' week. The idea was to remove her from her dressing room and drive her away from the theatre between the matinée and the evening show, returning her unharmed on payment of £25 from the theatre management, which would go straight to charity. But the stunt went badly wrong. The stage doorkeeper was tied up, and Miss Houston – 'scantily clad' according to the press – was bundled into a car. The driver lost his nerve and was hit on the head before he was persuaded to drive on. Miss Houston was fairly quickly allowed to return to the theatre, but there had been a scuffle and she complained that she had been roughly handled and had cut her lip; she was unable to appear in the day's second performance. Her husband threatened to charge the students with assault, though in the end the charges were not pressed.

Neither of my parents ever told me how close my father came to failing to complete his medical degree; it was something I discovered only after his death. There was always a secretive side to him. 'Your father doesn't always tell the whole truth,' my mother would say mysteriously. Indeed, the couple kept the fact of their marriage concealed for two years – not just from Jim's parents, but from almost everyone. They were in any case apart for quite long periods at the beginning of their married life – my father completing his term as a junior doctor in Scotland, my mother working in a hotel in London.

When war came in the autumn of 1939, Jim was working at the Head Injury Unit at the newly converted St Hugh's College in Oxford. This specialist unit, which had been opened earlier the same year, was the brainchild of Oxford's first Nuffield Professor of Surgery, Hugh (later Sir Hugh) Cairns, a brilliant neurologist whom my father admired enormously. Hugh Cairns had experience of treating head injuries from the First World War, and as early as 1935, when another international conflict looked likely, he began to plan the new specialist unit from his neurology department at the Radcliffe Infirmary. It was eventually to become an offshoot of the celebrated National Hospital for Nervous Diseases in Queen Square in London, where my father was to work after the war.

By the time war broke out my parents had made their marriage public and my grandmother's approval was finally gained. She had by then doubtless been charmed by my mother, who was taken to meet her on many occasions in the new family home, a mock Tudor house in Beaconsfield where Jim's sister Betty, her husband, my Uncle John, and their daughter Jane had moved in to live with 'Granny' on their return from Malaya. This was fortunate, for in the spring of 1941 my mother discovered she was pregnant; and when, soon after I was born, my father, who had joined the RAMC in 1940, departed for the far east as part of a mobile neurosurgical unit, my mother and I had no permanent home. So we stayed with my grandparents in Beaconsfield for some of the time; we also lodged with friends in Oxford, and for a year or two with Aunt Mona and her husband Malcolm in Elgin in Morayshire. For my mother, this must have been almost a return to her childhood, for Elgin is not many miles west of the old manse in Fordyce where she had been born. It is an attractive small town of grey stone houses above the River Lossie, and is proud of the ruined remains of its magnificent thirteenth-century cathedral –

once one of the finest in Scotland. Around it is rich farming country.

Uncle Malcolm, a large man with gently droopy eyes and a big grin, worked as a manager in Johnson's woollen mill in Elgin. It was his proud boast that he had not been south of Edinburgh since 1938. He was fond of children, though he and Mona had none of their own. I was rather a 'forward' child according to Aunt Mona, and not averse to giving advice. Once when I was in bed with a bad cough the doctor came to visit and conscientiously tapped away at my back with his stethoscope to test my lung function. 'If you're looking for my chest, it's here,' I announced, helpfully indicating the correct spot. I was sent to nursery school in Elgin, where I quickly acquired a Scots accent and an ability to say 'Wait a wee minutee' and 'Decht yer moo' – wipe your mouth – convincingly enough. In the eyes of Aunt Mona, who was more comfortable with the boxer dogs she owned and doted on than with children, I was continuously over-indulged. My mother dressed me as meticulously as she could with her ration coupons, and always made sure my auburn curls were shown to their best advantage. Aunt Mona, on the other hand, believed in plenty of spankings for bad behaviour. One of them was administered to me, much to my mortification, in Elgin's main street after she had saved me from certain death under a bus. Her dogs led a cosseted life; and after each one died it was buried at the bottom of the garden, wrapped in a length of cashmere from Johnson's mill. Now it was my mother's turn to be appalled: she could have made much better use of the cashmere herself. Malcolm in his spare time spent many hours drilling with the Home Guard, and when, at the war's end, the Home Guard marched triumphantly down Elgin's main street, he swept me up on to his shoulders so that I too could join the procession for the final march past.

Many years later I had the opportunity to discuss a very different wartime childhood experience with the *Guardian* journalist Hella Pick, whom I interviewed for *Conversation Piece*:

Interview with Hella Pick, broadcast 29.11.93

SM: Hella Pick, you came to Britain just before the war began, as a child, as a refugee, aged ten and quite on your own. Can you remember what you made of us when you got here then?

HP: Not very much, I have little memory of my early childhood and that includes being in Vienna and, again, the first few months in England. The one distinct memory I have is being put on to a train in Vienna to come to England and arriving at Victoria Station and being taken into some large waiting room and waiting to be picked up by the family who had volunteered to take care of me and my first words, my only words in English, which were to say 'goodbye'.

SM: But when you first came here it was without your mother, she followed later.

HP: She came a few months later in 1939. You had to do domestic service if you came as an adult woman refugee to Britain at that time and she had gone to cook for a family who had a house in the Lake District and they asked me to come along as well. So we spent a blissful month in the Lake District near Ambleside in a lovely house and this family they had three children and of course we all played and swam together and did all the things that little children do. And then when war broke out I stayed up there, I was put into a school there, and my mother went to work for another family because these people went back to London.

SM: She had to be a cook, which was quite a change in lifestyle for her?

HP: It was, but I think at that time people did whatever they could do. She'd been through a very difficult time in Vienna because she'd lost everything, virtually all her possessions, a lot of her friends, her mother – my grandmother – was left behind and she knew by then that she was in a concentration camp where she died. So in a way she felt fortunate that she had managed to come to Britain where she had a degree of security, that I was there, I had been put into a very good private school which gave me a free place in Ambleside in the Lake District. And I had a relatively untroubled childhood even though at that time we were both still labelled as 'enemy aliens'.

SM: Did you adapt quite quickly to the English way of doing things?

HP: Well, I think I adapted but it was in retrospect not a very easy period, partly because the family for whom my mother was working took domestic service still quite seriously. We were living in a large and beautiful house but I had to use the back entrance to the house! I could only go and swim in the lake (because the house was on the lake) when they were out because they didn't want to see me walk across the lawn.

SM: Was this because you were in effect the child of a servant?

HP: Exactly, and it meant that I was very embarrassed to invite some of my schoolfriends home because I didn't want to show this curious aspect of my life. So that left its mark.

But there were other compensations. I made a lot of friends. I was very impressionable then. Amongst my very close friends to whom I clung was a family who were very active members of Moral Rearmament. I was terribly impressed by the way they handled their lives.

SM: That Moral Rearmament was very much a Christian movement. Did people try and persuade you to leave your Jewishness behind at all?

HP: Well, I was really never very Jewish. My mother was very much an agnostic. Her own marriage had broken up because she had married into an Orthodox family and had really not been able to cope with that at all. And if she'd had her way I really would have ignored every form of religion. As it happened at an impressionable age I started going to a church in Grasmere because the vicar there seemed an amazingly attractive person and I really loved going to church but it didn't really bite deep. In retrospect I bitterly regret that I've had so little upbringing in the Jewish faith and that I've really missed out on a whole culture about which I ought to know a great deal more. But it took me years before I could even admit that I was Jewish. It was only the first time I went to New York when I suddenly realized that there are an awful lot of Jews in the world and they all live quite openly! It was really an awakening . . . a coming out which I found very difficult.

My father returned home after VJ Day, and, like many war children, I was quite taken aback by his sudden reappearance. I could see that my mother's attention was now thoroughly divided, and I turned up regularly in the morning at their bedroom door asking the identity of the strange man in her bed. But my father was devoted to us both, and besides he was a wonderful teller of bedtime stories. Gradually I came to accept him.

By the time I was five we had moved to Wheatley, just outside

Oxford. Now a sprawling place, almost an outer suburb of the city, it was then a small village consisting largely of a church, a manor house, a short high street and some attractive cottages built of warm grey stone. Here my father, now a lieutenant-colonel in the RAMC (he was not finally demobbed until 1947), continued his neurological work as head of the medical wing of the specialist Head Injury Hospital, treating former members of the armed forces. One of his patients there was the writer Roald Dahl, who had been badly wounded after being shot down over the north African desert. They became friends, and later Roald, after his first trip to Hollywood, sent me a sketch of Mickey Mouse signed by Walt Disney himself. It was a friendship which was to be renewed after Roald married the Oscar-winning American actress Patricia Neal and settled in Great Missenden, in Buckinghamshire – by which time he was an immensely successful writer of short stories for adults and of children's books. In the late sixties my parents and I visited the Dahl family in Great Missenden. Roald, tall and courteous, introduced us to the children and showed us the gypsy caravan in the garden and the shed nearby where he did his writing. Patricia was by then making a remarkable recovery from a stroke, helped by a roster of neighbours who came in daily to talk to her and stimulate her. She even went on to make one or two more movies. Sadly, they eventually decided to live apart and Roald married again.

Our home in Wheatley was Pound Cottage, which my parents rented. On a corner close to the edge of the village, it was a tiny eighteenth-century stone house with steep steps to a basement, where I was forbidden to go. In the field opposite stood the conical stone marking the village 'pound' – long out of use – which gave the cottage its name. My mother once said that the couple of years we were there were the happiest of her life. At weekends we went on expeditions. My parents brought out their bicycles and all three of us, I in a basket at the back at first, and later on a small bicycle of my own, cycled round the Oxfordshire villages looking at interesting churches. My father was still a good amateur watercolourist. He encouraged me, once we had chosen the right spot, to sit at his side with a tiny easel and paint my own impressions, and occasionally when local people came to look over our shoulders I was delighted to get as big an audience as he did. On weekdays I went to school: Miss Hamersley's in Headington. Miss Hamersley, who was in her thirties and lived with her mother, was adored by all the children she taught in her tiny schoolroom. I was soon convinced that the words of the hymn she thumped out each morning on the piano were 'All Things Bright and Beautiful, All *Teachers* Great and Small'. I made friends with the Hassall family who lived in Wheatley manor house, and Tom and Mark Hassall and I collected snails, which we called Kucka Joeys. Tom was fond of pointing out the dramatic stain halfway up the walls on the village high street; he said it marked the depth of the water when the Thames had burst its banks the year before we had arrived and nearly drowned them all. After that I monitored each burst of rain with special interest.

Then life became more uncertain again. We returned to a peripatetic way of living, mostly because of my father's medical work, and partly because he was reluctant to put down roots in austere postwar England. Like his father Tom, he had a restless nature. This meant that I went to several schools, including Barham Lodge in Weybridge, Surrey, where I was sent as a boarder when only six. I was convinced my parents had abandoned me forever. I wrote dutiful letters home – 'Dear Mummy. This week I'm having a Brownie Uniform for Brownies. Is it only two moor [sic] weeks till half term?' – but I loathed every minute of it. The Brownies were to be my downfall. During a game called 'Submarines', which involved running a gauntlet of blindfolded cross-legged Brownie harbour guards to the safety of the open sea, I wet my knickers. I didn't confess to it immediately, but there was ample evidence of what had happened. Brown Owl was not amused. Her contemptuous public announcement – 'Susan MacGregor! If you can't own up there's no room for you here' – led to my banishment from the Brownie pack and more misery. After this I think my mother realized that boarding school was not a good idea, and removed me to a day school called High March in Beaconsfield, near the house which my parents now shared with my grandparents – so near, in fact, that I could sneak out and run back home on a regular basis. I usually arrived before lunchtime, weeping with fury at the unfairness of life and being sent to yet another strange school. I do remember that when I did stay I was enormously impressed with our English teacher, who read poetry aloud to us, including parts of Bunyan's *Pilgrim's Progress*, some of which we were expected to learn by heart. I liked the adventures of the Pilgrim; and I learned too a healthy respect for fine writing and the well-spoken word.

The house in Beaconsfield was our last home in England, and the best thing I remember about it was the woods at the end of the garden. When I was much smaller and came from Wheatley to visit my grandmother, they were a good place for my father to plan adventures. One of them involved secretly hanging the entire contents of a box of chocolates by tiny threads from the lowest branches of several trees. He then proclaimed that it was 'Chocolate Tuesday' and that I might discover some interesting things in the woods. I found all the suspended treasures, wrapped in silver paper – just as the fairies had left them. By the time I was seven I was allowed, after supper, to sit with my parents and listen to the BBC Home Service, though I was always firmly consigned to bed before the nine o'clock news. After a vivid radio dramatization of Conan Doyle's 'The Speckled Band', which involved gypsies and snakes entering houses through tiny holes and slithering down the curtains to do their worst, I lay awake in my room terrified, gazing anxiously up at the airbrick four feet above my bed.

I did not know it then, but a few hundred yards away, in Penn Road, lived a teller of tales for children so successful that she eventually made a fortune: Enid Blyton. I adored her books. After I and my parents had left Beaconsfield, my grandmother boldly knocked at her door and asked if she would sign one or two of her books for me. I still have them. Fifteen years later, in the mid-sixties, I tapped at Miss Blyton's door myself, and recorded one of the few interviews she ever gave.

The winter of 1947 was the toughest Britain suffered in the twentieth century and followed a summer in which wet weekends had succeeded each other relentlessly. The deep snow and generally miserable weather were too much for my father, who longed for the warm sun. He decided we would emigrate, and chose as our destination South Africa. During the war the troopship taking him east had spent four days in Cape Town, and it had seemed like paradise after the rigours of wartime Britain. Table Mountain made a spectacular backdrop to a city of great charm, and the local people were highly hospitable to visiting troops on their way through. In the years after the war, Cape Town seemed a good place to settle. The weather was good, the scenery was spectacular, at least one of the languages was familiar, and there would be plenty of opportunities for long walks in the mountains at weekends. Politically, the country had not yet been consigned to pariah status. The former prime minister General Smuts had been an important wartime ally of Britain's, and his successor after the general election of 1948, the leader of the National party Dr D. F. Malan, though hardly pro-British, had yet to put in place the worst of the apartheid laws. In my father's mind there was only one argument against going. My mother had suffered from increasing deafness since childhood, and it was possible that her hearing would continue to deteriorate, though she seemed to be recovering well from a complicated inner ear operation in London. But the standard of medical care in South Africa was high; perhaps with the help of hearing aids things would dramatically improve for her. My mother herself was much less keen to start a new life in the Cape, but she managed to extract a promise that if South Africa didn't suit them, my father would consider returning to Britain.

A medical colleague had confirmed that there were plenty of

jobs in South Africa for specialist doctors, that accommodation was reasonably cheap, that the climate was indeed pleasant, and that it would be a good place to bring up a child. So early in April 1949 we set sail for Cape Town on the *Edinburgh Castle*, one of the Union Castle mailships which sailed weekly between Southampton and the South African ports. With some basic furniture and books stashed away in the hold, and several tin trunks containing our clothes stuffed into two small cabins, our new life was about to begin. My own belongings included some books, a watercolour painting set and a pink-cheeked china doll called Mary. I had been very fond of a beautiful dark-skinned doll whom my mother named Josephine Baker, after the black American singer, but sadly she could not be found before we set out. Perhaps my mother thought her presence in Cape Town might be unwise.

The mailships timed their arrival in Table Bay for around six in the morning, so that energetic passengers could see the spectacular panorama as the boat steamed towards the Duncan Docks. My father made sure we got up early enough to be at the railings to watch. Table Mountain rose high above a sleepy city, flanked by Devil's Peak to the left and Lion's Head to the right, the two smaller peaks perfectly framing the famous flat-topped centrepiece. As we approached I looked eagerly for palm trees and black faces, neither of which I had seen before. The palm trees had to wait until we were well on our way to our new home, but there were dark faces everywhere on the dockside: Africans clothed in shabby overalls and shouting to each other as they waited for orders to unload. It seemed wonderfully exotic. The day was warm; but after eleven days of rolling about on the ocean, dry land felt strange.

A former medical colleague of my father had found us a temporary home in a cottage at Miller's Point, beyond the British naval base at Simonstown. It was a few hundred yards from the sea, and forty minutes by car from Cape Town. My father and I were thrilled by the prospect of starting a new life here; but my mother immediately noticed there were ants everywhere and the place needed a great deal of cleaning up. I began to explore. Our new home had three intriguing features. There was a front door which was divided into two, South African-style, so that the top half could be opened independently to let in the fresh air; the house was surrounded by a stone porch, a 'stoep', a simple version of the traditional Cape Dutch verandah, on which one could sit and watch the local traffic – a few cars and a regular number of hawkers' carts; and, best of all, there was a flat-roofed garage, in which my father parked his shiny black second-hand Oldsmobile. I soon got to know the children of our neighbours – English-speaking South Africans of the second or third generation – and we discovered that, while lying unobserved on this roof, we could spit accurately onto the street below.

We stayed at Miller's Point for only a few months. My father needed to be closer to town, where he had set up his own neurology practice, sharing consulting rooms with a Dr Kooy, whose parents had migrated from the Netherlands. It would be useful, too, for him to be only a few minutes' drive from the university with its excellent medical school. So we moved to the outskirts of Constantia, a suburb of Cape Town dominated by whitewashed houses and rolling green vineyards – one of the most desirable areas in which to live. The house we rented, The Summit, lived up to its name: it was perched on a hill and looked down on other people's vineyards. But as Christmas and the heat of midsummer approached, it proved an unwise choice. The garden was treeless and the house hot and airless; my mother, who had just discovered she was expecting another child, needed somewhere less exposed and cooler. To add to her unhappiness, her precious collection of Victorian Crown Derby china had just arrived from England. It had been sloppily wrapped by the packers and much of it had been broken on the voyage. I can still remember her tears as the shattered cups and saucers emerged from the battered wooden crate.

I rather enjoyed The Summit. I learned to swim in a neighbour's sumptuous pool. My earlier attempts had involved suspension in a canvas sling over the brown and muddy Thames near Oxford, where every time you put a foot down to reach the bottom it touched something sickeningly slimy. This cool blue pool was incomparably preferable, surrounded by lavish sprays of crimson bougainvillea and bursts of blue agapanthus. Swimming became one of my favourite sports, one of few I was any good at.

I was soon successfully installed at my new South African school, an Anglican girls' school called Herschel, named after the British astronomer William Herschel. I began to make new friends, some of whom lived close by. I suppose they must have thought me rather odd, with my English accent and pale, freckly skin, but in the early evenings after school and at weekends we went exploring together in and around the local vineyards. This was then considered quite safe; only one area was quite forbidden to us. There was a Muslim tomb in a little wooded grove, only a hundred yards from our house, that was occasionally visited by the local faithful – Cape Malays, as they were called – but we children were told not on any account to go near it. This made it all the more intriguing, and we made regular nervous little forays inside the small stone building. It evidently housed the body of someone very important, for we discovered a small raised dais on top of which was something oblong covered with layer upon layer of highly embroidered silk We lifted the layers very gently – somewhere underneath, a corpse would undoubtedly reveal itself. But we always lost our nerve before we reached the final veil, and each tomb expedition ended with shrieks and a thrilling run home to safety. Our parents did not discover our secret expeditions.

Constantia was also home to a substantial population of Cape Coloured people – people of mixed race whose history went back to the years of early European settlement, when the seventeenth- and eighteenth-century Dutch colonizers intermingled with local Hottentot people. I was aware from the beginning that the Coloureds lived in areas segregated from us, either in rather soulless small brick houses or, if they were really poor, in tin-roofed shacks at the edge of the vineyards. Many of the men were agricultural labourers, while the women generally took on domestic work. African faces were much less common. The number of black people who were allowed to live in the Cape Peninsula was strictly controlled, and those who came to seek work in urban areas could stay only for a limited time. The black people with a claim to residential status lived in the stark and impoverished 'townships' near the airport.

My mother, like most white women, employed a maid – a woman who was called rather grandly a 'cook general' – but never really discovered the secret of being a successful 'madam'; we had a high turnover of domestic help. A succession of cooks general lived in a small room at the back of the house, and did the cleaning and some basic cooking. There was usually a gardener, too, to do the heavy work outside. Sometimes they were Cape Coloured, sometimes black; often they were a couple. The regular comings and goings of staff may have stemmed in part from communication problems arising from my mother's deafness and their sometimes rudimentary English; it may also have been because of the high Atholl Crescent catering standards she was determined to keep in her kitchen. I began to get used to seeing, on my return from school in the evenings, yet another couple on the way out, the woman with an enormous bundle of belongings on her head, African style, and the man swinging a stick. In my friends' houses servants seemed to stay for years and were almost part of the family. They were usually paid a rudimentary wage, but if they lived in and were decently treated I suppose it was a preferable life to a permanent home in a run-down shack.

My parents began to make their own circle of friends, and I regularly accompanied them in the back of the Oldsmobile and waited for them there as they did the evening rounds of the medical cocktail parties. One gin and tonic was usually enough for Mother, after the second, she was liable to be indiscreet. I remember one evening a more rapid than usual return to the car, my father furious and my mother a little crestfallen. On her second gin, apparently, she had asked the wife of the dean of the medical school, who was wearing a copiously decorated cocktail hat, whether she suffered from greenfly. This had not gone down well either with the dean's wife or with my father, who feared it might spoil his chances of a teaching appointment in the neurology department. In fact it did not; he was offered a post and remained on the neurology faculty for over forty years.

It was impossible to grow up as a white child in South Africa in the 1950s without being aware even at the simplest level of the apartheid system and how it worked. The prime minister Dr Malan, a former minister of the Dutch Reformed Church, was succeeded in 1953 by the hard-eyed J. G. Strijdom, who increased his party's majority and its commitment to segregation of the races. He was followed by apartheid's real mastermind, Dr H. F. Verwoerd, a former newspaper editor and an academically brilliant man, chillingly convinced that apartheid was not only sensible but morally justifiable. Even in the days of Dr Malan I could see for myself how well entrenched the system was. There was no social mixing between whites and black or brown people, who were confined to their own living areas and types of work. Schools, parks, post offices, cinemas, restaurants and beaches were rigidly segregated. The 'Blankes Alleen' – 'Whites Only' – notices were everywhere, in Afrikaans and English. Black people could be seen in the parks and on the beaches only if they were domestic servants in charge of white children. The post offices and banks had separate queues for the 'Nie-Blankes' or 'non-whites'. Coloured or mixed-race people had certain privileges over blacks; postmen, junior policemen and – perhaps a quirk of the more liberal politics of Cape Town – some traffic police were Coloured, for instance. And there were residential areas, as I was to discover later, where the segregation rules were still distinctly blurred.

The buses on which I travelled to and from school were racially divided in a curious way. Notices proclaimed that the space between points A and B was for whites only. Between points B and C all races could sit. Between points C and X, at the back of the bus, space was reserved for non-whites. In defiance of all this, black women often sat at the front of the bus, conversing at high volume in the Xhosa language with their friends at the back. Sitting close by in my neat blue school uniform, I felt a strong sense of admiration for these women. I cannot recall any of the white passengers complaining, or the bus conductor insisting that the segregation rules be obeyed; Cape Town was sometimes like that. Trains, on the other hand, were completely divided: first-class carriages were reserved for whites, second- and third-class reserved for Coloureds and blacks. Third-class carriages had wooden seats and were generally shunned by the Coloured population, who did not, on the whole, mix with blacks. Their languages differed, for a start. Coloured people spoke Afrikaans; black Africans in the Cape spoke mostly Xhosa, and lived further away from the white suburbs. They were, naturally enough, often resentful of the easier relations Coloureds seemed to have with the whites; until the early 1950s the Coloured people even had the vote. At the massive Groote Schuur hospital where my father worked there was a small relaxation of the rules: at the insistence of the academic staff the outpatients' department was unsegregated, and so was the medical school. But this liberal-mindedness did not extend to the hospital's wards; here black and white patients were kept rigidly apart, according to the local authority rules.

I was also aware of the intense importance of 'politics' to most of the white South Africans of my parents' generation. It was the subject of endless discussion, and sometimes argument, at any sort of grown-ups' gathering, and the newspapers at home were full of political comment. The political leanings of the parents of most of my contemporaries were liberal in white South African terms – they voted for the opposition United party, and later for the breakaway Progressive party. This was not always a vote against apartheid. It was a gesture of solidarity with fellow English-speakers against the increasingly powerful Afrikaners. Few of them would have entertained, at that stage, the idea of universal suffrage. In white politics only the Liberal party preached the rightness of one man one vote, and many of their members were exiled, banned or languishing in gaol. The African National Congress, not yet banned, was a political movement rather than a party; none of its black members had a vote.

After 1955 a number of the mothers of my schoolfriends belonged to a white women's organization called the Black Sash, formed as the Coloured population lost their right to vote. These women were to be seen draped in their wide black sashes, in mourning for the constitution, at almost every ceremonial occasion, and were much mocked by government supporters. My parents did not vote, which rather disappointed me. They preferred to hang on to their British nationality, which made them ineligible. They voted for the first time in the democratic elections of 1994 when the only qualification for voting rights was residence. In the fifties and sixties my father would have described himself as politically liberal, and actively supported objections by the university and the medical school to further discriminatory legislation as it affected non-white students. My mother was more conservative: I don't think she would ever have called herself remotely radical. Nevertheless, when the election of 1994 came round – it was just before she died and she was in her eighties, very frail and in a wheelchair – she determinedly got to the voting booth and put her 'X' on the ballot paper for the Progressive Reform party. For both my parents, it was their first vote in any election in almost fifty years.

In 1950 we moved from Constantia to the middle-class white suburb of Rondebosch. Our new house was a fairly simple affair, whitewashed, single-storeyed and shingle-roofed, but it had more than half an acre of shaded garden. At the bottom of the garden was a large oak tree – perfect for climbing – and just beyond it a stream, a tributary of the nearby Liesbeeck river, which was easily reachable through the fence. The house had belonged to the local

29

vicar, a Mr Tiarks, and he and his wife had driven a hard bargain over price. On their departure they took every plant from the garden, every light bulb from each room, and even the wooden lavatory seat. But in thirteen years of married life it was the first house my parents had owned for themselves, and my mother set about ordering new curtains, sorted out my father's huge collection of books and displayed her remaining Crown Derby in the corner cupboard.

In July 1950 my sister Kirsty was born, and I was no longer an only child. She was placed in my arms as my father drove us all back from the nursing home. If it was intended as a canny form of early bonding, it worked: I decided I would do my best to look after this red-faced and wrinkly baby. She was nine years younger than I; I enjoyed the business of helping look after the new baby, and feeding her, and I even quite liked changing her nappies. She was what the Scots call a bonny baby, and as soon as she had enough hair our mother encouraged it into the sort of flaxen curls that made her look just like her almost exact contemporary, Princess Anne. I envied her being a natural blonde; my own red hair was firmly woven into plaits which stuck out unbecomingly from beneath my school hat.

By now I had settled happily into my new school. Herschel was considered a 'good' school; indeed, it liked to think of itself as the best in the Cape. We wore uniforms in the British tradition: dark blue blazers, lisle stockings and felt hats in the winter, and pale blue cotton frocks, short socks and panama hats in summer. We walked to church in crocodiles. 'Games' were compulsory four days a week. The headmistress, Miss McLean, a fierce Scot with pale red hair, ran the school rigidly, and any transgression from the rules meant detention, learning lines or – for boarders – not being allowed home at weekends. I was put straight into Standard Two as a day girl and the youngest in the class: it was assumed that my English education, despite its many disruptions, had put me at an advantage over the local girls. The classes were not arduous: there was quite a lot of reading aloud by our class teacher, Miss Taylor, who was from Yorkshire and was particularly fond of Frances Hodgson Burnett's *The Secret Garden*. I had my first Afrikaans lessons. Such was the enthusiasm of our specialist teacher for the language and culture of the Afrikaner that she organized Boer folk dancing displays on the school cricket pitch. This involved the whole of the junior school dressing up as nineteenth-century *Voortrekkers* – pioneer Boer settlers – to perform strange gavottes to traditional South African tunes. In every other respect the school was proudly English-speaking. Elocution lessons were on offer once a week, though few of my classmates could manage the test phrase 'Little Noddy Nine Pin' to the satisfaction of Miss Maas. It usually came out as 'Luttle Noddy Nahn Pun', South African vowels intact. I was not popular for managing it correctly.

The black Oldsmobile was swapped for a Humber Hawk, and each January it was packed high with suitcases, blankets and tinned food as we set off to drive a couple of hundred miles up the Cape coast for a fortnight's summer holiday. In the early fifties not all the rural Cape routes were tarred, and the journey involved bumping over miles of rutted, hot and dusty roads. Once we had left the main route, regular cattle grids increased the car's rattling: my father never drove across the grids sufficiently slowly to please my nervous mother. We carried spare water in a large canvas bag fixed to the car's radiator, where the wind kept the water cool, and there were frequent stops to swig from the emergency supply. We usually stayed in modest seaside hotels, from which I happily trotted each morning with my wooden surfboard – useful not only in crashing breakers but also for smashing down on blue jellyfish called Portuguese men o'war. They had air-filled bladders which exploded with a most satisfying 'pop'.

Once my father booked us sight unseen into a remote cottage high on a bluff overlooking the sea. When we arrived we discovered that the only way down was by a perilous path, and the cottage itself was sparsely furnished, dirty and insect-ridden. It was clearly unsuitable. My father remonstrated with the owner, another recent immigrant from Britain. 'We can't stay here till you've cleaned it up.'

'Sorry, mate,' said the owner, 'you've sent your deposit and now you're committed.'

'No fear,' said my father. 'You can keep it. We're off.' And we repacked the car and began to drive away. The owner shouted after us, 'There's one born every minute!' – an insult which had to be explained to me. But the expedition had a happy ending. A few miles further on we found rooms in a charming hotel on a lagoon at the mouth of the Breede river. Here I learned to manage a rowing boat and to feed the hotel's pet penguin without getting pecked; and at night, as I lay in my bed, I could hear through the thin walls the hotel owner's daughter playing 'The Tennessee Waltz' and 'Beautiful Brown Eyes' over and over again on her wind-up gramophone.

After school in term-time I often went home with friends, and stayed there until my father could collect me after work. Going home with Gay Beresford was a special treat, for she lived with her grandmother, who owned a pianola, and after tea we were allowed to insert the perforated paper rolls and play the tunes. The pianola library contained an enormous popular repertoire from Chopin to Cole Porter; 'In the Still of the Night' was one of our favourites, and we learned the words by heart. As her grandmother was often out at bridge parties, Gay and I were supervised by her black maid, Ellen, a large Xhosa woman who was considered to be highly reliable. One afternoon she scooped us up and took us in an ancient battered car crowded with her friends to the largest of the black townships – Langa – for a visit and afternoon tea. I can still remember the rattletrap journey and the exciting and dangerous feeling of being in forbidden territory. Soon we were sitting in Ellen's neat front parlour, two small white girls drinking large cups of sweet tea. Ellen introduced us to her extended family, who I think were as intrigued by us as we were by them. By the time we were deposited home, safely, Gay's grandmother had returned too, and there was a huge row. I think she thought we had been kidnapped; when she discovered we had been taken into an African township she was beside herself. Ellen was shouted at and my mother summoned and reassured; she must have thought that we were lucky to have escaped with our lives. Most whites had never been near a black township, and considered them distant and dangerous places. But we told Gay's granny and my mother that we had had a wonderful time. We feared Ellen would be dismissed, but her employer was fond of her and forgave her – as long, she said, as there were no more spur-of-the-moment trips.

Shortly after this episode I gave my parents another nasty turn. I had gone home from school with another young friend, Caroline Syfret. We had spotted a fierce dog in the driveway of the house across the road, and I offered to go and pat it, to see if it really was as ferocious as it was said to be. It was, and lunged towards me snarling. Next moment I was flying through the air: a car, fortunately travelling not very fast, had come round the corner and hit me as I ran back across the road. I landed on my back and was knocked unconscious. The poor driver thought he had killed me. As it turned out, I was merely badly concussed, but I had dislocated two vertebrae in my neck and done some damage to my spine. This meant many weeks lying flat on my back at home, and then wearing an elaborate brace made of leather and wire to support my head and neck.

Spending a long time at home in bed was no real hardship to me, for it meant I could read for hours – I devoured all the Arthur Ransome books and discovered Bulldog Drummond – and listen to the radio. I loved the endless afternoon serials on the local commercial station, Springbok Radio. Some of the stories had a strong medical slant. 'Mary Livingstone MD' and 'Doctor Paul' were populated by selfless doctors and devoted nurses. Others were even purer Mills and Boon. 'Portia Faces Life' at lunchtime was introduced in a breathless preamble as 'the story taken from the heart of every woman who has ever dared to love [pause] completely'. I tolerated the saccharine romances, but much preferred the hinted horrors of 'Death Touched My Shoulder' and 'The Creaking Door' at night. Judging from the actors' accents, most of these productions were imported from Australia. I suppose this was the beginning of my lifelong devotion to radio.

When I returned to school wearing my strange neck contraption I was the object of a great deal of teasing. I didn't much like this; I was already quite self-conscious enough, with my pale freckly skin next to the golden-brown limbs of my classmates. Still, at least it got me out of the one form of physical exercise I loathed – gym. I had also discovered that I was a poor tennis player, and joined the band of those fairly hopeless at most organized ball games and the last to be picked for anyone's team. The great advantage of this was being able to slip out of sight and climb up one of the gum trees on the periphery of the games field, from which cool and leafy vantage point it was pleasant to watch the others exhaust themselves. The massive pine trees nearby were too rough-barked to climb, but they did provide edible pine kernels. We called them by their Afrikaans name, *donnapits*. They were delicious – pale and soft – and I can still taste their slightly bittersweet nutty flavour.

I stayed at Herschel for the rest of my schooldays. At the age of eleven, when I moved up to the senior school, I became a boarder, although the school was only a few miles from home. I think my parents thought it might have an improving influence, as I was beginning, they said, to be resentful of the attention lavished on my baby sister. I don't think this was true – though Kirsty was certainly a beautiful child, with her golden curls, and much admired by all who met her; I think I had simply reached a rather bolshie pre-pubescent stage, and our house was getting a little crowded. It was not large by the standards of middle-class white South Africans, with four small bedrooms and a bathroom; but our household had recently expanded with the arrival of Miss Williams, a woman in her sixties, to help look after Kirsty. She was originally from Mauritius, and I loved to hear her announce to my baby sister in perfect French that her *bain* was *prêt*.

The conditions in the boarding-school dormitories were spartan. Cape winters can be cold and wet, there was no heating, and our sleeping area had only a large flapping wet canvas sheet between us and the beating rain. But in most respects living away from home suited me well; I discovered I enjoyed communal living. We were given pocket money of sixpence a week, splurged on Saturdays on large gobstoppers called Golden Balls which scratched your tongue until you reached the smooth chocolate centre. The food was as bad as boarding-school food could be, but at teatime supplies of sliced white bread were limitless. In the summer months at weekends we could loll around the school pool for hours. I became a willing ringleader for anything out-of-bounds, from midnight feasts in the school library to climbing trips around the walls of the school quadrangle after 'lights out'. Once or twice we were discovered, and eventually Miss McLean sent a letter to my parents threatening to expel me for these irresponsible nocturnal activities. 'Should anything further of this nature occur, I shall be unable to accept the responsibility of having her in the boarding house.' I stayed, but only after an intervention from my father, who somehow placated her; he had charm. To their credit, my parents were unperturbed by the incident; like me, they thought Miss McLean a tyrannical figure. Years later I came to feel desperately sorry for her, when I visited her after she had been incapacitated by a stroke and suddenly rendered helpless.

On Saturday nights there was ballroom dancing in the school gym. This was strictly a single-sex affair, girls dancing with girls and taking it in turns to 'lead' a partner: it was considered useful preparation for the real thing. The music on the wind-up gramophone consisted of anything we could retrieve from record collections at home, which meant an eclectic mixture from Ivor Novello to Guy Lombardo. As the 1950s progressed, we began to add our own music to the collection – Frankie Lymon,

Little Richard, Paul Anka and, most blissful of all, early Elvis Presley.

South Africa may have been run by the white Afrikaners, but our culture – that of English-speaking Capetonians – was largely rooted in Britishness. In the local cinemas before the main feature we watched British newsreels as well as the local version, the *African Mirror*. At the end of the performance 'God Save the Queen' was played – though not everyone stood to attention: non-royalists, mostly Afrikaners, stayed firmly in their seats. For the coronation of the new Queen in Westminster Abbey in June 1953, we had a day off school. I lay on my stomach on the shiny parquet of my bedroom floor at home listening to the commentary fading in and out on the BBC's World Service. I could follow the entire ceremony as if I were there, peering through the peep-hole of my special cardboard pop-up model of the Abbey. In Cape Town, Union flags flew over public buildings next to the familiar orange, white and blue South African flag. There was much grumbling in the Afrikaner press.

In the senior school I was allowed to give up Afrikaans lessons in favour of French, which my mother thought would be more useful to me if I returned to Europe. Madame Polaciewicz, a refugee from Poland, taught us; as there were only four of us in her class – three girls from Rhodesia and me – she generally left us alone so that she could get on with more important matters. 'Ven you haf finished your set work, girls, come to the staff room and knock me out.' We sniggered nastily. Nevertheless, I still had to sit through the Afrikaans classes – I and the three girls from Rhodesia were permitted to sit at the back of the class – so I suppose I absorbed quite a lot of the language fairly painlessly. In any case we heard it around us all the time. Afrikaans literature was taught by a remarkable woman called Sarah Goldblatt, well into her sixties and sporting wildly henna-ed red hair. She was said once to have been the mistress of a famous Afrikaner writer, C. J. Langenhoven – the man who wrote the words to the national anthem 'Die Stem' – and she was fiercely protective of his literary reputation. Her pupils had to learn much of his poetry off by heart, and she bullied them, lining up her class at the end of the lesson in strict pair formation to go off to their mid-morning break. 'Meisies! Voorentoe! Links, reg, links, reg . . .' (Girls! Forward march! Left, right, left, right.) Nobody dared giggle: she was the one member of staff who struck real fear into our hearts, and she was a good teacher. The others ranged from excellent to barely tolerable. English classes were in the charge of Mrs Pierce-Jones, a plump and moustachioed woman, far less terrifying than Miss Goldblatt. I looked forward to her lessons as they involved much reading aloud, which I was reasonably good at, and she helped us dissect Dickens, Shakespeare and the major English poets with some skill. Miss Mulliner's history classes consisted chiefly in copying her well-worn notes off the blackboard. It was rumoured that her passion for the whisky bottle was greater than any she had for teaching, and we seldom strayed beyond the American Revolution and early Cape history: I left school without having reached the Anglo-Boer War. Music was taught by Miss Sweet, whose speciality was choral singing; she persevered with us and made the school choir rather good. I became part of it. My parents, who were not habitual churchgoers, came loyally to St Saviour's Anglican church to hear us sing. My father passed most of the time in church reading the New Testament in Greek. Entirely self-taught, he could follow the classical poets in the original, and enjoyed making his own translations from them, which he recorded in a series of closely written notebooks. My mother gave our choral performances her undivided attention, half-moon hat well anchored on her head.

'Current events' were in the hands of one of the more politically liberal teachers, Mrs McCormick, who also organized the school debating society. Here was a chance to follow South African politics with a teacher who treated us as young adults. I see from my school 'Civics' notes, written when I was thirteen, evidence of the way Cape politics differed from those of the other South

African provinces. There was, I have written firmly, 'No Colour Bar' in the vote for members of the Cape provincial government, nor was there within its membership. This was to change the following year: in 1955 the government removed Coloured people from the electoral roll. It was an iniquitous act against which the white opposition both within and outside parliament protested vehemently. Members of the Black Sash movement, including the mothers of several of my schoolfriends, lined the streets outside the House of Assembly. Henceforth Coloured people were represented there by white members only.

A thousand miles to the north, the forcible removal of large numbers of black people from their homes had begun. In some areas near Johannesburg houses were razed to the ground. Their former owners were placed in segregated 'townships' or 'locations', though in the Cape, the removal of Coloured people into their 'own areas' had barely started. Education was another target. The concept of 'Bantu education' – separate schools for blacks – was initially introduced by Dr Verwoerd, then the minister of education. This meant that black children were condemned to an inferior system funded with the slimmest of resources; Dr Verwoerd made it clear he believed that it was pointless teaching Native children mathematics if it was not to be useful to them in practice. To him black people were the biblically ordained hewers of wood and drawers of water.

But these injustices, though we may have learned about them at school, were happening in a world far away from our comfortable white surroundings. The only black people we met on a daily basis were the school's kitchen staff or gardeners, or our servants at home. We were encouraged to be polite but not over-friendly. I remember noticing that one or two of the Rhodesian girls in the boarding school had a rather different attitude to black people from the rest of us. There was no official apartheid in Rhodesia, but they referred to their farm workers contemptuously as 'munts' or 'muntu boys' – an equivalent to the pejorative South African 'kaffir'. I found both the words and the tone in which they were uttered odd and rather disturbing, but I never discussed the matter with them.

My immediate concerns were less political. During the school holidays there were opportunities to get to know the local white boys. This I was keen to do, though in the company of adolescent males I was painfully shy. I envied my best friend June Jeffrey, who had a wide circle of male admirers. This she achieved despite the fact that she, like me, had no brothers. June also had a collection of popular records far larger than mine, and a rather more impressive wardrobe. Full skirts with wide elasticated belts were the height of fashion, further puffed out by many layers of stiff petticoats beneath, kept at their crackling best with a mixture of warm water and sugar. June taught me at the age of fourteen how to smoke filter-free cigarettes without coughing, a skill we practised behind the large oak tree at the bottom of our garden. And she got us tickets for the Tommy Steele show, in Cape Town on tour all the way from London. Here in the fourth row we showed off our newly acquired powers of inhalation, and screamed appreciatively between puffs.

By the time I was fifteen I had managed to acquire a male admirer of my own: Helmut Losken, a boy from the local Catholic Marist Brothers college. We met at a schools' seminar organized by Barclays Bank, who must have imagined some of us were recruitable material. As Helmut was extremely tall my parents insisted on referring to him as Helmut the Pelmet, which was annoying, but he was a gentle sort of fellow, and I achieved the desired rite of passage – my first kiss – on the *stoep* at home well before my sixteenth birthday. During school holidays, midnight was the witching hour by which I had to be home – without fail: if it was five past when I returned, my father would be standing on the doorstep in an embarrassing fury. Kirsty, I always felt, when she reached the age of fifteen or so, got away with murder by comparison. Most of us were still thoroughly virginal in our mid-teens, though there were exceptions. One girl at boarding school regularly sneaked out at night to meet her boyfriend in the park, got pregnant and had to leave; another daringly spent all night on the beach with her boyfriend over the Christmas holidays. But ours was on the whole a chaste generation: teenagers just before the pill.

It was of course easier to hang on to your chastity at boarding school. The one occasion when boys were permitted on to the premises was for the annual Matric Dance – the final party of the school year for school-leavers. Six months in the planning and carefully supervised by Miss McLean, it was a decorous affair. No plunging necklines were permitted; prim three-quarter-length dresses and low-heeled silver shoes were *de rigueur*, as were boys with decent haircuts. Slicked-back 'ducktails' were frowned on. It was also preferable that our dance partners should come from our brother Anglican school, Diocesan College, known to everyone as 'Bishops'. My mother thought that I could do better than poor Helmut so, coward that I was, I invited instead a Bishops boy called Rab Shiell. The band hired for the night played quicksteps and foxtrots and their versions of what we called the Hit Parade; there were no slow smoochy numbers, nor anything stronger to drink than a weak fruit punch. Miss McLean in her long-sleeved velvet gown stalked the perimeter of the dance floor to make sure the rules were observed. At midnight our parents came to scoop us up and take us home. I'm not sure we thought that the weeks of preparation and anxiety about whom to ask had been worth all the fuss; parties at home were more fun, and if parents kept out of the way you could turn the lights out for the slow numbers.

An alternative to clutching your loved one on the dance floor was to meet him in a bio café – a tea-room cinema (cinemas in South Africa in the fifties were still quaintly called bioscopes). Here feature films played all day, and you could stay as long as you liked if you bought refreshments for one shilling and ninepence. These consisted of a pot of tea or a 'cool drink': a huge glass of liquid, very sweet and bright red or green. Bio cafés were also popular places of gay assignation, though at the time I failed to notice the unusual number of male couples in neighbouring seats.

I went back to being a day girl for my final year at Herschel, as my parents thought that this would give me more time to swot. I was ready to come home for what proved to be my last extended period of living with my parents. A little more free time was only one of the bonuses. I was, at the age of fifteen, given my first adult-sized bicycle – something that up to then had been forbidden me after the accidental brush with a car some years earlier. I could cycle to school each day along the same route as the Bishops boys, and discuss them with my friends as they whizzed by in the opposite direction. The one we voted the best-looking, John Clare, ended up years later as an education correspondent for *The Times*, the *Telegraph* and the BBC. Another advantage of living at home was that I got closer to my sister Kirsty. She was now six and at school herself. I knitted her a cardigan in her school colour of dark blue – a superhuman effort, as I was a poor knitter and collected her from her ballet lessons on the back of my bicycle. We shared a passionate love of the family cat, a fluffy grey tabby called Chotty who had an unfeline enjoyment of games. I sensed that Kirsty had an easier relationship with our father than I did, which I envied. In the weeks before the final Matric exams I had to shut myself in my bedroom for hours of revision; Kirsty, who couldn't understand this state of purdah, posted me notes and peppermints under the door in the vain hope of luring me out.

In the summer holidays and over most weekends there was the Western Cape to explore. My father was a keen walker and regularly took himself on all-day expeditions. He enjoyed what was locally called bundu-bashing, which meant avoiding main paths for the hardier pleasures of getting up mountains through the undergrowth. The Cape Peninsula, topped by Table Mountain and ending spectacularly thirty miles further south at Cape Point, is said to be the most floriferous area of the world, with more plant species in just under 200 square miles than the whole of the British Isles. It was a happy hunting-ground for my father: he knew the names of almost all the species, and in Greek or Latin too. He always went with the family dog. His favourite, Sadko, was a bull terrier and Irish setter mix: a tireless walking companion, gentle with children but a fiercely protective guard dog. The rest of the family was happy to join him on an occasional day's walk if it was on decent paths. Sometimes scrambles on Table Mountain turned into climbing expeditions, at which point my mother retreated. They were not too taxing, but they did involve ropes and sheer drops; at one point on one of our regular routes we had to shuffle across the top of a dramatic overhang. There were birds wheeling in the updraught below us, and beneath them tiny cars glinted on the dual carriageway into town. Further afield, beyond the vineyards of Stellenbosch, there were endless mountainous areas to explore. We went on weekend expeditions with tents, and sometimes it was warm enough at night to sleep out under the stars. Their brightness in the southern skies, even seen from the city, was dazzling: today's pollution haze was still years away.

My matriculation exam results were good enough to get me into university: somehow I had scraped into the first class despite my lamentable maths. I was only sixteen, and not very keen to go; I would have much preferred to go abroad immediately. But my mother – in whose hands plans for my future rested as my father had no strong views – thought me too young for university, and certainly not equipped for a British one. She probably thought, too, that I'd have hated 'cramming' in Britain – and she was probably right. So, with her acquiescence in my short-termism, I signed up for an arts degree without telling the university authorities that I intended to drop out.

The University of Cape Town, set on the lower slopes of the mountain away from the city, considered itself in the 1950s a politically liberal institution, and there were a number of black students on most of the courses – though the government's separate education policies and the high student fees kept the proportion tiny. The black students were actively supported by the local branch of the National Union of South African Students. Many

NUSAS office-holders went on, in the sixties and seventies, to more active anti-government politics, and were as a result banned or exiled. The university had an excellent medical school, and decent teaching in other departments, but I was ill prepared for the sort of unsupervised study that a university demanded. I spent a large amount of time in local cafés with old schoolfriends drinking 'brown cows' – Coca-Cola ice-cream sodas – really wanting to be somewhere else. But NUSAS did enable me to pay my second visit to the black township of Langa. The union ran evening classes here, and I joined a busload of young undergraduates who went in once a week to help coach black students for their Junior Certificate. As a very new BA student I did my best to enthuse a bored-looking group of twentysomethings with a description of the geography of the British Isles. Nothing I told them can have seemed remotely relevant to their lives, but, I told myself, if they were prepared to give up their evenings to come to extra classes, then I should do my best to help. And yet already I could see that the apartheid system had crushed out of most of them any hope of real achievement.

My parents finally agreed that I was too young to benefit from a university course, and that I could go abroad as soon as we could arrange it. The large cabin trunks were pulled out again and packed. My mother would accompany me on the voyage; my father would follow later, by plane. My mother had now been in South Africa for almost ten years, and it seemed unlikely now that she would return to England on a permanent basis: the promise about repatriation if she wished it had been quietly forgotten. I knew she still felt out of place in South Africa, and, despite her many warm friendships with local people, she longed for the Britain she had left behind: for a village near Oxford, and grey stone cottages. I could sense her excitement as we headed with our luggage down to the Cape Town docks and the sharp smell of an oily sea. Several months in Europe lay ahead for her; but I was not to return to South Africa for three years. At sixteen, I felt almost ready to grow up.

CHAPTER THREE

Civilizing Influences?

Thought you might like to see how disgustingly fat I look in a ski outfit – baggy pants and all! Unfortunately I couldn't go up to the Jungfraujoch today, so I got prosecuted for sledging down the railway line instead.

Photo postcard from the author to her parents, Wengen, Switzerland,
9 January 1959

My mother and I shared a tiny cabin on a compact and comfortable Dutch liner belonging to the Holland–Africa Line. It did regular trips along the route between Africa and Rotterdam, putting in a stop at Southampton, and it was a popular way to travel. The food was good, the journey was smooth for most of the way and the company was usually reliably entertaining. As I watched Table Mountain recede gently over the horizon, I was aware that at the age of not quite seventeen I was about to leave the parental nest for a very long time. We hadn't explicitly discussed exactly how long I was going to be away, but I think my mother knew it would be at least a couple of years. I was to be delivered into the care of a series of friendly guardians: Prunella Stack, who had recently left the Cape herself with her two teenage sons, and Aunt Topsy, a friend of my mother's since the war; there was also my father's sister Aunt Betty in Beaconsfield. All of them had offered to keep an eye on me.

Meanwhile there was fun to be had on board ship. These were not cruise ships so much as commuter ships: a cheaper and more relaxing alternative to an air passage to Europe. Nevertheless it was a shipshape world of white-uniformed officers and organized entertainment, including a band to dance to in the evenings. There were deck games, a daily mileage sweepstake, and the Crossing the Equator ceremony, where novices were dumped in the swimming pool by King Neptune wearing a green seaweed wig. In the evenings you could lean over the rails and hear the waves slap against the ship: sometimes if you looked carefully you could see flying fish skimming over the foam. The sun shone on shiny white paint and gleaming wood; you felt enclosed, and safe.

Passengers were not allowed to fraternize with any of the ship's officers except the captain, the doctor and the purser. But younger officers and teenage girl passengers inevitably eyed each other up, and I managed to form a brief attachment to a junior officer called Otto. Our romance consisted merely of innocent kisses behind a lifeboat after dark, but we wrote to each other for months afterwards. Helmut the Pelmet had not been much of a correspondent, and I kept Otto's letters, with their neat sloping writing, in a wallet for years.

As the ship neared Southampton I began nervously to wonder who, and what, I was exactly: British, as my passport declared me to be, or South African? In Cape Town my contemporaries thought of me as not quite one of them, I knew that. On the other hand, so much of what I remembered about England seemed strange to me. I had left only nine years before, but to a teenager that was more than half a lifetime away. My childhood memories of England had blurred into a shifting picture of poor weather and some rather miserable schooldays, and I could still remember the houses sliced in half by wartime bombing on either side of the railway line between Beaconsfield and London. I wasn't entirely sure how different it would all feel, or whether I belonged there. My picture of postwar Britain since our departure had been gleaned largely from the *Illustrated London News* at home, bound editions of the *Daily Mirror* at the hairdresser's, and gently satirical films like *Genevieve* and *The Lavender Hill Mob*. I had a penfriend called Wendy who lived in Doncaster, with whom I had exchanged letters for several years. But though from her photographs our neat school uniforms looked remarkably similar, her world of brief summers and long, damp Yorkshire winters would take some getting used to.

There was also the question of how British people looked on white South Africans. By this time most politically aware people had heard of apartheid, and had more than a vague idea of what it meant. The Afrikaner National party had been in power for ten years. Jobs, schools, housing and leisure facilities were now rigidly segregated by law. Black women as well as men now had to carry the hated 'pass book', an identity document without which they were summarily arrested and could be sent back to their so-called 'homelands'. Opposition to the system outside parliament was fragmented. Those black people who demonstrated publicly against the system were dealt with ruthlessly, though the notorious legislation allowing detention without trial had yet to be introduced. I was not prepared to defend apartheid, as I had heard so many people of my mother's age do on board ship, but at the same time I thought it unfair that all white South Africans should be lumped together as racists. Many whites were appalled by the system. There was some opposition to apartheid within the all-white parliament, most notably from Helen Suzman, then a member of the United party. The English-language press was on the whole highly critical of the government. The women of the Black Sash kept up their vigils. But in the 1958 general election the Nationalist government increased its majority, and later that year Dr Verwoerd became the new prime minister. The real suppression was only just beginning.

We were met off the ship by Prunella Stack. She had bought a large and attractive house in Uckfield in East Sussex, and said we might use it as our base for as long as we liked. Prunella was the president of the Women's League of Health and Beauty, a popular keep-fit movement founded by her Irish mother in the thirties. League members participated in mass displays of choreographed exercises once a year at the Albert Hall, dressed in white tops and black satin knickers; there were also successful branches in South Africa. Prunella had twice been tragically widowed: her first husband, David Douglas-Hamilton, was killed in a flying accident during the war and her second, Ally Albers, had been fatally injured in a fall while climbing Table Mountain. After Ally's death she and her sons Diarmaid and Iain Douglas-Hamilton had become close friends of our family: they had often joined us on walking and camping expeditions in the Cape, and had provided us with a great deal of entertainment. Diarmaid, a year older than me, was a keen chemist and a tireless maker of small explosive devices. These could be placed strategically so that each time a visitor drove through their front gates there was a massive bang: loud enough to give a fright but not quite powerful enough to damage the car. He was also rather good at designing aerial railways. His most impressive was built at a height of about fifteen feet from the ground and slung from one pine tree to another at the end of their garden. His younger brother Iain was usually the guinea-pig, but occasionally I too could be persuaded to test the design. This involved a leap off one tree towards a trapeze-like device which then rushed down the wire towards the second tree. Occasionally I missed and fell off. As she sipped tea with Prunella one afternoon, my mother spotted me sailing through the air unattached, and I was forbidden any further role as test pilot.

Diarmaid, Iain and I were also enthusiastic explorers of the extensive cave system in the mountains of the Cape Peninsula. Some of the caves were flat and dry, and with a good supply of candles could be negotiated by simply crawling along the dark passages. The sand scraped one's bare knees and sometimes the candles blew out, but they were otherwise quite safe. Others, like Bats' Cave, meant steep descents with ropes and powerful torches, trying to ignore the large clusters of bats hanging from the roof. My father could sometimes be persuaded to accompany us, and we came to no harm, though there were many nervous moments when I looked up and felt the weight of thousands of tons of rock poised above my head.

Diarmaid eventually moved to the United States with his partner Meg and became a successful research scientist near Boston; Iain and his Italian wife Oria settled in Tanzania, and campaigned extensively and successfully for the elephants of Lake Manyara National Park. As boys, having barely known their real father, they were immensely fond of Jim. They admired his energy and sense of fun, and they provided the sort of boisterous company he enjoyed at weekends; in many ways they became the sons he never had. For me, they were almost brothers and though I was now beyond the stage of wild tree-hopping and scraped knees, I was anxious to see them again.

But, as we drove with Prunella from Southampton to her new house, there was something else I was even more anxious to see. For me, this was a prospect even more exciting than a year or two in Europe. I had never in my life watched television. There was none in South Africa: indeed, it was not to arrive till the mid-1970s. The government considered it politically undesirable: it would be too much of a window on the world for the black population. If television came the Afrikaner would be at an immediate language disadvantage: half the imported programmes would have to be dubbed or subtitled. Besides, Dr Albert Hertzog, the minister of posts and telegraphs, genuinely believed that television 'would be absolutely fatal for the intellectual future of our country' – he often referred to it as 'the devil's box'. The pictures it brought were too awful to contemplate. 'Friends of mine recently returned from Britain', declared Dr Hertzog in parliament, 'tell me one cannot see a programme which does not show Black and White living together; where they are not continually propagating a mixture of the two races.' I couldn't wait to see my first programmes on the small screen, and insisted that we stop Prunella's car outside the first rental shop we saw. It was the end of June, and Wimbledon was on. I gazed through the shop's plate-glass window enchanted: the tiny black-and-white figures darting across the screen seemed magical to me. To my immense disappointment, I found when we reached the house in Uckfield that Prunella did not own a set. This was not unusual in the late fifties: there was still some resistance to what was perceived as an expensive and time-wasting device. Fortunately the woman who lived next door said I could come and watch Wimbledon as often as I liked.

We settled in happily. My mother was able to renew her acquaintance with the England she had left nearly a decade before, and she introduced some of it, and her dearest friends, to me. We visited Oxford and Wheatley again, and found them hardly changed. My grandmother was still living in her house in Beaconsfield, together with Aunt Betty and Uncle John and my cousin Jane; Granny, we found, had mellowed into a rather charming old lady. The following year she was to visit the Cape to celebrate her eightieth birthday. There she enjoyed the first party that anyone had ever given her, and ascended Table Mountain in the cable car. She had, as she said later, the time of her life.

On our first trip up to London together my mother and I were intrigued to see young West Indian men happily walking in Hyde Park with their white girlfriends: a colour combination unthinkable in the Cape Town we had left. But the New Commonwealth immigrants were not universally welcomed: there were still 'No Blacks Need Apply' notices to be seen in the windows of the seedier boarding-houses of Notting Hill. There were Teddy boys, drainpipe trousers, beehive hairdos and winkle-picker shoes: but these exotic fashion statements were largely confined to working-class people. Middle-class teenagers still dressed in rather dreary versions of what their parents wore: variations on the well-cut suit for both sexes. Carnaby Street was yet to make nonsense of the class divide.

At first the sheer size of London and its crowds were a little frightening. It was strange to get on a bus, or travel by tube, or simply walk along a crowded pavement, and not recognize a single soul. In Cape Town it was difficult to avoid meeting someone you knew even on the briefest of shopping expeditions. But I eagerly lapped up the London theatre. We saw Agatha Christie's *The Mousetrap*, only in its sixth year, and Fenella Fielding and Kenneth Williams in a wonderfully funny revue called *Pieces of Eight*, some of it written by a clever young Cambridge undergraduate called Peter Cook.

By the time we arrived, the *London A–Z* was the ubiquitous guide to the capital's maze of streets; but not much more than thirty years earlier newcomers had no such reliable companion. For *Conversation Piece* in 1989, over half a century after she started the first modern street mapping of London, I talked to Phyllis Pearsall, founder of the Geographers' A to Z Map Company and asked her how she came to undertake such an ambitious project.

Interview with Phyllis Pearsall, broadcast 9.11.89

PP: I saw that the maps of everywhere – including the Ordnance Survey – hadn't been brought up to date since nineteen-eighteen or nineteen, and I lost my own way because of that. I went to some local authorities so that they could give me information about their particular borough. Several had no information and several didn't want to give it to me: here I was, a stupid woman coming in and asking them stupid questions. So where I couldn't get the information I walked. It wasn't easy, as when you go off left or right you don't know which streets you're leaving out. After I had done all the streets I handed it over to a draughtsman, and to pay the draughtsman I painted portraits at the weekend. I had to learn about card indexes in order to index the maps. I also thought I had to do the house numbering along the main roads, so I walked all the main arteries and got the house numbers. And today they are just as confused and muddled as they were in my day. By the way, I nearly lost Trafalgar Square in the first A to Z, because I lost the index cards out of the window. I managed to scrabble back all the cards except those on the top of a bus, and Trafalgar Square ended up on top of a bus. And the printers' reader said, did you leave out Trafalgar Square on purpose?

SM: How did you go about selling it?

PP: I did the walking of the streets of London again to try and sell it. I went round and they all said we don't want it. Finally I went to a little tobacconist in Clapham Common and the lady there said no, the only chance you have is to go to the wholesalers, but I'll give you lunch, you look worn out. She gave me lunch and she bought the first A to Z. I went to the wholesalers and they hadn't a moment to talk to me. I then went to W. H. Smith and Son and the cubby-hole where reps had to go, which was opened for exactly an hour and shut an hour later, and nobody thought I was a rep because they hadn't seen a woman rep before. When I was eventually shown in a very nice man gave me an order, sale or return, but our shops pay within thirty days. I went home quickly to get a barrow to put all these maps on, because this was a big order, and I got a barrow from the pub next door. The man from W. H. Smith was just coming out [of the office] and patted me on the shoulder, and said it's all right, you'll be successful, you don't mind what you do. And that's how we sold the first A to Zs.

SM: Have you ever thought of retiring? You're eighty-three, and I know you whizz about in a fast car quite a lot. Perhaps we shouldn't say that.

PP: I keep within the speed limit since a very nice chap on a motorbike, a policeman, stopped me and said do you know what speed you're doing? And I said I'm trying to avoid you. I'm always nervous that I might upset a motorbike so I've been going as fast as I could.

We had been in London only a few weeks when my father arrived and whisked us off in a hired car on a high-speed journey through Europe. I think we managed a breathless total of six countries in seventeen days. A century after the Crystal Palace extravaganza, huge international exhibitions – or 'expositions' – were still a massively popular draw, and one of our first stops was the Expo '58 site in Brussels, with its striking new gleaming Atomium representing the workings of an atom. Here people were willing to queue for two or three hours to see the Russian Sputnik, the world's first space satellite, which had beeped its extraordinary way around the skies the year before. Prunella and Iain joined us for the first few days, after which we left them in a canoe on the Moselle river at Trier, mother and son paddling off bravely downstream. In our hired car we sped on through Luxembourg, France, Switzerland, Austria and Italy. My father was an enthusiastic traveller, and a willing if occasionally slightly erratic driver. I was allowed to try out my rudimentary language skills when we looked for hotel rooms each evening. The thick wad of travellers' cheques diminished rapidly. Even Jim could see that his beloved Greece could not be on this itinerary, but Paris, Rome, Florence and Venice were good consolation prizes. He took us round the Louvre, the Sistine Chapel and the treasures of the Accademia in Venice, and we shared in his delight. Some of the buildings and paintings felt like old friends, for I had pored over their images in his large collection of art books at home. Virtually all the original European art I had seen in Cape Town had been connected to Dutch colonization: charming marine pictures with strangely contorted versions of Table Mountain. The museum in Cape Town had a small collection of African artefacts and several life-size models of members of a Bushman tribe, but little else. The history of the Cape with which we were familiar went back a mere three hundred years: in Europe, the past felt infinitely longer.

Once our family Grand Tour was over, my father returned to South Africa to resume his work. He didn't seem to mind being away from my mother for a few weeks at a time – and I think she enjoyed being back in Britain more than she missed my father. She remained with me for another few weeks as I approached my seventeenth birthday and the next stage of my patchwork education. A series of alternatives had been laid out to keep me in Europe for a year or two. I was rather keen to go to a British university, but my mother had different ideas. I think she thought learning to type would be more immediately useful, as would improving my French. So my mother and I had a tearful farewell at Heathrow Airport – after she had made sure I had all my travel instructions in a safe place. I was destined for Geneva and on from there by train to the city of Neuchâtel and the Ecole de Commerce where, someone had told her, they taught the best French in Switzerland. Someone else in the Cape had recommended a delightful *pension* on the edge of the lake, run by the de Meuron family. I was to stay there for six months.

The de Meurons had recently returned to Switzerland from Tunisia, where Henri de Meuron – Monsieur – had run a business which had been nationalized by the government of Habib Bourguiba. At the *pension* Monsieur's cousin the Comte de Meuron, an amiable fellow who wore a beret at all times, did the cooking and largely kept himself to the kitchen. Most of my fellow *pensionats* were young English-speaking Canadians in their final high-school year, on a six-month exchange visit. They were a lively lot, with names like Martha and Stu and Mary-Ellen, and I took to them instantly. Eighteen of us sat round the table for evening meals, which were enlivened each night by fierce political arguments between Monsieur and his elder son Gilles. Anything Gilles said was instantly contradicted by his father. '*Mais non!*' he shouted furiously across the table. His other object of contempt was Bourguiba himself – '*cet espèce de cochon*'. This sparring may not have done a great deal for our conversational French, but it improved our knowledge of French colonial politics, and the family arguments made mealtimes hugely exciting. It was understood that we should speak French at all times; this was less of a struggle if meals regularly turned us into spectators at a battle.

The Ecole de Commerce was less daunting than it sounded. I joined an intermediate French class, did my homework assiduously, and grew fat on Swiss chocolate; Madame de Meuron was related to the Suchard family, and it seemed appropriate to sample as much of the family product as we students could afford. But I was also terribly homesick. Phone calls home were expensive and required booking well ahead; even then, a call on Christmas Day meant hours of waiting, and finally a rather meaningless shouted exchange, largely about the weather, on a crackly line. Christmas in Cape Town had been a traditional one, with turkey and plum pudding and crackers. If the sun was beating down outside, we would simply draw the curtains so that we could see the brandy flames on the pudding. There was nothing like this in Switzerland. But the Canadians took me firmly under their wing and cheered me up; and gradually my homesickness lessened. In the last weeks of summer we swam in the lake at the end of the garden, and when winter finally arrived there was ice-skating at the local outdoor rink. We saw dozens of movies badly dubbed into French from the cheapest seats in the front row. As they were only about three feet from the screen, we had an interesting view of the latest releases if we really craned our necks:

Hitchcock's film *Vertigo* took on even more surreal dimensions. It was necessary to economize in other directions, too. Madame de Meuron charged two Swiss francs for a bath, so there was a great deal of surreptitious consecutive sharing until the water got too dirty or went completely cold.

Just before Christmas there was enough snow in the mountains above Neuchâtel for the Ecole de Commerce to give us a day off to try a bit of skiing. They organized a bus trip into the mountains and absolute beginners were encouraged to hire the right equipment. I was excited by the prospect of a scary, if brief, slither down the slopes. We hired our lace-up boots and wooden skis and poles, and, after some instruction on how to negotiate the T-bar drag lift, I set off on a wobbly course upwards, partnered by a girl who introduced herself as Georgie. She was an English fellow student from the Ecole and she assured me she had tried skiing before. Alas, my companion turned out to be as much of a novice as I: about halfway up the slope, at its steepest point, we fell off the draglift, and watched as the dangling T-bar continued its progress without us. We spent the rest of the afternoon slowly and carefully negotiating our way sideways down the mountain, while the rest of the class enjoyed themselves beyond the crest of the slope. Despite this unpromising beginning to our acquaintance, Georgie, and her twin sister Nonie, turned into lifelong friends.

A few weeks later in Wengen I managed to try skiing properly for the first time, and decided that despite my natural lack of athleticism it was a wonderful way of getting down a mountain. I have been devoted to it ever since, and each winter for the past two decades I have returned to ski from the tiny Austrian village of Gargellen, whose permanent population numbers only just over a hundred. Here the Rhomberg family have run the comfortable Hotel Madrisa for generations, and my companions have regularly included Georgie and her family, Jane Glover, Richard Kershaw, Jürgen Mittelstrass – professor of philosophy at the University of Konstanz – and his wife Renate. When Horst and Gisi Kraft from

Hamburg joined us they were especially welcome on cold and miserable days, for Horst's ski poles were hollow and filled with the best local schnapps. In the winter in good conditions you can ski over to Klosters; in the summer there is magnificent walking. Even in August patches of snow remain to tramp through on the higher peaks. I am, though, still a little wary of T-bars as a means of upward transport.

Slowly I got used to being on my own away from home. My mother, father, Kirsty and I exchanged regular letters which kept me in touch with their lives in Cape Town. My parents seemed to lead a pretty active social life. My mother overcame her deafness to an impressive extent with the help of a hearing aid, and she enjoyed both entertaining friends at home (their house, curiously after Pound Cottage, was called Farthings) and going out to parties, of which there were a great number. Their closest friends were largely local writers, artists and musicians, and included the novelist Mary Renault, who with her friend Julie Mullard had moved to the Cape in the late 1940s. Her meticulously researched novels set in ancient Greece, including *The Last of the Wine* and *The King Must Die*, became best-sellers. My father and Mary were delighted to meet again in the Cape, having last seen each other at the beginning of the war, when she and Julie were nurses at the new neurosurgical unit in Oxford. Mary had since won a valuable literary prize with an early novel on a modern theme which had enabled her to leave England and settle in the Cape. She gave no interviews to the British media: it was said to be something to do with a bad review she had once had in the *Observer*. But she agreed, years later, to talk to me both on South African radio and for BBC Radio Four's *Kaleidoscope*.

Interview with Mary Renault, broadcast 4.12.79

MR: I wrote one absolutely terrible historical novel [when she was a student at Oxford University] about the middle ages. Thank God nobody published it. It was about knights bashing about in some kind of Never-Never Land. I don't know why, seeing I was at Oxford, and I knew what research was, that I seemed to think you could spin this thing out without ever doing any. I never really got down to doing a sound job of getting my facts right. So it was a very, very good thing that nobody wanted this thing. Then I decided that I wanted to nurse. Because you weren't wasting your time, you were doing something for somebody, and it seemed a useful way of spending one's time and getting to know about human beings.

SM: Now that you've written eight successful novels set in ancient Greece, I wonder whether you would ever want to live in a period of ancient Greece even for a day, and which period you'd choose?

MR: Well, in the first place I'd take very good care to be a man if I was reincarnated in ancient Greece. You know what Pericles said, don't you, in his great funeral oration. He turns, after praising the dead, to their friends and relations, and incidentally finally to their mothers and wives, and says, 'It is the glory of a woman never to be spoken of, either for praise or blame.' I don't think I have the vocation to be a *haitaira* [a courtesan] and that is the only kind of woman's life in which you have any fun or any mental stimulus at all. But perhaps I shouldn't say that because in the Ionian islands women were very much freer, and they produced Sappho, who went about giving recitals as if she were a male Bard. But I don't think one could go back at all, because remembering one's present life so much would seem crude and barbaric. I mean the way they treated animals one doesn't like to dwell on. And the smells. When I think the Greeks went to market keeping small change in their mouths. If I had to be born as a Greek not having come from the twentieth century, having no standards of comfort, cleanliness, hygiene, kindness to animals or any of these things, I suppose the time would be in the Great Age of Pericles, or again possibly after the Peloponnesian War, when Greece was trying to find its feet again in the time of Plato, which is when I made my actor live in *The Mask of Apollo*.

SM: Why did you choose South Africa [to settle]?

MR: Well, it was in the sterling area. This to me was the country of Rider Haggard and Kipling and all the writers who wrote the boys' adventure stories of my childhood. And the present political situation hadn't even developed. I remember when we were in the plane coming down, the news was flashed through that there had been an election and that the Nationalist party had got in, and a lot of people in the plane were jumping up and down and saying 'My goodness, what will happen now?' And having been used to the rather staid quality of British elections we rather thought, 'So what? These South Africans – what a thing they're making of an election.' Funny now.

After six months at the Swiss Ecole I emerged armed with a certificate in intermediate commercial French. I wasn't sure where this would lead me, but I hugged the de Meurons and my Canadian friends goodbye and returned to England. The ferry crossed from Calais to Dover in a fearsomely choppy sea and everyone was sick, bar a young New Zealander and me; we survived by standing out on deck, buffeted and sprayed by the mountainous waves. On dry land I was back in the nominal care of Prunella, but also now of Aunt Topsy, who had a house in Shropshire. I made my way to Shrewsbury by train.

Aunt Topsy, otherwise Lady Holcroft, was a member of the Swire shipping family and was comfortably off. She lived with her husband Rex and the youngest three of her five children in a large Victorian house in the village of Pulverbatch near Shrewsbury. There was a small farm attached to the house; my mother had met Topsy during the war when her sister Sheila worked on the Holcroft farm as a Land Girl. Sheila went on to marry an American and settled in Indianapolis, but after my parents moved to South Africa Topsy and my mother kept in touch by letter. To me she was a warm-hearted, welcoming, maternal figure, if a slightly eccentric one: broken zips on skirts were liable to be pinned together with a diamond brooch. From her and other members of the Holcroft family I learned something of the ways of the British upper classes. Breakfast consisted of huge mounds of kedgeree, laid out each morning in their chafing dish: kedgeree at home had been a special treat, and here there was as much as you could eat on a daily basis. Topsy employed an elderly butler called Deacon, thought by then to be well into his nineties, who tottered into the dining room at mealtimes bearing huge salvers of over-boiled cabbage and Brussels sprouts. If you didn't eat them at lunch, Deacon would produce them again for dinner: no fresh vegetables were allowed before the old lot had been consumed. He ignored me completely, and I didn't blame him. It must have been plain to him that I wasn't used to living in such a grand house.

Aunt Topsy owned a magnificent diesel-engined Mercedes, though she seldom drove it herself as she was considered rather too hazardous on the narrow Shropshire lanes. Instead she handed me the keys. Could I, she asked one morning, go into Shrewsbury and do a little shopping? It shouldn't take long. I pointed out that I had no driving licence, although I had had a few driving lessons in South Africa. This was quite sufficient for Topsy, and within minutes I was gingerly steering the huge Merc along the nine-mile route into Shrewsbury to pick up the groceries. Somehow I found a parking spot, did the shopping, and got everything back intact. Fortunately the roads were relatively clear and I committed no further offences; no one asked to see my licence. But I made up my mind to pass my driving test before my next visit.

This was 1959, and Aunt Topsy's youngest daughter Virginia, who was a little older than me, was the proud possessor of one of the first Mini Minors off the production line. She had also done the London Season the year before, when the *Daily Mail* had declared her Deb of the Year. Both these achievements led me to regard Virginia with some awe, even though on one of her test runs with the new Mini she had sneezed on rounding a corner and had ended up in a hedge. The Season at that time still involved dozens of 'coming out' balls, though the debutantes were no longer presented to royalty in long white gowns. Ginnie was very attractive and had an impressive number of admirers and social invitations. She was told to look after me, and Aunt Topsy made sure I was taken along to all the best local events, like point-to-points and hunt balls and cocktail parties. Each one of them presented a minefield of social traps for me. 'Indian or Earl Grey?' asked one kindly hostess, as the teapot hovered. I had never heard of such choice – at home it was simply Five Roses tea out of a brown china pot. And I misheard her. I took a stab at the one which sounded more exotic. 'Old Gray,' I said, 'thank you very much.'

I marvelled at the cut-glass accents and utter self-confidence of Ginnie and her friends. I tried out the accent myself, not very convincingly, and gave up. I was aware I had a tinge of South African in my vowels, and I knew these girls could spot me as Not One Of Them. I was happy to observe from the sidelines. The Season was still about meeting the right people – and especially the right man, the sort of man you eventually might marry. With her deb year behind her, Ginnie had no difficulty at all in achieving this. A year after she shepherded me through a small part of the

Shropshire social calendar, at the age of twenty she married Willie Trotter, who was in the army. I was astonished and delighted when she chose me as one of her bridesmaids. The wedding photographs show three slim bridesmaids and one plump one – me, still fighting the Swiss chocolate effect.

My Neuchâtel certificate in commercial French was not, I decided, in itself likely to open too many career doors for me. Some extra qualifications might not be a bad idea. I knew I would have to pay my own way quite soon, for my father, although a highly esteemed medical man, and fondly regarded by most of his patients, was not really interested in making money. In fact he rather despised any such ambition: money was simply of no consequence to him. The drawers of his desk overflowed with unpaid bills and, my mother always suspected, unsent invoices to his paying patients. His attitude to financial security was always a source of deep anxiety to her. He spent an enormous amount on books, or so my mother always claimed, leaving not very much for her housekeeping or for the rest of us. She found it difficult to understand how the man who was thought to be the best neurologist in Cape Town was so bad at asking his patients for payment. Naturally enough, his Coloured and African patients were treated free at the outpatients' sessions at Groote Schuur hospital; few of them could have afforded to see him privately. But he was also immensely generous to his friends, seldom sending them a bill if they came to him in his professional capacity, and always insistent on picking up the tab over dinner or at the theatre. As a result my poor mother was always rather short of cash. I think her uncertainty about funds transmitted itself to me at an early stage: I was determined to pay my own way from the moment I could.

The next part of my mother's alternative plan was that I should spend a year at an educational establishment called The House of Citizenship. Based in a beautiful part eighteenth-century building, Hartwell House, close to the village of Stone near Aylesbury in Buckinghamshire, The House of Citizenship was the creation of an extraordinary woman, Dorothy Neville-Rolfe, whose mission it was to prepare girls not for marriage but for Life. Hartwell was not, she said, a Finishing School, it was a Beginning School. She was herself, she told us, an Unclaimed Treasure, for after the First World War there were tragically far too few young men available for all the girls of her generation to get married. Miss Neville-Rolfe worked hard to make sure that enough fee-paying parents around the world knew about her school to keep it going. She went on worldwide trawling expeditions in the long holidays, making sure she stayed with local ambassadors and high commissioners who had wide contacts and might recommend local girls to her care; she had trawled in South Africa, and word had got about. The idea was to give her students a stimulating year in attractive surroundings, with plenty of lectures on British, Commonwealth and international affairs. That was the citizenship course, on top of which you could concentrate on the arts or take a secretarial course. I chose arts.

My first term at Hartwell coincided with the glorious British summer of 1959, when the sun shone without interruption for five months. Between lectures, students could laze on the lawns, admiring the topiary and the fine proportions of the house itself. Half the college's intake was British, one or two were American, and the rest from the Commonwealth. This meant that I could meet on an equal basis and become friends with black and Asian girls for the first time, which was thrilling for me. None of them was from South Africa, but all the same I was astonished by their lack of resentment towards someone brought up in the apartheid system. This generosity of spirit applied, I remember, even on the day in March 1960 when I spotted the awful newspaper headlines proclaiming the horrors of the Sharpeville massacre, revealed in a graphic photograph on the front page of the *Daily Mail*. The papers told the terrible story. A large crowd of black people had converged on a police station in a township south of Johannesburg to hand in their pass books in a new protest against the hated identity documents. A policeman panicked and fired into the crowd; other shots followed. Sixty-nine black people were killed and 130 injured. The pictures ran round the world. A few days later, more pass books were burned in a public demonstration of contempt for the apartheid laws. In Cape Town, a thousand miles to the south, there were violent confrontations between the police and blacks in the local townships, including Langa, but fortunately nothing happened remotely close to the scale of the Sharpeville tragedy. At the beginning of April, the African National Congress was officially banned under the Suppression of Communism Act. Nelson Mandela and his fellow protestors became outlaws.

By lucky coincidence my new friends from the Neuchâtel Ecole, Georgie and Nonie – the Crossman twins – were at Hartwell House too. Their parents, Austrian Jews called Grossmann, had left Vienna early in the 1930s and had settled in Moor Park, near Rickmansworth in Middlesex. They were not practising Jews and the twins had been brought up as Catholics. Edith and Victor, their parents, were immensely hospitable. They invited me home for weekends and introduced me for the first time not only to a regular glass of wine with meals but also to dumplings, Sachertorte and Wiener schnitzel – which Mitzi, their mother's elderly Viennese cook, made to perfection. Edith was a small, quiet, neat woman who was impressively well read and did occasional research jobs for the BBC's German service at Bush House. Victor was a successful businessman who drove a Bentley in which he took great pride. His work in the veneer business frequently took him into the East End of London, where he found a garage good enough to look after the car. One afternoon, just before collecting it after one of its regular services, he stopped for a cup of tea in a local greasy spoon. He overheard two men talking as they collected their order from the counter. 'Did you 'ear about that geezer's Bentley dropping off the ramp this morning? It didn't 'arf make a racket.' Victor, astute as ever, was able to come to a good arrangement with the offending garage about its repair bill.

Most exotic of all to me was the fact that Victor had a 'girlfriend', whom he visited twice a week. It was an arrangement which had long been accepted by Edith. Each time he was likely to come home late she would leave out cheese and fruit as a snack for him. When he was in his seventies his failing eyesight meant that Victor was no longer permitted to drive the Bentley to town or anywhere else. This looked as if it might put an end to the visits to his girlfriend. Edith, ever accommodating, offered to drive him there herself. He thought about it, declined, and took a taxi instead.

We were fortunate that Dorothy Neville-Rolfe's considerable powers of persuasion provided us with some spectacularly good visiting lecturers at Hartwell House. They came unpaid, but with the promise of a decent supper and what she assured them would be an appreciative audience. One of the speakers she cajoled into talking to us was an impressive young Labour candidate called Shirley Williams; another the eminent architectural historian Nikolaus Pevsner. Peter Wilson, the chairman of Sotheby's, was a regular lecturer. In return for the privilege of being addressed by such luminaries, we were expected not only to introduce the speakers to their captive audience and ask them intelligent questions at the end, but to go out into the community ourselves on a weekly basis to talk to local women's groups about our own lives. Heaven knows what the poor women of the Aylesbury and Stone Women's Institutes made of us, but it probably gave us some sort of early self-confidence about talking to strangers.

Dorothy Neville-Rolfe herself was supremely unembarrassable. She claimed that on one of her trawling trips to Ghana she had been made an honorary tribal chief, and she entertained new Hartwell pupils with a fierce Ghanaian war dance, stamping the floor enthusiastically with her heavy brogues. She had written a formidable guide to being a perfect secretary (inevitably nicknamed the 'perfect secs guide' by the girls), and disbursed gems from this compendium in her own weekly lectures. The arts course interested Miss Neville-Rolfe less than the secretarial, but it meant for us coach trips once a week to London and the National Gallery. Twenty of us collected little collapsible stools and sat in front of the chosen picture as the lecturer traced its most important features with his little finger. Over the course of the morning the group gradually diminished in size as girls slipped away on assignations. The lecturer did his best to ignore the steady haemorrhage of listeners, even when eventually there were only two or three of us left. To the annoyance of the diligent few, the bunkers-off always made it back on to the return coach with seconds to spare. We were also taken as a group round some grand stately homes, or those that would let us in on private visits. Once the bus took us to Claydon House in Buckinghamshire, the home of the Verney family and, for all her long invalid years, of Florence Nightingale. Sir Harry Verney, Claydon's owner then, was a delightful old man who could remember sitting on the end of Florence Nightingale's bed while she told him her stories of the Crimea.

University receded still further. After I left Hartwell House in the summer of 1960 my mother made a further long-distance arrangement for me: I was to live in Oxford to take a six-month course at Miss Sprules' secretarial school. Shorthand and typing seemed a good alternative to three years at university, and might lead to interesting things – primarily, in my mother's mind, meeting a nice intelligent man who would make a suitable husband. But even then, she said, I was 'too fussy', and indeed I wanted a paragon: clever, kind *and* good-looking.

Miss Sprules was a reserved elderly lady with manicured white hair. Together with the dark and slightly forbidding Miss Glyka, her partner in life as well as in business, she ran the college with stern efficiency, ensuring that after six months at their establishment you could dash off shorthand at 120 words a minute, and type at fifty. It was rather hard work for me, and I loathed the boredom of typing out letters until they were perfect, but the secretarial grind was largely compensated for by the chance to watch undergraduate life at Oxford from the fringes. My fellow typists and I were invited to a string of parties in college. I longed to be one of the 'proper' Oxford students; but the next best thing was to meet and mix with them.

It turned out that Miss Sprules and Miss Glyka had other ideas for their pupils: to the dismay of us all and with very little warning, they moved the entire secretarial school down to Winchester in Hampshire. In frustration, and also because I didn't like like her very much, I'm afraid I chained my bicycle across the gate of my landlady in Banbury Road, Mrs White, before I crossly caught the train from Oxford. I saw out the second half of my six months' course in a state of some gloom, at the wrong end of the line from Waterloo.

So here I was at eighteen: not yet ready to go back to South Africa, not quite brave enough to try for a British university, armed with a vague qualification called Citizenship and a certificate in shorthand and typing. I think my parents would have liked me back home; but I decided to move up to London. I arranged to share accommodation with some of the ex-Hartwell girls who had found a tiny flat in Edith Terrace, just off the Fulham Road. Here five of us – Jean and Eve Shaw-Mackenzie from the Black Isle, Penny Lunn from Hartlepool, Shelley Andrew from Hertfordshire and me – turned a blind eye to the cramped conditions and enjoyed our first taste of real independence. The Shaw-MacKenzie sisters were rather glamorously wild and enjoyed their whisky: when we were still at the college we paid regular visits to the local pub, the Bugle Horn, and afterwards danced down the white line in the middle of the road. Miss Neville-Rolfe would not have been amused. When we moved in the flat was filthy, with dust everywhere and indeterminate oderiferous stains on the carpet, but we cleaned it up and made it tolerably decent. There were two bedrooms: one was just big enough for three small beds, while the other had a double-decker wooden bunk jammed into a corner. The kitchen was tiny and poorly equipped. The bathroom was airless and steamy, and permanently draped with damp underwear. The black-and-white television set showed the BBC through a snowstorm, and ITV only if you gave it a good kick – as I discovered one night when, after a particularly hefty blow from me to improve the reception on BBC, ITV's *Emergency Ward 10* suddenly appeared. After that I was glued to it twice a week.

I knew I would have to go back to South Africa eventually, probably within a year or so; but in the meantime, in order to pay my share of the rent, I had to find a proper job. It was at this point that the BBC loomed into view as a possible employer. I had a godmother in London, Yvonne Pulling, who lived in an apartment block in Sloane Street. Yvonne was Belgian and cooked the most delicious meals, rich with creamy sauces. Her husband Martin held an executive job in the BBC's television engineering division, and to me was almost synonymous with the BBC. He had joined the engineering department before the Second World War, and had an old-fashioned reverence for Lord Reith and his concepts of what broadcasting should be about, disapproving strongly of the *laissez-faire* liberalism of people like Hugh Carleton Greene, the director-general in the 1960s. One of his pet projects was Eurovision, which linked television stations throughout Europe. He had also helped organize the BBC's televising of the coronation in 1953, and once proudly shown me round the enormous hole in the ground near Shepherd's Bush which was to become Television Centre. I asked his advice about working for the Corporation; he was encouraging, and offered to act as a referee for me in any job application. So I wrote to the BBC's appointments department.

Meanwhile I scoured the *Evening Standard* in search of more temporary employment. It wasn't long before I spotted an ad that sounded quite intriguing: Australia House needed typists to help them process a new wave of immigration from the United Kingdom. This was at the height of the Ten Pound Passage scheme, under which, for ten pounds a head, whole families, if they were accepted, could board a ship in Southampton and end up six weeks later as potential new Australians in Perth, Sydney or Melbourne. They filled in application slips and sent them in to Australia House with their postal orders; we neatened up their details and passed everything on to the next department. It was not demanding work, and the head of the typing pool, who enjoyed the eminently suitable name of Miss Remington, kept a benign eye on us.

My first pay packet contained the enormous sum of just over seven pounds: what was left of a weekly wage of nine guineas, less tax. After paying my share of the rent, I had about three pounds spending money. Once I'd handed over my share to the food kitty, I had about a pound a week to spend for pure enjoyment. It was enough – just – for the odd bottle of Spanish wine (about six shillings) and occasional paperback book (about the same), but left nothing for new clothes or shoes. My father agreed to subsidize me at a rate of about two pounds a week so that I could replenish my wardrobe.

On the whole, I now thought I was pretty well off. There were parties at weekends, accompanied by the Spanish plonk, and during the week young men could usually be persuaded to take us out for at least a sandwich at the pub. I was briefly heavily smitten by an Australian called Alan, who seemed a lot older than me at almost thirty. He was attractive and amusing, and I was intrigued by what we would now call his laid-back charm. Our affair lasted only a matter of days, after which, having relieved me of my virginity, he quickly moved on to a more enticing prospect in South Kensington. He specialized, I learned later, in girls from South Africa. I picked myself up and concentrated on finding a job away from the world of the temps' typing pool.

After a week or two the BBC replied to my general job enquiry. There was the possibility of a post working in the Light Programme's headquarters in Aeolian Hall in Bond Street – a great rabbit warren of a building, much larger than one would have supposed from its front entrance. Its concert hall had seen the first performances of William Walton's *Façade* in the 1920s, when Edith Sitwell had bellowed the words through a megaphone. The job on offer was that of junior secretary to Peter Duncan, who edited and produced the radio version of *In Town Today*, a programme based on interviews with visiting celebrities. It had a long and illustrious history, each half-hour edition introduced by Eric Coates's 'Knightsbridge March' as it went out on Saturday. I eagerly snapped up my chance. By 1960 the programme was no longer in its heyday, but in Tony Bilbow and Nan Winton it had a good pair of interviewers. Tony was a friendly young man who went on to become one of the regular hosts on BBC2's *Late Night Lineup*. In June 1960 Nan had the distinction of being the BBC's first woman television newsreader, but her promising career in news lasted only six months, after which the head of her department decided that women carried too little authority and she was dropped. She was married to Charles Stapley, the actor who understudied Rex Harrison in the original London stage version of *My Fair Lady*, and impressed us all by arriving to work in a chauffeur-driven car.

My duties were to consist of working under Peter Duncan's senior secretary, Wendy: typing letters, fetching the tea and filling in Peter's expense claims. These included his regular application for a quarterly evening dress allowance, which even then seemed an anachronism – a hangover from the Reithian days when radio newsreaders wore dinner jackets to deliver the nine o'clock news. Before I could get to grips with any of this I had to go on what the BBC called an induction course. It lasted two weeks, and consisted of shorthand and typing practice, and learning not only how the BBC worked but also what its plethora of abbreviations stood for, from HLE (Head of Light Entertainment) and AHAR (Assistant Head of Audience Research) to DCEng (Deputy Controller of Engineering) and the DG (Director-General) himself. There was even rumoured to be someone with the initials EIEIO, but I never discovered where he lived. Most of these important people were based at BH (Broadcasting House). A fortnight later I was officially a member of the BBC's staff.

Peter Duncan was a large, affable man with a clipped moustache. We were all on first-name terms in the office, which was unusual in the wider office world forty years ago; we thought it rather racy. Each day I was allowed into the studio's control room to watch parts of the programme being recorded; soon I was timing the interviews with a stopwatch so that accurate editing could be done. I observed the techniques of the two professional interviewers. Their task on *In Town Today* was not hugely demanding. Peter was keen on showbusiness interviewees and there was a heavy sprinkling of old reliables like Vera Lynn, Peter Ustinov and Arthur Askey, mixed in with newly discovered stars. Adam Faith came in to talk about his first record, and so did the fourteen-year-old Helen Shapiro, immaculately coiffed in an impressive beehive. Most of their conversations were carefully prepared in advance, which left little room for spontaneity; today they sound almost comically overproduced. But here was a procession of famous people trooping into a radio studio, and I was thrilled to be sitting only inches away from them, close enough to see for myself how they reacted to being questioned. It did not occur to me that I would ever talk to them across a microphone myself, but I could see the attractions of becoming a producer, or perhaps a producer's assistant, and playing some part in a programme's creative process. I could also see that to progress up the job ladder, if I stayed at the BBC, would take a very long time, especially for someone of my age with no university degree.

In South Africa things might happen a little more quickly, and I continued with my arrangements to return. In any case, I missed the wide skies and the Cape's magnificent mountains; I longed for warmer weather and a more relaxed and outdoor life. In summer in the Cape it was often warm enough, on weekend expeditions into the hinterland, to sleep in the open. We had once spent five days in the Cedarberg, a range of mountains a few hours' drive into the Cape's vast interior. Here you could hire a Coloured man and four donkeys for a camping trip: the donkeys carried the tents and the heavy cooking equipment, while you spent all day walking at your own pace along rugged paths admiring the fynbos – the indigenous scrub and bushes. You moved from one glorious campsite to the next, all of them close to clear streams or dark peaty rivers. At night there were dazzling stars, and close by the rustling sounds of the bushveld and the occasional plop of a frog in the river. In the spring the fynbos was dotted with bright wild flowers. The Cape was a heavenly place to be, and I wanted to be back again, although the South African political climate was becoming fiercely confrontational.

I had been following events closely in the press. In the aftermath of the Sharpeville massacre the prime minister, Dr Verwoerd, held a referendum on whether or not the country should become a republic: few of his supporters felt any sort of allegiance to the Queen. It was an all-white affair, of course, with the opposition parties campaigning for a 'no' vote. The result was as expected: Verwoerd won. He came to London to attend the Commonwealth prime ministers' conference, reportedly believing that he could keep South Africa within the Commonwealth as a republic. His arrival at Heathrow gave the Anti-Apartheid Movement, and South Africans in London who supported it, a splendid chance to demonstrate against him. I joined them, waving my 'Verwoerd Out' banner on the side of the A40 as his car and its outriders swept by. I imagine he barely noticed us; but that evening on ITN there was a recognizable flash of me and my banner on the six o'clock news. I was delighted, but from their remarks afterwards I knew that not all my expatriate South African friends thought it a decent thing to have done. As it turned out, the majority of Commonwealth leaders were so fiercely against Verwoerd after the events at Sharpeville that he decided to pre-empt their inevitable decision to throw him out, and announced South Africa's withdrawal with immediate effect.

Just after I had booked my passage home on another Union Castle mailship, I was strongly tempted to change my mind and stay. A few weeks before I was due to sail I met a journalist called Peter at a party given by my friends the Crossman twins. Peter was twenty-four. He was good-looking, witty, and had an impressive job in Fleet Street editing a long-established gossip column. He had light brown floppy hair and smoked a pipe; he wore slightly old-fashioned bespoke tweed suits with a waistcoat and a gold watch-chain; he was evidently a bit of a dandy. He had many interests outside journalism and pursued them with huge enthusiasm: these included working for the Liberal party and collecting original Dixieland jazz recordings. He also had a large taped collection of old BBC radio programmes – including bootleg episodes of the *Dick Barton* and *Paul Temple* serials. He asked me out to dinner. We went to a French restaurant in Soho, Chez Victor, and I was highly impressed by the enormous bill at the end of the evening – five pounds. I was also bowled over by Peter's chatter, his talent for mimicry, and most of his enthusiasms. He, flatteringly, seemed to be quite taken with me. But to my intense dismay, aside from Soho dinners *à deux*, it was extraordinarily difficult to be alone together. He shared a flat in a Mayfair mews with two other journalists, and they always seemed to be there when I visited in the evenings. Although I had by now moved to a rather better flat in South Kensington, it contained several South African girls and a constant stream of friends 'passing through', so there was little privacy there. The new and better flat naturally meant a higher rent, and the bedrooms were divided up according to how much the residents could afford to pay. I shared one of them with an old schoolfriend: she had the bed and I had the mattress on the floor. It was the cheaper option, and, as a temporary arrangement, it suited me well – except for the lack of privacy.

Not long before my scheduled departure, Peter suggested I join him on a weekend in Paris that he'd had planned for a while. It was hardly a romantic tryst, as both his flatmates and some of their friends were coming along too. As there was no room for me in their hotel, a bed was found for me in an otherwise empty apartment. The weekend was not a success. Peter and his friends insisted on spending the Saturday night touring the bars of Montmartre; I opted instead to return to my apartment early. I was woken in the middle of the night by the sound of someone climbing through the bedroom window. It was not Peter, but an opportunist thief; I had foolishly left the window half open. Rather than cower beneath the sheets, for some reason I flung back the bedclothes – fortunately the intruder took this as a cue to change his mind, hop back out of the window and flee. In the morning I got little sympathy when I told the others of my narrow escape; they had ended up making too much noise in the street and having water poured over their heads from a high apartment window. And yet my adoration of Peter was in no way diminished. We resumed our relationship back in London; I longed for him to ask me to cancel my passage to the Cape and stay on, but he did not. Perhaps I thought he might follow me; but I was beginning to realize that my feelings for him were a great deal stronger than his for me.

So in the late autumn of 1961 I set sail for South Africa, counting the days till landfall. There would surely be some sort of communication from Peter waiting at the other end. The voyage took eleven days, quite long enough, I calculated, for an airmail letter to overtake me. As the ship nudged the Cape Town quayside I spotted my parents in the crowd below. We waved excitedly at each other. 'Any letters from London?' I shouted. My mother shook her head. I waited in vain over the next few days for any communication from Peter; international phone calls were still difficult to arrange, and expensive. Weeks later, a letter in the familiar florid handwriting arrived. It was affectionate and full of London news, but there was no urgent plea for me to come back. Many years later, my mother told me that she had always thought I was wasting my time with Peter. She claimed to have 'known' our relationship would never come to anything. Still, we stayed in touch for many years, occasionally meeting for long Sunday lunches when I returned to London. Gradually being smitten turned into fondness and then to simple friendship. One day when I was in hospital recovering from an operation the phone rang next to my bed. It was Peter, to tell me that a newspaper columnist had written something deeply unflattering about me. In my fragile state it pierced me with a shaft of dismay. I snapped that he had chosen an odd moment to pass on bad news; he was genuinely astonished that I had taken his cheery snippet of information so badly. After that there seemed little point in continuing our sporadic meetings, and I decided to bring our friendship to an end. But that was some years later.

Cape Town in 1961 was a sleepily beautiful city. The high-rise buildings which have since marred so much of its profile were not yet there to spoil the gentle symmetry, and the majesty of the great mountain behind still caught the breath. After three years in Europe I was ready for Africa again. I had worked for the BBC in London as a very junior secretary. Perhaps South African broadcasting could offer me something a little more exciting. And I had not seen my parents for two years. It was good to be home.

CHAPTER FOUR

A Long Way from Toyland

SM: How do you actually write your books?

EB: Well, I take my typewriter, and I put it on my knee, and then I think for a little while. Then my hands go up, my fingers go on the keys, and I go straight on typing out the story without a stop. I think straight on to my typewriter. I find it's the best way of getting a story through vividly.

SM: How long would it take you to write an average size book?

EB: A week.

Interview with Enid Blyton, recorded Beaconsfield, England, 1966

S outh African broadcasting was government-controlled; everyone knew that. The news bulletins reflected the thinking of the ruling National party, and since the early 1960s the membership of its governing board and the management of most of its important internal departments consisted of politically reliable Afrikaners. The chairman of the South African Broadcasting Corporation,

Dr Piet Meyer, was a member of the Broederbond – literally, the 'bond of brothers' – a secretive grouping which had its roots in the assertion of the rights of Afrikaans-speakers after the defeats of the Boer War. When the National party was voted into power in 1948 the Broederbonders pledged to gain control of all the most important strands of political and economic life in South Africa. Its members – they were always men – could be found within all principal sections of government, as well as in the civil service, the police, banks, building societies and Afrikaner cultural organizations. The SABC's higher echelons were an important stronghold, and Piet Meyer was a close friend of cabinet ministers. It was said he had a son called Izan. The name was a grim joke: you only had to read it backwards to see where his real sympathies lay. But the SABC's headquarters and most of its controlling Broeders were in Johannesburg, which is a thousand miles to the north of Cape Town. It was possible, if you lived and worked in the Cape, to feel that the Broeders and their nasty controlling hands were a distant threat, and to look on the SABC, if you ignored the editorials, as a useful source of entertainment and information.

In the 1950s the SABC's Cape Town offices were moved from the centre of town to the pleasanter aspects of Sea Point, a few miles further south. Whoever chose the spot chose well. The building itself is unremarkable: a postwar concrete block five floors high, with a bronze goddess plunging down the wall next to the main entrance, and a tiny pillared car park to one side. But the inhabitants of its foursquare little offices gaze out on to a seductive view: across the road, past the neat green lawns with their windblown palm trees, is the sea. On a calm morning the sun glints off it enticingly; on stormy days the wide blue Atlantic hurls itself against a retaining wall. Occasionally a rusty shipwreck is revealed a few hundred yards off the shore. These can be treacherous waters. In the 1960s the southern sea route between Europe and the far east was still extremely busy. When the Suez Canal was closed during its nationalization crisis, dozens of ships a day, from luxury liners and tugs to tankers and freight carriers, had to go the long way round Africa, and slipped into Cape Town's docks. Regularly, during local storms, one or two of them came to grief. Their ageing and rusty remains reared up out of the water as a reminder of their perilous voyage.

Cape Town is not like the rest of South Africa. It is the country's founding city – the Dutch used it as a staging post to the far east from the 1650s – and in the apartheid days it prided itself on its easy-going attitude to two of South Africa's great problems: 'race relations', as they were officially called, and the relations between the two main white groups, the English and the Afrikaners. This was just as well. In the Cape it was not simply a case of white versus black, or Boer versus Brit. There were subtle gradations of belonging and prejudice. The Coloured people, those of mixed race, had much in common with the majority of the whites: a language, Afrikaans, and a nervousness about the threat to them of the black population, numerically the largest grouping in South Africa. 'Swart gevaar', it was called: literally, 'black danger'. The Coloured people were certainly better off than their black compatriots. The Western Cape was a 'Coloured preference area', which meant that certain jobs and housing areas were reserved for them. Worse off than the whites they might well be, but they were enormously better off than the blacks. Black people were only tolerated in any part of South Africa because the whites needed their labour, and Dr Verwoerd's Grand Apartheid plan assumed that one day it might be possible for them all to be removed and sent back to their 'homelands'.

If there was a liberal element to Afrikaner nationalism, it was based in the Western Cape, which was the home of the country's oldest and most respected Afrikaans university, in the charming old town of Stellenbosch. Stellenbosch has oak-shaded streets and whitewashed houses with pretty Dutch gables. Its university was the alma mater of every South African prime minister in the twentieth century, but it also educated many of the Afrikaner intellectuals who later opposed the government's Grand Apartheid plan. So as one gazed at that solid set of offices in Sea Point, knowing it was ultimately run by the Afrikaner political elite, it was possible to believe that one might not feel entirely alien there. The country's real political battles were being fought elsewhere.

The SABC had a lively English Service, much of it unashamedly modelled on the BBC's old Home Service. Some of its programmes were identical, imported with special permission. They included *The Goon Show* and later *Round the Horne* – until the gay couple Julian and Sandy were deemed a little ripe for South African audiences and it was taken off the air. But generally the programmes, and the voices, would have sounded quite familiar to listeners in Surbiton or Sunderland. In the early 1960s the SABC's English Service ran a competition to find 'the Voice of South Africa'. The winners were a recent immigrant from Britain called Michael Todd and an Irishman, Paddy O'Byrne. They hadn't a single South African vowel between them, but the locals liked the way they sounded, and they became two of the most popular announcers in radio.

Armed with the details of my brief spell as a BBC employee back in London, I applied for a job at the Sea Point studios in 1962. A family friend gave me an introduction to a man called Jack Morel, who ran a programme for teenagers, *Calling to Youth*. He looked at my curriculum vitae, spotted the letters BBC and invited me to try my hand at doing an interview using one of their portable tape-recorders. I gulped. The recorder was portable only in comparison with a studio console: it was a huge, heavy green beast of a thing, lifted by large webbing straps, and extremely cumbersome to operate, with tiny handles to wind back the tape after the recording was completed. Fortunately I wasn't expected to operate the machine entirely by myself: an engineer was delegated to help me on my debut interview, and together we were despatched to the Cape Town docks to meet some French officer cadets who had just arrived on board a vast aircraft carrier, the *Jeanne d'Arc*, on a brief goodwill visit to the city. The French senior officers were welcoming and helpful, and produced a couple of young men who spoke passable English. Nobody had told me what to do or how to prepare myself for this first interview; I barely knew how to hold the microphone. Back at the BBC, sitting in a purpose-built studio, it had all seemed much easier. I pointed the microphone at the cadets and asked them where they came from and about their impressions of Cape Town. Their answers were polite. I ploughed on until the tape looked as if it was coming to an end, and then stopped. We returned to the Sea Point studios to try to edit the rambling mishmash into something crisper. Judicious cutting, I knew from my London experience, could radically improve a recorded interview. Jack Morel was kind, and did eventually use my efforts. On the day the piece was broadcast my mother and I crouched beside the radio set in a state of high excitement. The whole thing was over in about a minute and a half. Jack Morel did not suggest any further assignments.

If radio interviews were not to provide the career break I needed, I would have to look elsewhere. My funds were low, and I decided to get a temporary job as a typist until something more enticing turned up. A fruit-exporting firm in Cape Town took me on as a clerk and part-time switchboard operator – a brave experiment on their part, as most of their clients were from the hinterland and spoke only Afrikaans, and my command of the language, despite Miss Goldblatt's classes, was rudimentary. So were my switchboard skills: I managed to cut off most of the firm's incoming calls. But they kept me on for a month or two, and I found a place to live: one of my old friends from Hartwell House, Sue Little, needed someone to share the costs of a flat. For the first couple of months back in South Africa I had stayed with my parents; I was very happy to be back with them and with Kirsty, who at eleven was now a proper little person, full of confidence and her daddy's approval. But I knew that it was time I struck out on my own again, and so I joined

Sue in her small maisonette high in the upper reaches of the city, in Kloof Street, where the old trams still ran. The apartment block was heavily exposed to the sun in the summer and to the regular blasts of the seasonal south-east wind, but it was convenient for the centre of the city. Living here was much less expensive than London: fruit and vegetables were plentiful and cheap, and huge flagons of wine for parties could be bought for less than a pound. We settled in and I waited for something to turn up.

My brief encounter with the French sailors, it turned out, had not been quite the disaster I had feared. I was invited to return to the Sea Point studios to meet the head of the English Service, a well-known and popular broadcaster called Dewar McCormack. I sat nervously in his office as people bustled in and out with important-looking pieces of paper. He told me he was looking for someone as an assistant on *Woman's World*, an afternoon magazine programme quite closely modelled on the BBC's *Woman's Hour*. Daphne Shackleton, its main presenter, needed extra help: someone with secretarial skills who could be taught to edit tapes, and who might even be able to take over some of her production work. It sounded just the job. Would I be interested? I certainly would; I said I could start immediately. My salary was to be just over forty rands a month, the equivalent of about twenty pounds. It would be just about enough to get by on. Two months after arriving back in Cape Town I was solvent, employed – and even mobile: my father had lent me the money to buy a small car, and I had acquired a bright red Hillman Imp of which I was immensely proud.

Daphne Shackleton turned out to be the perfect boss: not only bright, cheerful and chatty, she was also happy to hand over a great number of her production tasks to me. She was a divorcee and, she told me, soon to marry again; within two months she was to leave the SABC for good. Dewar McCormack called me back into his office and asked me if I would be interested in replacing her. This meant, at the age of twenty, taking on the whole of *Woman's*

World myself – presenting the programme live each day as well as supervising all of its contents, taking on most of the interviews and editing the serialized book. It was an astonishing offer to make to an inexperienced youngster. Rather pleased by my own audacity, I accepted. It would be hard work and it wasn't well paid, but I was young, I told myself, and I had plenty of energy. I went through the formality of a 'microphone test' and worked my way down a tricky pronunciation list, and somewhat to my surprise I passed. Now that I had the title 'announcer/producer' on my pay slip, my monthly salary would go up to fifty rands – twenty-five pounds. This was not quite the breadline salary it sounds, but – not for the last time in my career – it was less generous than the remuneration of my male colleagues, for the SABC paid its women employees less than the men as a matter of course. This was perfectly legal, and I can't remember that we women felt particularly strongly about it; it was simply an irritating fact of life. But for other employees lower pay was not just a matter of gender. Coloured people got paid considerably less than whites, and black people less still. It would be another thirty years before all South Africans could claim equal pay.

I couldn't quite believe my luck. Here I was, barely out of my teens, catapulted into running my own radio programme on a national network. And my base for this was a sunny office with a wonderful view of the southern Atlantic Ocean. I even had my own secretary – who, to my relief, did not seem to mind taking dictation from a woman several years her junior. My boss, Dewar McCormack, kept a careful eye on me from his office three doors down the corridor. We were all a little scared of him, for he did not suffer fools at all. He had a loud laugh, an Irish temper and a fondness for small glasses of gin at the end of the day. He expected impeccable standards at all times. We had to dress formally at work: all the men wore suits on weekdays, and one of my female colleagues was instructed to wear a hat and gloves each time she went down to the docks with her tape-recorder to meet the Union Castle mailboat.

Dewar was also a stickler for what he called 'correct microphone technique', and I had to be given a crash course in live broadcasting. I was exceedingly nervous, and it was several weeks before I relaxed sufficiently to unwrap my fingers from their grip on the studio table. Dewar taught me how to read from the page without sounding too 'scripted', where and how to breathe (through the nose and not the mouth), and how to turn the page without making a noise (turn it up at opposite corners and lift carefully). I was taught the importance of watching the clock during live interviews, and also how to listen to the answers to your questions, which was a great deal harder than I had imagined. I learned about producing scripted talks, and how to edit them both on paper and on tape. The instruction was basic and rapid, but it was a distillation of some essential broadcasting skills, and I lapped it up.

Woman's World was cosy stuff by today's standards: local celebrity interviews, talks on cooking and child-rearing, regular taped letters from correspondents overseas and a serial reading at the end of the programme – an idea copied from *Woman's Hour* on the BBC. I had to select the book, cut it down to a fraction of its original length and choose the reader. We also quite often used material from what the BBC called its 'Topical Tapes': a monthly miscellany of BBC interviews sent to radio stations around the world. The material was usually good, and sometimes even inspiring. I heard Prokofiev's *Romeo and Juliet* ballet music for the first time on one of these tapes, followed by an interview with Rudolph Nureyev and Margot Fonteyn, who had just performed in the première of Kenneth Macmillan's new version of the ballet at Covent Garden. As the tape spooled past me on the massive playback machine I listened enchanted, and made sure there was a large space in our programme for the whole sequence. I remember, too, an interview with the brand new member of parliament for Finchley in north London, Margaret Thatcher, who spoke about the poor representation of women at Westminster. She sounded young and enthusiastic – almost girlish.

My fellow broadcasters turned out to be a friendly and easy-going lot. One or two of them were conspicuously British. The most eccentric was John Reeves, a florid-faced man with iron-grey hair and pebble glasses who had once, as he constantly reminded us, been Her Majesty's Consul in the Portuguese enclave of Macao in south-east China – where, we learned, he had almost single-handedly fought off the communist insurgents. He and his wife Tess gave riotous parties to which we were all invited: plenty of cheap booze and grilled chicken were served, with rice dyed in patriotic stripes of red, white and blue. One of John's broadcasting jobs was to compère the live Sunday afternoon classical music recitals in front of an audience. He welcomed them into the foyer at Sea Point wearing a black opera cloak lined with red silk, and twirling a silver-topped cane. During the week, less flamboyantly dressed, he introduced the daily classical record requests which preceded my programme, and as I waited for four o'clock I listened to John's adventures in the consular service. Once in Macao he had escaped death by inches when the whole place was shot up by machine guns. Keeping his eye on the door and his back to the wall, he had dived under the table just in time. We all imagined that John, of whom we were very fond, had spent too long reading the Macao section of Errol Flynn's autobiography, My Wicked Wicked Ways, in which some remarkably similar incidents took place. Another émigré from Britain, Ralph Elliot, had served in the Royal Navy during the war and had found himself in Cape Town as part of the crew of a tugboat. He was said to have stepped straight off the boat into a successful audition for the SABC.

One of the daily duties Ralph and John Reeves shared was the reading of the regional news. This required a decent grasp of Afrikaans place names and surnames, which neither of them had. They discovered a fine disguise: a difficult word would be rendered virtually inaudible if you allowed the corner of your script to brush the edge of the microphone at the appropriate moment. Their Afrikaans avoidance technique was successful for years; there were no complaints – indeed, few people bothered to listen carefully to the local news, which consisted largely of an endless list of agricultural prices. It was a ruse I never had a chance to attempt, as women's voices were deemed inappropriate for reading even the regional news.

We assumed we were broadcasting to a largely white audience. The SABC had a separate radio service for blacks called Radio Bantu, staffed largely by black people but under close white supervision. It produced, as its own publicity material had it, 'talks of an informative and educational nature ... including Bantu speakers discussing the Homelands [where Dr Verwoerd wanted them all to end up], and valuable gardening and agricultural hints'. Their carefully controlled agenda was quite different from that of the programmes aimed at whites. The minister of posts and telegraphs, Dr Albert Hertzog – the man who rejected television – had assured parliament in 1960 that 'the taste of a white man is not the taste of a Bantu. We live in totally different spheres; you can almost say that we live in different civilizations.' White people did listen to Radio Bantu, however, and did so for its hugely enjoyable music programmes. It was a way of hearing the latest 'township' jazz or 'kwela' music – the sort of music you could hear in the city streets, where it was often played on a simple penny whistle. The music programmes were lively and addictive, and it didn't matter to white listeners that they were introduced in a language they could not understand. Sadly, none of them was produced in the Cape Town studios; Radio Bantu was broadcast from Johannesburg. The only brown or black people we saw worked in the canteen, or among the cleaning or messenger staff.

At that time – and right up to the 1980s – it was not unusual for whites to refer to middle-aged black employees as 'girls' and 'boys' – as in 'my girl in the kitchen' and 'the garden boy', though I don't recall my parents using those terms. In return the employers

Colonial life – my father, his mother and sister Betty, about 1917.

My father and the stuffed alligator: Kuala Lumpur, about 1918.

My maternal grandfather, the Reverend J. C. MacGregor, in Fordyce, Banffshire, Scotland, about 1912.

Taking a bath – aged two.

Aged six with my mother: Wheatley, near Oxford.

A letter to me from my father and one home from boarding school, aged six. Somehow the second line does not have the ring of truth.

Page 1.
THE NATIONAL HOSPITAL.
QUEEN SQUARE. W.C.1.
FOR THE RELIEF AND CURE OF DISEASES OF THE
NERVOUS SYSTEM INCLUDING PARALYSIS AND EPILEPSY.

Wednesday 29th September 1948

My Darling Susie,
          We miss you so much. You
must have been much _much_ bigger than we thought
you were as the house seems very _very_ empty
without you--just like that hungry horse.
     I expect the next time we see you that you
                    will look something like this:-

Oct: 2nd   Barham Lodge
                              Weybridge

Dear Mummy,
          I hope you are well.
I love this School very
much. How is Daddy ? We
have a lovely Climbing
Frame, and two swings !
I'm doing Jim on Tuesday..
How many more day till
the end of term ? I think
46. Please send my Plast-
acine (or bag).

     Love
     Susan M.

MENU
VEGETABLE SOUP.
COLD CHICKEN SALAD
CRÊME A LA SUDDIE
COFFE
NUTS
DRINKS — SHERRY, WHITE —
WHINE, GIN, BRANDY,
RUM, PASSION FRUIT
AMEN
S.M.

My suggested menu, aged eight,
showing an early interest in alcoholic
refreshment.

My father and me: Miller's Point,
South Africa, 1949.

My mother, me and the black Oldsmobile,
on holiday, probably in 1950.
Aged ten, with Kirsty aged thirteen months.
Me and chubby Kirsty.

My father and the ever-affectionate Sadko.

HERSCHEL SCHOOL
CLAREMONT
CAPE

February 14th, 1956

Dear Mrs MacGregor,

       I regret having to let you know that on Saturday night after "lights out" Susan, with others, climbed over the balcony rail, walked round on the outside of it and then across a narrow wall with no hand-hold, to the other side of the quadrangle.

       This I consider to have been most dangerous to herself, apart from the responsibility devolving on me, should an accident have occurred and I feel it only fair to let you know that it happened and that I think it sufficiently serious to say that should anything further of this kind occur, I shall feel unable to accept the responsibility of having her in the boarding house.

       In view of the lack of responsibility for herself I shall be unable to allow her to go out other than with you or me (with Mrs Steyn as my deputy).

       I have told her all this and that I should let you know what I had said to her.

       I am more than sorry that this has happened, but I know that I shall have your support and co-operation.

       With kind regards.

       Yours sincerely,

My headmistress and her unruly pupil.

Presenting *Woman's World* in
South Africa. Mid 1960s,
judging by the hairstyle!
(Bryan Wharton)

Leaving Cape Town, 1967.

With the writer Mary Renault and her
musical box: Cape Town 1965.
(James de Villiers)

The egg-frying incident at Piccadilly Circus, 1969, with a
colleague guarding the Uher tape recorder.
(Mirrorpix 2002)

My mother, circa 1970.

My friend Desmond Bowes-Taylor
took this 'glamour' pic in about 1973.

were always addressed as 'Master' and 'Madam'. It was 'Master' that I objected to strongly when I first came home from London in 1961; after that the 'maid', whoever she was, was encouraged to call my father 'Doctor'. A tiny semantic triumph, but I thought it an important one.

The control of the Afrikaner elite over the majority black population in South Africa in the 1960s was absolute. Few of us imagined that this could be changed overnight. In the early sixties not even Helen Suzman's Progressive party – she had broken away from the old United party in 1959 – wanted immediate universal franchise. In white politics, only the Liberal party was unequivocal in its promotion of universal suffrage, and many of its members were technically banned, which meant they were prohibited from being in gatherings of more than two people. I cared deeply about the country and its politics, but in one very real sense I wasn't a true South African: I had not been born there. My passport was British and I had no vote. This annoyed the local SABC regional director, Dr Burgers, who called me up to his office at least once a year to discuss the matter. 'Susan,' he said, staring hard at me, 'don't you think it's time you got rid of that British nationality and applied for a South African passport? Why don't you do it? It makes sense.' I always made some vague reference to giving the idea my full consideration, but the truth was that I could not contemplate swearing any sort of allegiance to the South African state of the 1960s. I also wanted to hang on to a passport that was acceptable around the world.

If you lived in South Africa it was not possible, whatever the colour of your skin, to avoid the laws of separation, but none of us openly criticized 'the system' at work: like most of my contemporaries, I reserved conversation about the absurdities and injustices of apartheid to safer ground. It was easier to express disapproval sitting with close friends around the supper table; otherwise 'politics' could soon deteriorate into the sort of furious argument that ended with doors slammed and friendships ended. Apartheid was an unjust system, certainly, and often a brutal one, but one was constantly reminded at election time that most white South Africans supported it. We who opposed it, but not bravely enough to go to gaol for our opposition, tried our best to treat black and brown people with courtesy and sympathy, but few of us knew a single black or Coloured person as a friend. Active opposition to apartheid offered three options. You could fight from within the system, and support a legal political party – but one step over the line and you risked gaol. You could leave the country voluntarily to fight apartheid from abroad, as many did. Or you could stay, wholeheartedly reject the system, and take part in activities which would inevitably end in banning, gaol or enforced political exile. This had happened to several people we knew. It was dangerously conspicuous to be a politically active radical in the South Africa of the sixties.

There was one white politician my close friends and I strongly admired: Helen Suzman. She seemed to us to be the only MP with the courage to speak out against the injustices of the system – indeed, at one point she was the sole member of her party in parliament. She took a particular interest in black political prisoners and campaigned for them to receive more humane treatment. In this she was eventually remarkably successful. Through her intervention and her personal visits to Robben Island, including to Nelson Mandela, prisoners were allowed to read books for the first time, to enjoy a slightly improved diet and to receive visitors more often. Virtually all her campaigning work was ignored by the SABC news bulletins: opposition politicians were seldom given airtime. The news editors' idea of a politically important story generally meant an unedited version of a cabinet minister's latest pronouncement.

Years later I spoke to two Afrikaners of different generations, both of them former SABC staff members, about how they had viewed the political control of the Corporation's news output, and the iron grip of the Broederbond over current affairs broadcasts. One former news editor was an unreformed supporter of the old system. 'We believed', he told me stiffly, 'that the news must not be used by anyone to foment friction between different communities. Remember, the nineteen-sixties was the period of Uhuru in Africa – emancipation for blacks north of our borders. We supported apartheid because it was a way of avoiding sharing power. We also believed in respecting authority.' A woman of a younger generation who had worked as a parliamentary reporter in Cape Town was appalled, she said, by the memory of her family's support for apartheid; but – her voice shook as she told me – it was simply not done for Afrikaans-speaking journalists working for the SABC to question the status quo. Such was the acceptance of the system that politics were simply not discussed, not even round the family dinner table. 'As an Afrikaner you felt you were a soldier. If you loved your country, you would do anything to fight the spectre of communism. You had an absolute duty to do so. The alternative was chaos – the destruction of your beloved country. We complied.'

One SABC announcer who broke the rules just before I joined the corporation experienced the wrath of the authorities within minutes of his transgression. Robert del Kyrke was a former actor, good-looking, with a mellifluous voice. He had his own record request programme broadcast countrywide from the Cape Town studios. One afternoon he read out a greeting from a listener to fellow members of the Black Sash organization – the group of women who protested regularly at official events. 'Well done, girls,' said Robert, 'keep up the good work.' The telephone rang in the office of the regional boss on the fifth floor. It was Johannesburg on the line: head office. Had he heard the appalling gaffe in studio P2? Del Kyrke was sacked the moment the programme came to an end. He never broadcast again, and lived on in Cape Town in circumstances of some hardship.

The main news bulletins of the day, in both English and

Afrikaans, were produced and read in Johannesburg. Each evening the national radio news at seven o'clock was followed by a five-minute talk, anonymously presented. This slot, called simply *Current Affairs*, gave a chilling insight into the government's thinking. In 1963 these talks were written and introduced by a man called Ivor Benson, or 'Dr Ivor Goebbels', as the South African *Sunday Times* called him. He was later to move to Rhodesia, where as Ian Smith's information adviser he was paid by the Rhodesian government a salary more generous than that of the prime minister himself. In South Africa he was employed to convince the English-speaking radio audience of the inevitable rightness of apartheid – although curiously it was never called apartheid on the SABC. A couple of years earlier the director of programmes, Douglas Fuchs, had ordered that the term should be replaced by the phrase 'separate development', which was used by Dr Verwoerd himself during the Commonwealth conference of 1960.

Ivor Benson delivered his message in clipped and sneering tones. He regularly referred to South Africa's 'difficult' role in the world, and to the necessity of closing ranks against the communist enemy. Pulling together like this was 'an exciting and inspiring' idea: 'that our little nation should have been called upon by Providence to stand in the very front lines of a struggle that involves the fate of all mankind . . . it is a thought that should make us proud and happy to be South Africans . . . When we fight communism, or liberalism, which is a diluted form of the same thing, we fight for our own faith. The war against communism is ultimately a religious war in which the very thing which makes life worth living is at stake.' I often visited my parents for an evening meal, and whenever we heard Ivor Benson's opening sallies after the news bulletin one of us would rush to switch him off; but he no doubt had his many thousands of devoted listeners among the white population. The SABC published his five-minute talks, perfect reflections of government thinking, for sale in booklet form under the title *Know Your Enemy*.

Blatantly biased broadcasts such as Benson's were relatively new to the SABC. The Corporation had been set up in 1936 with the help of the BBC's John Reith himself, who had visited South Africa to advise on how a national broadcasting organization could be put into place. During the Second World War the SABC – like General Smuts' government – had been firmly on the side of the allies: so firmly, indeed, that German music was forbidden. Hundreds of recordings of works by Bach, Beethoven and Brahms were deliberately ruined by having their surfaces heavily scratched with a sharp instrument; other recordings were simply dropped from a height on to a concrete floor. In its annual report in 1950 the SABC stated that its news service had 'no editorial angle or policy'; its aim was 'presenting South African and world news correctly and objectively'. By 1961, with Dr Verwoerd heading the government, things were very different. The annual report now announced proudly that Radio South Africa was taking steps 'to promote the survival of the bounteous heritage of the White people of the Republic of South Africa'. In 1964 this became a mission to reflect the 'increasing parity of thought, action and sentiment of [the] two equal cultural components of one White Christian-Western African nation'. Clearly the culture and aspirations of the black people of South Africa were now deemed largely irrelevant in a world ruled by whites. To minimize the temptation for blacks to listen to the anti-South African broadcasts coming from across the border on shortwave, the government arranged that FM frequency radios would be available cheaply on which you could hear only the SABC, and no foreign broadcasts.

There were parliamentary objections to the way the Corporation was going: one member of the United party, Etienne Malan, kept up a chorus of criticism of the SABC for being an agent of Nationalist propaganda, but the government retorted that the broadcasting organization was perfectly entitled to defend South Africa 'against the Frankenstein monster of one man one vote'. The press, particularly the English-language press, did report these parliamentary debates, but the restrictions on quoting 'banned' people meant that most of us had only a hazy idea of the names of the political radicals. Robben Island, where so many of them were incarcerated, was only a few miles out to sea from the Cape Town docks: you could see its bleak, flat shape quite clearly from the slopes of Table Mountain. The stretch of sea between the island and the shore was cold and treacherous, and the currents were strong: it was impossible to escape.

At first we knew next to nothing of Nelson Mandela, apart from the fact that he was a prominent member of the ANC; we had read his name in the newspapers, but knew little of what he stood for. He had been arrested in 1962 after a secret visit to Europe, and sentenced to five years in gaol for incitement and leaving the country without a passport. In 1963 he was imprisoned on Robben Island, and less than two years later his sentence was increased to life imprisonment. He was found guilty with half a dozen others of planning sabotage, and might well have been given the death sentence. Several of Mandela's co-accused members of the ANC had been arrested on a farm in Rivonia, then a quiet suburb to the north of Johannesburg. In what became known as the Rivonia trial, Mandela made from the dock his famous and moving reference to the fight for a democratic and free society – an ideal for which, 'if needs be', he was prepared to die. The speech was reported in full in the English-language press. In 1963, just before the second batch of arrests, I had spent a long weekend in Rivonia with my old friend Caroline Syfret, now newly married to an Englishman, Bob Kingdon. As we walked their basset hound down a peaceful road in the autumn sunshine, we had little idea of what momentous political plotting was going on in the small farmhouse building a few hundred yards away.

After a year of living in the hot little flat in Kloof Street I moved into Claremont, a suburb of Cape Town on the far side of the mountain from the city, where a journalist friend, Gorry

Gordon-Bagnall, had found a charming and slightly dilapidated five-bedroomed Victorian house. It was big enough for four young women, including me, to join her there, and Claremont was a pleasant place to live. Parts of it were still multiracial: Coloured families, many of them from the Cape Malay community, lived in little pockets of houses next to their white neighbours. There was a mosque on the main street, and you could hear the muezzin call the Muslims to prayer each morning from the top of its tiny minaret. This call was, unusually, played on an old gramophone record; you could hear a tiny repetitive click behind it each time the faithful were summoned. From the Vineyard Fruit Supply in Protea Road opposite the house, run by Mr Mohamed and his family, we could buy grapes, avocado pears, melons, mielies – South African corn – and peaches. In the busy main road a couple of hundred yards away there were tiny shops and cafés, Cape Malay tailors and dry cleaners, and an old fashioned department store called Henshilwoods, from which a few years earlier my mother had obtained my school uniform and ordered Cash's name tapes.

Our house, number 1 Kildare Road, had a sheltered patio at the back with an old fig tree. Three of the five of us had been at school together, so had no objection to sharing a small kitchen and one bathroom. I ran a taxi service into town each morning for as many as could squeeze into my tiny Hillman Imp. We entertained regularly and quite a number of boyfriends were in evidence, though 'staying over' was usually confined to Saturday nights. The sun warmed the house and made it seem a benign old place; we acquired a tabby cat called Wolsey who lazed about on the patio.

The population of 1 Kildare Road changed gradually as residents came and went. Gorry Gordon-Bagnall was not with us for long – she left to marry a successful local photographer, Desmond Bowes-Taylor, who was as different from the average white South African male as it is possible to be: a firm royalist who wore a waistcoat, bow tie and watch chain, and was a very skilful cook.

Everyone else in the house, including my closest remaining friends, Joy Forwell and Sally Williams, eventually left to get married: only I stayed resolutely single. One of the early residents, a journalist from Rhodesia called Kathy Bowman, was friendly with a quiet young lawyer called Albie Sachs. We all knew Albie was a committed political liberal, but it was not until we read one morning in the papers that he had been arrested that we knew how deeply involved in radical politics he was. Polite, almost shy, he had seemed reluctant to discuss his own political ideas with us in any detail; now we learned that Albie was an active member of the banned African National Congress. He was held without charge for 168 days under the so-called 'ninety-day' law, which meant that detainees could be released and immediately re-arrested. Eventually he went into exile in Mozambique, where the South African security police sent him a letter bomb that blew off his arm; he almost lost his life. He is now a judge and a member of the Constitutional Court of South Africa.

Albie Sachs has written movingly about his experiences in gaol, but at the time we faint-hearted liberals knew little or nothing of what he had gone through. It was an offence to publish any honest account of conditions in South African prisons; in 1965 the *Rand Daily Mail* and its editor were prosecuted for a series of articles giving a graphic account of life as a black political prisoner.

For whites who were not prepared to commit themselves to the struggle, it was possible to make tiny gestures of defiance. It was a sign of the more relaxed attitude to apartheid in some parts of Cape Town that multiracial cafés and nightclubs existed. They did not advertise themselves, but could be found through word of mouth; they were popular with both students and some of the more adventurous white adults. The Naaz Café in the vibrant neighbourhood known as District Six was owned by Cape Malays and served excellent curry; after the more conventional forms of segregated entertainment closed down it was possible to dance and drink at the Naaz till the early hours. The lighting was dim, but any visitor could see that the clientele was racially mixed. It was wise to keep an eye on the door, for the police raided it from time to time, and thought nothing of piling half a dozen people into the back of a van and incarcerating them overnight for flouting the segregation laws. There was also Marguerite's, a cheap nightclub run by a burly transvestite who pretended to be French. Here I ate my first and I think only plateful of horsemeat, after ordering what did seem remarkably cheap fillet steak. It had an interesting taste – tender and rather sweet. Down near the docks there was an altogether rougher place, the Navigator's Den, where visiting sailors came and where prostitutes did good business, and where you had to take your glass of wine with you on to the dance floor: anything left on the table disappeared. But wherever we spent our leisure hours, at the end of the evening it was time to return home, back to our segregated lives.

Sometimes the local social scene was further enlivened by a distinguished visitor from abroad. When the Irish actor and writer Micheál Mac Liammóir came to Cape Town with his one-man show about Oscar Wilde, he was introduced to my parents, and he and my father took to each other immediately; it became what Micheál called 'the strangest and swiftest friendship I have ever known'. He spent many evenings at Farthings, a flamboyant figure always fully made up and with carefully dyed black hair. He entertained my parents with theatrical stories, sitting with the family cat on his knee. Chotty, the grey tabby to whom I was specially attached, impressed Micheál sufficiently – 'a profound and handsome cat' – to merit a mention in one of his autobiographical books. But it was my father who impressed the Irishman most of all; for years afterwards he wrote assiduously to Jim, and sent him a fond telegram each Christmas. In his book *An Oscar of No Importance* he described my father as 'a shrewd, outwardly unremarkable, pleasant-featured Scot; a typical doctor, a typical family man, with a delightful wife and two intelligent children. Our views on life were as opposed as views can be,' he wrote.

'He was a man of science, I an avowed, old-fashioned aesthete. He was an atheist, I a believer in God . . . there was a great deal to talk about. We talked, endlessly, about art and life and death and friendship and love and all the rest of it. And with him I was shown all the natural beauties of that Eden-like country.' He was just in time: by the mid-1960s the cultural boycott ensured that almost no one of his stature was to visit South Africa for another quarter of a century.

Only one theatre in Cape Town was determinedly multiracial. The Luxurama in Plumstead, which was built and owned by the Quibell brothers, was a huge place, garishly decorated with highly coloured stained glass. It was really a local variety theatre, but visiting British artists performed here too, taking advantage of its multiracial status and hoping that the British actors' union Equity would overlook their appearances in segregated theatres elsewhere. (What became universally known in South Africa as the 'Equity ban' had begun in 1961 with a prohibition by the Musicians' Union on its members playing in segregated venues, and was taken up by British playwrights in 1963.) At first this seemed to work. Dame Vera Lynn came to the Luxurama, while Cliff Richard and the Shadows did a season at the segregated Alhambra theatre in the centre of town. I managed to get a backstage pass to the Alhambra and watched the whole Cliff Richard show from the wings, and was thrilled when the drummer Bruce Bennett winked at me. Kirsty, now thirteen, was hugely envious.

Things got more difficult when Dusty Springfield and Adam Faith came over. I was sent by the SABC to interview them in turn soon after their arrival. Faith was all easy charm, but Springfield, who was famously 'difficult', was less willing to talk; she gave the impression of someone trapped in a schedule – part segregated, part multiracial – which she had not fully thought through. As she began her tour at the Luxurama, she declared that she would continue only if she performed before mixed audiences. Her local promoter had other ideas: she must complete her contractual obligations, which included some segregated theatres. In the face of protests from Equity at home and local activists in South Africa, she and subsequently Adam Faith cut short their visits and went home, pursued by the local and foreign press. Soon after this brouhaha all visits by popular British artists, including theatrical troupes, stopped altogether. It was the beginning of a long period of cultural isolation for South Africa.

Apartheid in entertainment had its bizarre and wretched implications for local people too. Mixed audiences and mixed casts were generally forbidden, except with special permission from government. Permits were granted from time to time, though usually with great reluctance. In 1965 the SABC's director of programmes requested permission for a Coloured baritone, Victor Swartz, to sing with the all-white SABC Orchestra in a concert in a Coloured township; special dispensation was requested for a similar date for a Coloured pianist, Jan Volkwyn, with the all-white Johannesburg Symphony Orchestra.

Eventually permission was granted for both artists, provided no social mixing took place and that there were separate toilet facilities. The Cape Town branch of the Union of Jewish Women had no such luck. For twenty years they had organized an annual concert in the City Hall to which physically handicapped and underprivileged children and orphans of all races were invited. Now all sorts of new rules were insisted upon: separate entrances for the white and non-white children, separate seating, separate toilet facilities and no refreshments for the non-whites. The UJW decided not to attempt to comply, and arranged separate parties at private homes for the Coloured and African children.

Two regular light entertainment broadcasters at the SABC studios in Cape Town, Donald Monat and June Dixon, came up with their own solution to the 'no mixing on stage' problem. They had hired a Coloured singer, Maude Damons, for a regular slot in their new series of variety shows recorded before an audience. When they were told Miss Damons could not perform on stage with white musicians before a white audience, they recorded her contributions separately and spliced them into the taped show. The listening audience at home had no idea she was Coloured and probably few of them would have cared; but the sensibilities of the SABC's management had been catered for. I can remember laughing with colleagues at the madness of all this. Soon afterwards, Monat and Dixon left South Africa, and what had been a financially rewarding career for them, to try their luck in Canada.

By the mid-1960s the Group Areas Act – the law which ensured separate living areas for whites and blacks – was beginning to bite hard. In the Cape this particularly affected the Coloureds, many of whom had for generations lived in 'mixed' areas. Black people, rigidly controlled by the hated pass system, were largely kept out of the way in their own townships. Now Coloured people began to be systematically dispossessed of their homes in the 'mixed' areas, and this affected our neighbours in Claremont. Hundreds of families who had lived next door to whites were forced to move either to areas already designated as 'Coloured', or to brand new townships on the sandy, windswept Cape Flats, a long way from decent amenities. The original Group Areas legislation, which dated back more than a dozen years, was given a strange moral justification by the government: it would 'remove friction' between the races. In reality it caused desperate misery.

Some of our Coloured neighbours quietly went to other 'mixed' suburbs in poorer areas, only to be moved again. Mr Mohamed left Protea Road, though he continued to run his business in the Vineyard Fruit Supply. White property developers seized the opportunity and moved in: attractive cottages were renovated, whitewashed, given a small garden and a patio, and sold at a huge profit – to whites. One energetic renovator was Joyce Waring, the wife of the minister of tourism Frank Waring, one of the few members of the Nationalist government with an English-speaking background. Two families defied the apartheid laws and stayed, and got away with it: the Laloos, who were Indian, and Abdullah Tief Dawood, a Cape Malay, who ran a general dealer's store a hundred yards from our house and lived above the shop. He stayed, prospered, and sent all his children to university. More than three decades later Mr Dawood and his shop are still there.

The most notorious mass forced removal in Cape Town involved District Six, an area close to the centre of the city regarded by most Capetonians with a mixture of nervousness and affection. Since the nineteenth century it had housed a polyglot and multiracial community, though most of the people there were Coloured. On the streets of District Six you heard both Afrikaans and English, and a mixture of the two known locally as *straattaal* – 'street language' – all spoken with a distinctive sing-song local accent. The square mile of streets was narrow and messy; many of the buildings, both commercial premises and private homes, were in a poor condition, owned by absentee landlords who collected the rent and did not bother with maintenance. There was certainly crime there, and organized gangs – but there were also plenty of shops, small businesses, cafés and noisy hawkers, and District Six was a cheerful place to live. Many of its families had been there since the nineteenth century. In 1966 it was declared a white area, and over a period of fifteen years the entire population was removed. Sixty thousand people were rehoused on the Cape Flats, and the whole square mile of District Six was gradually demolished and flattened. All that was left was desolation, rather like a poorly cleared bomb site, with two churches and a mosque sticking up above the rubble. This time, though, the developers were denied their profits. There were too many influential protestors, appalled by what had happened, to allow the local council to create a smart new suburb; everyone knew that any new business would be boycotted. A brand new technical college crept into one corner of the site, but otherwise the area has remained empty for over twenty years. A process is now under way of recognizing land claims by the original residents, and there is hope that eventually District Six will be at least partially restored.

The way the South African state classified its racial groups would have been comical if it had not had such devastating impact. Your racial status defined your life, but there were many hundreds of thousands of people who did not obviously belong to any single group. If someone's ancestry was racially mixed, it was not always possible to say if he or she was white, Coloured, black or Indian. It was even whispered in the 1960s that Dr Verwoerd's wife Betsie had Coloured blood: you only had to look at her. The same muttered taunt was applied to many 'white' members of parliament on both sides of the House. The all-important Population Registration Act of 1950 (amended in 1962) defined a white person as 'a person who in appearance obviously is, or is generally accepted as, a white person, but does not include a person who although in appearance obviously a white person, is generally accepted as a Coloured person . . . [provided that] . . . a person who in appearance is a white person shall for the purposes of the Act be presumed to be a white person until the contrary is proved'. In 1967 these tortuous definitions were expanded to include the provision that 'the Cape Coloured group shall consist of persons who are, except in the case of persons who are members of a race or tribe referred to elsewhere, generally accepted as members of the race or class known as Cape Coloured.'

Many South Africans applied to be reclassified as a member of a different racial group, most frequently from Coloured to white. But if one parent was white and one Coloured, then the person was likely to be 'downgraded' to Coloured. If one parent was Coloured and the other black, then the person might be 'downgraded' to black. The reclassification process involved the careful examination of hair, earlobes, eyes and fingernails. One of the early tests was called the 'pencil test': if a pencil was inserted in wiry black hair and stayed there, then the owner of the hair was black; if it fell out, he or she was probably Coloured. It was no exaggeration to say that upon the decision of the examiners depended someone's entire future happiness: if the decision went the wrong way, total disruption of your life followed. Your job, where you lived, whom you could marry – all depended on your racial status. It was not unknown for the victim of a decision that went the wrong way to commit suicide. Sometimes brothers and sisters in the same family had different racial classifications. This tragic theme was taken up by Athol Fugard in his first popular play, *The Blood Knot*. After it was produced in England in 1961, Fugard's passport was taken away and he was unable to travel. The restrictions were not lifted for another ten years.

Nineteen sixty-six marked two extraordinary events in South Africa. In June that year Senator Bobby Kennedy came to Cape Town, having been invited to address the university students by the president of the National Union of South African Students, Ian Robertson. The visit caused intense excitement among liberal South Africans. At that time few internationally known political figures visited the country: South Africa's isolation had increased to such an extent that Dr Verwoerd proudly referred to the country as 'the polecat of the world'. That the brother of the assassinated American president, a man closely associated with the American civil rights movement, should come to address what was essentially a student gathering was astonishing. The students of Cape Town University had a long record of protest against the apartheid regime, and Kennedy was invited as keynote speaker at a meeting in the university's main hall marking seven years since the passing of the University Extension Act. Despite its name, this was a piece of legislation which further restricted the admission of Coloureds and blacks to South African universities.

On the night of 6 June 1966 the university campus was seething. The Jameson Hall with its Corinthian columns, where the Kennedy speech was to be delivered, was packed, and thousands more had gathered outside to listen on the public address system. I was there with three SABC colleagues. We had been unable to get tickets for seats in the hall but were happy to wait with the crowds outside. Students from the rival Afrikaans university Stellenbosch arrived in large numbers – mainly, we assumed, to make trouble. Inside the hall the academic procession was led by a symbolically extinguished torch of academic freedom. The student leader Ian Robertson was unable to be present, for as a 'banned' person he was forbidden to attend any sort of gathering: an empty chair was left on the platform as a reminder of his absence. Bobby Kennedy was introduced to the packed hall by the head of the students' representative council, Charles Diamond. Outside, we strained to hear what was being said. Then suddenly the public address system stuttered and fell silent: someone had cut the wires. Was it the security forces? Or the Stellenbosch students? We never found out, but the Kennedy speech was published the following day. Today the words sound unremarkable, even trite, but they moved his audience deeply: there were echoes of Mandela's courtroom speech of three years earlier. 'This is a day of affirmation,' he said,

> a celebration of liberty. The enlargement of liberty for individual human beings must be the supreme goal and the abiding practice of any Western society. The first element of this individual liberty is the freedom of speech, the right to express and communicate ideas, to set oneself apart from the dumb beasts of field and forests, the right to recall governments to their duties and to their obligations. Above all, the right to affirm one's membership and allegiance to the body politic, to society . . . All this can be swept away by a government which does not heed the demands of its people, and I mean all of the people.

It was heady stuff, and his audience in the hall held their breath. But the police remained outside; I expect they, like the rest of us not in the hall, had heard not a word of it.

Afterwards an official motorcycle escort took the senator and his wife Ethel back to their Cape Town hotel. My three friends and I followed in a state of high excitement and we managed to reach the Mount Nelson Hotel shortly after he did. Bobby and Ethel came out and chatted to us briefly. It was an extraordinarily emotional moment for me: here I was grasping a Kennedy by the hand. I told him that I had once caught a glimpse of his brother Jack when he and Jackie had visited London and waved from a motorcade. After we slipped away, I wondered how the SABC would cover the senator's brief visit, and the speech itself. As it turned out, they ignored it. They simply airbrushed Robert Kennedy out of their news and current affairs schedules. Not a word about his presence in South Africa ever made it on to the airwaves. Like the black political prisoners, he had become a non-person.

As for where had I been when President Kennedy was shot, two and a half years earlier, I can recall exactly: I was sitting in a kitchen in a simple house in Knysna, a pretty coastal town a few hours' drive from Cape Town. I had been sent by Dewar McCormack on a five-day trip along South Africa's 'Garden Route' – an area of great natural beauty, dotted with forests and cut through by rivers and lagoons – to record interviews with some of the local 'characters', including Anne Ziegler and Webster Booth, two popular British singers who had retired there. My recording engineer and I based ourselves in a hotel on the Knysna lagoon, and attempted some water-skiing between assignments. We had an appointment one evening with a local man, Jalmar Thesen, who ran a well-known timber firm and had written a book about some of the early inhabitants of the area, the *strandlopers* or 'beach-walkers' – indigenous people who survived off what they could catch from the sea shore. He insisted we stay for dinner. His radio was on in the kitchen as we sat down to eat around nine. Halfway through the meal our conversation and the radio programme in the background were interrupted by a series of loud beeps.

An emergency announcement told us that President Kennedy was dead: he had been shot by a sniper in a Dallas motorcade. I caught my breath in shock; it was momentous news. But my two companions continued eating their supper as if nothing had happened. To most white South Africans JFK had been a distant and not particularly sympathetic figure. Like a lot of young people of my age around the world, I admired him greatly. While I was still in London I had watched the series of televised debates between him and Richard Nixon during the 1960 presidential campaign. But Dr Albert Hertzog had been depressingly right: with no television, the outside world – its personalities and its ideas – made little impact on most South Africans.

Three months after Bobby Kennedy's visit to Cape Town, something happened which not even the SABC could ignore; it was to change South Africa's political history. On the afternoon of 6 September 1966 the lower house of parliament, the all-white House of Assembly, was packed to hear what would undoubtedly be a long speech by the prime minister Dr Verwoerd. He did not address parliament all that frequently, and whenever he did, he usually had something important to say. At about a quarter past two, as members were settling into their seats, a parliamentary messenger approached the prime minister; he seemed to have a note in his hand. It was not a note. The man produced a knife, raised it above his head and stabbed Verwoerd four times with huge slashing strokes. The prime minister slumped to the floor, bleeding heavily; his attacker was pulled away and punched by members of parliament so hard that his nose was broken. P. W. Botha, then minister of defence, rushed across the floor to the opposition MP Helen Suzman and wagged his finger in her face. 'You did it!' he screeched at her. 'It was you liberals who did this!' Verwoerd was rushed to an ambulance, but he was declared dead soon after he arrived at the hospital.

By this time it was a quarter to three in the afternoon. I was in my office out at the Sea Point studios of the SABC preparing my programme when word spread of the astonishing news about to be broadcast on all the networks: the prime minister had been assassinated. I could not pretend I was sorry. I visited my colleagues in their offices along the corridor. Most of them were shocked, and some of them even wept in their distress. Normal programmes were hurriedly cancelled and replaced by solemn music. There were tales later of jubilation among the Coloured people in the streets of Cape Town, but I never met anyone who witnessed it; they were probably careful to preserve their joy until they were comfortably at home. BBC television accidentally omitted to broadcast the news as it flashed around the world: the caption 'South African prime minister assassinated' was about to be superimposed on pictures of a race meeting when someone noticed that the caption writer had left one 's' out of 'assassinated'. It was two hours before the news broke in a BBC television news bulletin.

The assassin turned out to be a half-Greek, half-Swazi Mozambican called Demitrio Tsafendas – Verwoerd's killer was of mixed race, though he had presumably been passed as white when he applied for the job. He had a history of mental illness and imprisonment for illegally crossing borders; it was almost unbelievable that he had been taken on as a temporary messenger in the parliamentary building. It was arranged that Tsafendas would go on trial on 17 October in the Supreme Court in Cape Town before the judge president of the Cape, Andries Beyers. Beyers was a great bear of a man, a rough Afrikaner often mistaken for a Coloured fisherman when he was off duty and wearing his battered shorts. He was a brilliant lawyer and considered to be a fair judge – and he was no supporter of apartheid in his court: for years he had allowed Coloured people to sit in areas normally reserved for whites, and for this momentous trial things were to be no different. He ordered the court officials to allow anyone to sit where he or she wished.

The world's press descended on Cape Town, expecting a long

105

drawn-out legal affair, and a fascinating one. Here was a murder trial for the connoisseur: the prime minister of South Africa killed by a knife-wielding messenger of mixed race as he prepared to speak in parliament. Tsafendas' defence team was led by a distinguished liberal lawyer, Wilfred Cooper; he needed a first-class medical expert on his side, and my father agreed to appear for him. Cooper's main argument was that Tsafendas was mentally disturbed and therefore not fit to plead: the defence medical team established that he was convinced his body had been taken over by an enormous tapeworm which talked to him. On the third day of the trial it was my father's turn to enter the witness box to be questioned by Judge Beyers. 'It did not take me long', said my father in his evidence – he had examined Tsafendas several times – 'to realize that this worm was the central theme of his thoughts. It had disorganized his real personality.' Other medical experts told a similar story. The judge president was convinced. On the fourth day he made a dramatic announcement: Demitrio Tsafendas was not fit to plead, and would from now on be held at the state president's pleasure. In other words, he was to be confined to a secure institution for the rest of his life. The trial was over. The whole process had taken well under a week, and the world's press in great disappointment packed up their typewriters and went home.

Tsafendas spent the next twenty-eight years of his life in a series of mental institutions. When the new democratic government came to power in 1994 he was moved to his last place of confinement just north of Johannesburg. There he died, almost forgotten, in 1999.

I made two trips abroad during my time with the SABC. One was to South West Africa, the country that is now Namibia, across South Africa's north-western border. Fortunately, portable tape-recorders had by then become much lighter; I used an efficient German-made machine called a Uher which was easy to operate, weighed a little over twelve pounds and could be slung over your shoulder, though it was still hard work carrying it for any length of time. Dewar McCormack sent me to the country's capital, Windhoek, a town of some anachronistic European charm, set in a bowl of mountains. Its few thousand inhabitants included a thriving German-speaking community, largely left over from the days when South West Africa was a German colony. Each year they laid on a full-dress Munich-style beer carnival, complete with oompah bands and drinking songs, and large flagons of Windhoek beer, and this provided a handy peg on which to hang a series of interviews. I stayed in a miniature Rhineland castle in the centre of town owned by the Levinsons, Jack and Olga. Jack, who had just stepped down as mayor of Windhoek, was a well-to-do businessman with a big interest in industrial diamonds. Olga enthusiastically ran the local arts association, and was a regular correspondent on tape for *Woman's World*. They were generous hosts and lent me their shiny Mercedes with its black chauffeur Johannes. I took my Uher along to the carnival evenings and tried to weave a sound picture out of it all. I also discovered there was a Hollywood film crew working somewhere out in the nearby Namib desert. If I liked, said the Levinsons, I could visit the set. I was flown in a tiny plane across the vast rolling dunes of the Namib to observe some of the filming of *Sands of the Kalahari*, an adventure movie starring George Baker and Susannah York. As I stepped out of the plane the temperature was just under 110 degrees. The actors sat around dressed in tiny cotton towels, while I, still obedient to Dewar McCormack's dress code, tottered about in high heels and a tight cotton suit. Someone took pity on me and I completed the recordings in a towelling dressing gown.

My other trip I arranged myself. It was early in 1966; I was beginning to feel that I had had enough of South African broadcasting and wanted a break in Europe. I took six weeks' leave and boarded an Italian liner, lugging my precious portable Uher with me. I had written careful letters to half a dozen British writers who I hoped might talk to me, despite my South African connections: among them the *Observer* columnist Katharine Whitehorn; the novelist Mary Stewart; Richmal Crompton, the creator of *Just William*; and Enid Blyton. They all agreed to see me – even Miss Blyton, who seldom gave interviews to journalists. Richmal Crompton, who many of her devoted readers must have thought was a man, turned out to be an amusing elderly lady living in Chislehurst. She was still writing her William books, more than forty years after she had created the boy she called affectionately 'my Frankenstein monster'. A former Classics teacher in a girls' school who had taken up writing after a bout of polio had left her partially disabled, she was quite as I expected her to be: warmly humorous and very civilized company. She was particularly proud of the fact that her William books, despite William's idiosyncratic use of the language, were official school textbooks in Germany.

My visit to Enid Blyton's house in Beaconsfield was a great deal more daunting. Miss Blyton's husband, a retired Harley Street consultant who took a keen interest in his wife's literary reputation and her earning ability, insisted on being present throughout our interview. After each of my questions he raised an admonishing hand, preventing his wife from saying anything until he had decided what the answer should be. It was distracting, especially as my questions were utterly innocuous – like 'How did you come to give Noddy his name?' and 'How many languages are you translated into?' One of the most startling responses my questioning elicited was the calm revelation that Miss Blyton's writing method consisted of thinking a bit, and then 'typing out the story without a stop'.

An altogether more complex method of writing was described to me twenty years later, when I spoke to Ruth Rendell for *Conversation Piece* and discovered how one of Britain's foremost detective novelists constructs her work.

Interview with Ruth Rendell, broadcast 24.8.89

SM: How do you plot [your Inspector Wexford novels]? You have a crime. Do you always have a perpetrator in mind when you begin?

RR: For the Wexfords I do have a rather strange technique, since to me the mystery is all. So I have an idea and I have a perpetrator, and I write the book along those lines. And when I get to the last chapter I change the perpetrator so that if I can deceive myself I can deceive the reader. That means that I am obliged to go back and change things. But I do a lot of rewriting anyway. I haven't always done that, but I have for the past few Wexford books, and it works.

SM: To the extent that you're never going to be allowed to let Wexford go, are you?

RR: I'll never kill Wexford, unless I kill him in a novel to be posthumously published. I have thought of doing that, but I've done no more about that than think about it. I'm not going to kill him and get myself in the Sherlock Holmes situation of having to resurrect him. We know what happens when detectives are resurrected. They are never the same.

SM: One feels perhaps that you have more sympathy with the women in your [Barbara Vine] novels? Even if they're the perpetrators?

RR: Well, I am a woman. I like women. Do I like women better than men? You know, I suppose I do. If I had a whole lot of them together in a room and I had to choose one camp I suppose I'd go with the women, yes. It's awful to be the sort of woman who doesn't like her own sex and identifies with the men and wants to please them. So yes, I suppose I feel more sympathy with the women, which seems to be a natural thing to feel.

SM: You also have a keen eye for young people, in particular. Do you do that from observation, from a distance, or do you talk to them about their lives?

RR: I don't ever go out to talk to people in the way an investigative journalist would, for the purposes of my books. For me that would destroy it. If I talk to young people it's just because it happens in one's social life. We have all been young, and really the emotions of young people don't change. What changes is the manners and the customs [of the times] in which they live. I try to be aware of what happens in the world to the young. I have a dread of what happens to ageing writers – which is that they people their novels with old dodderers, which is terribly boring. You should have a big spectrum of ages really in fiction.

SM: People don't mind talking to you about themselves, because at some later time you might take that and put it into a novel?

RR: Well, that's very interesting. You would think that people would never talk about themselves and their personal things to somebody like me. In fact they do it exhaustively; they wait for an opportunity to tell me all. They don't know this, but I don't put real people into fiction unless they're dead. But I do think there may come a time when fiction will be hard to write. Because sadly, when you get old you lose touch, however hard you try to hold on. And I think you see it in the fiction of even really great very old writers. Well, I'm not very great, but I may one day be very old and then I shall give it up and write real things, facts.

Back at Beaconsfield, despite the interruptions, Miss Blyton and I eventually recorded enough questions and agreed answers to make a coherent piece, and I sold the result to *Woman's Hour* in London. It is still in the BBC archives. Listening to the recording now, I'm struck by my 'upper-crust' vowels and the formality of the questioning: but that was how most BBC interviewers sounded at the time. Perhaps I was trying to sound just like them, in case I got the chance to join their ranks one day.

By the beginning of the following year I had made up my mind to return to Britain, at least for a couple of years, and see if I could find some interesting work with BBC radio. It was a decision my parents approved; we were all increasingly unhappy about the political climate in South Africa. Most of my friends and contemporaries had now married, and I was beginning to be very aware that I, in my mid-twenties, had not. I had enjoyed several not very serious love affairs, including one with a handsome young Welsh anaesthetist who was on a year's work experience at Groote Schuur hospital. I had also met and fallen for an officer in the Royal Navy called Richard, who spent two terms of duty based at Simonstown, the local naval headquarters. He, unfortunately for me, was married; but I was very taken with him. In Cape Town in the 1960s it was not unusual for naval officers, stationed there for some months and plied with generous local hospitality, to have affairs with local girls. Usually they came to nothing; but what started as a bit of fun became more important to both of us, and Richard and I grew increasingly attached to each other. There was never any question of his leaving his wife, and I was (as usual) happy to be a free agent; still, we did not assume that our relationship would end when I left the country, and he told me there might be opportunities to meet in London.

I told my bosses at the SABC that I wanted to spend some time in Europe, but that I had every intention of returning. This was not entirely true: I was not at all sure that I would come back. On 12 April 1967, clutching a fat book of press cuttings and a warm letter of recommendation from Dewar McCormack, I set forth on the mailship the SA *Vaal*. On the quayside, as I was about to board, Kirsty hugged me, sobbing, 'Don't go!' We were both surprised by the intensity of her feelings. Twelve days later I was again watching the unloading of a pair of cabin trunks at Southampton docks; but this time there was no one to meet me. I arranged for the trunks to be sent on, and boarded the train for London.

CHAPTER FIVE

The World At One: Enter Sue

Dear Miss MacGregor, We have been informed by Mr Harvey of our Appointments Department that you are interested in the possibility of working for the BBC. Mr Brian Bliss who is Editor of Radio News Features would be pleased to meet you and discuss whether there are any openings in his programmes. Please telephone his office – LANgham 4468 extension 3065.

Letter from BBC Administrative Officer, 15 June 1967

In the spring of 1967 most white South Africans regarded Harold Wilson's Britain as a perpetually gloomy and strike-bound place. They had some reason: the Labour government was battling with the trades unions and an ailing economy, and by the end of the year the pound had been devalued by over 14 per cent. South Africa, to the white supporters of the new prime minister John Vorster, seemed in contrast a paradise: cheap labour, warm sunshine and an efficient infrastructure all made their life exceedingly comfortable, and it looked as if things would stay that way for another generation. To liberal whites, however, those smug certainties were almost as oppressive as the apartheid laws. Thousands chose to leave, and Britain, where so many had roots, seemed a sensible place in which to start again.

I was glad to be back in London, where I found myself a small bedsit in South Kensington. The previous occupant had kept a bush-baby as a pet and there were some curious stains at picture-rail level on the walls: something to do with its nocturnal prowls. Otherwise the place was comfortable. I set about preparing myself to apply for a job at the BBC, making a point of listening carefully to as many programmes as I could on what were then the Light Programme and the Home Service. Few of them were cutting-edge stuff and some seemed familiar, for virtual copies had been broadcast by the SABC: *Housewives' Choice*, *Down Your Way* and *Mrs Dale's Diary* had their equivalents on the South African airwaves. I had been told that *Today* and Jack de Manio were doing something rather different, and I tuned in eagerly.

Jack was evidently considered a bit of a card and was held in deep affection by a huge number of listeners – largely, as far as I could tell, because of his complete inability to tell the time correctly. I enjoyed *Today* and the fact that it didn't appear to take itself terribly seriously – we had nothing like it in South Africa – but I was irritated by Jack's erratic timekeeping, and by his golf-club bore attitude to anything foreign. This was decades before the era of political correctness, and Jack could refer on air to John Lennon's wife Yoko Ono as 'Yoko Hama or whatever her name is' without the skies falling in. But once on the BBC Home Service, filling in a gap between the end of a live concert and the nine o'clock news, Jack had announced a talk to be given later in the evening by the governor of Nigeria, called *The Land of the Niger*. Unfortunately, Jack pronounced Niger with a hard 'g'. His announcement was heard throughout Nigeria, where there was a royal tour in progress, and the Queen, the Duke of Edinburgh and a number of top Nigerian officials had been brought together specifically to hear the broadcast. There were appalled gasps all round. History does not relate how quickly diplomacy smoothed ruffled feathers, but an abject apology was made by the BBC.

Although Jack's gaffes on *Today* were frequent, his editors were supportive of him as long as he was considered to be an asset to the programme. But he was fond of his whiskies and increasingly unpredictable, and eventually was demoted to hosting a short-lived programme on Radio Four called *Jack de Manio Precisely* – in case anyone had forgotten his arm's-length relationship with the clock.

The idea that I might one day be fronting *Today* myself didn't occur to me as even a remote possibility; at the time I didn't see myself in 'hard news' and was thinking about attaching myself to a magazine programme of some kind. I made my bid to the BBC appointments department in Portland Place, just across the road from Broadcasting House, filling in a form giving details of my experience in South Africa. I said I would like if possible to work in front of the microphone rather than in a production job. A swift reply warned me that it might be weeks, even months, before I heard anything concrete from them at all, so I decided to pay my first visit to North America. I had longed to see New York and spent a week there, quite on my own, staying in the cheapest half-decent hotel I could find, in the rather sleazy area just off West 44th Street. The curtains were so threadbare that my bedroom glowed blue all night from the hotel's neon sign just outside the window. I had been warned to lock, bolt and chain my bedroom door before retiring. On the first morning, at six-thirty, I got the fright of my life. Despite all my precautions, the entire centre of the door swung open and, as I stared up in horror, a cheerful black face popped through, enquiring, 'Any laundry? Just checking.' I sank trembling back on to my bed. Outside, I explored as much of the city as I could; I was told that nobody would bother me if I walked fast in a determined manner, and nobody did. New York was an astonishingly vertical city: its soaring buildings, as I gazed up and further up to their summits, really did seem to touch the sky. At night I was happily aware of the honk of yellow taxi cabs and the squeal of police sirens echoing through those concrete canyons. Even my hotel bed produced its own little thrill: insert a quarter, and it trembled and shook for fifteen minutes, as if to remind the occupant that lying still was a waste of time. Somehow it didn't seem odd to be alone here. I fired off a series of postcards to South Africa, and felt rather pleased that I had managed this adventure all on my own.

Aunt Sheila was still in Indianapolis, and I flew west to see her and meet her husband, Lyndon K. Beals. Lyndon was a keen freemason who insisted on showing me the only local landmark he deemed worth visiting – a massive masonic building called the Scottish Rite Cathedral. I also flew north to Montreal and took in another Expo, this one celebrating Canada's hundredth birthday. It attracted huge crowds, but almost bankrupted the city. The Expo, however, was not my primary reason for visiting Canada: I had a rendezvous with my naval friend Richard in Ottawa. For our two days together we were based at an enormous turn-of-the-century Canadian railway hotel, rather loosely modelled on a Scottish castle and heavily ornamented with turrets. We promised to meet again in England when his tour of duty ended.

On my return to London there was a letter waiting for me from the BBC, offering me a chance to audition for a department called Microphone Publicity. The vacancy was for a job as a continuity announcer on the Home Service: it might turn out to be a stepping stone to something a little less anonymous. I attended the audition, and faces smiled encouragingly at me through the glass; but a few days later I was told by telephone that after a process of elimination which had got me into the last three, they had chosen a man. Male voices, they said, in the end carried more authority.

In the late sixties this was a widely held view. Despite Nan Winton's breakthrough almost a decade earlier, there were still no women newsreaders on radio or television. It was not until 1974 that Sheila Tracy became the first woman to read the news on Radio Four. Female voices in the late sixties were reserved largely for programmes like *Woman's Hour*, *Housewives' Choice* and the rather arch discussion programme *Petticoat Line* – one of the stars of which turned out to be the woman who had been the object of my father's kidnapping prank in Edinburgh thirty years earlier, Renée Houston. Thus rejected, I sighed, and began to contemplate the more precarious life of a freelance contributor, or even returning to South Africa. I rented a tiny flat up many stairs in Cornwall Gardens in South Kensington and persuaded another expatriate South African girl to share it. This was convenient for us both: she was working for the French jazz pianist Jacques Loussier, and as she spent most of her time on the road with him I barely saw her.

Many of my London friends were, like me, newly arrived from South Africa. We swopped horror stories of flat-hunting and high prices, and I enjoyed their company all the more as the novelty of being back in London began to wear off. They understood my slightly semi-detached feelings. Two of my Cape Town friends, Brian and Anita McMinn, had moved to a studio flat in Hampstead, where Brian painted enormous impressionistic landscapes. They gave regular parties and invited an engaging mixture of writers, artists, actors and South African immigrants. Their guests included the novelist Bernice Rubens, the young actor Tim Curry, soon to star in *The Rocky Horror Show*, and several South African political exiles, including the Cape Coloured writer and academic Kenny Parker. The company was amusing, and the occasional shared 'joint' was passed around after supper – though it was not, I was told by the experts, as good as the South African variety. One South African already well established in London, Pauline Vogelpoel, was especially kind to me. Pauline, who ran the Contemporary Art Society, gave glittering parties in her Little Boltons flat. Here one could meet more Establishment rising young artists and successful writers, as well as a series of Pauline's snuffly pugs, all called Lucas. Eventually, in her late forties, she married a banker called David

Mann and went to live in Switzerland, from where she would dash
into London several times a year and cheerfully sweep together all
her old friends.

As it turned out, the BBC's rejection of my services had not been
so final as I'd thought. Within a month of my audition another
letter arrived from Portland Place – this time inviting me to go
and see Brian Bliss, editor of Radio News Features. He would like
to discuss the possibility of giving me a short-term contract in
his department. Mr Bliss lived up to his name: he was friendly
and charming, and turned out to be rather keen on young South
Africans. In his experience, he told me, they were hard working and
reliable. I had not heard this before; indeed, I had been warned back
home that most white South Africans were considered an untidy
and lazy lot by their British hosts, used as they supposedly were to
dozens of domestic servants back home. Mr Bliss could offer me
a one-month holiday relief contract producing *Radio Newsreel* –
a round-up of foreign correspondents' reports, transmitted on the
World Service but produced at Broadcasting House – though there
would be no guarantee of any extension of the contract.

It was the toehold I needed. I turned up for work a couple
of weeks later and was given a large stainless steel stopwatch.
Producing 'the *Reel*' as it was called – a programme heard by
millions – consisted largely of carefully timing each item and
writing two-line introductions. The *Reel* went out live several
times a day, and I was to be responsible for three consecutive
editions. I was put in the charge of Eric Stadlen, an émigré
from Vienna with very firm ideas about the most effective use
of the English language. Written introductions on the radio should
contain just enough information to keep people listening. It was
no good saying, 'There has been a political upset in France. Over
to our correspondent Thomas Cadet in Paris.' It was more elegant,
and intriguing, to say something like, 'The pressures on General de
Gaulle's foreign minister have increased. Some within his own party
want him replaced. Our correspondent Thomas Cadet in Paris has

been following the events of the weekend.' Eric's fierce blue pencil scored through all my efforts with great regularity; he was seldom satisfied.

At the end of the month I was relieved to be offered another BBC contract of thirty days' duration, this time in domestic radio as producer of a regional news programme called *South East*, which followed the Home Service *Six O'Clock News* each evening. This was a bit more complicated. It was twenty minutes long, consisted of short reports and live interviews, and was edited by Marshall Stewart, a good journalist – he went on to edit the *Today* programme – but a man of rather elusive habits. *South East* came from a studio on the seventh floor; Marshall's office was on the fourth, and he seldom left it. Messages about changes in the programme's running order, or instructions to drop items and add others, were typed on flimsy sheets of pink paper and conveyed to the studio by his secretary, who had to rush her way up several flights of stairs to deliver them. For most of my time as a studio producer – the only woman on the production team, apart from the fleet-footed secretary – I was in a state of utter panic, clutching Marshall's latest pink slip. Instructions about editing an item or removing it altogether often arrived just as the offending item had gone on the air; all I could do was plough on, and await Marshall's disapproval at the end of transmission.

Somehow I managed to stumble my way through to the end of my second month with the BBC. As well as the challenge of a new job and a new programme, there was an element of culture shock to cope with. Some of the men I met in the studios were fairly hostile, and when I tried to 'produce' a home correspondent he clearly resented it. This had never happened to me in South Africa. And then there was the business of expenses. On the days when I was not producing in the studio I was sent out to record interviews with a portable tape machine. In my innocence I totted up the cost correctly to the nearest penny: five shillings and sixpence on a taxi, tenpence on a bus ride down Oxford Street.

119

My more experienced colleagues were appalled: 'It's no good you putting in your weekly expenses at six shillings and fourpence if everyone else's are twenty quid!' I learned that it was far better to nod in the direction of what my next boss was to call 'creative fiction'.

One of my assignments involved spending half a day at the old Shepperton Studios in Middlesex, snatching conversations with Dick Van Dyke and Sally-Ann Howes on the set of *Chitty Chitty Bang Bang*. By chance, the result – an unremarkable little radio picture of the making of a new British musical film – was heard by Andrew Boyle, a former *Radio Newsreel* man and now editor of *The World At One*. He was looking for a new reporter to join his team; he gathered I had some experience of interviewing and working to deadlines, said he'd liked what he'd heard of my work and offered me a three-month contract. Things were looking up; I might not have to go back home after all.

The World At One had begun modestly enough in 1965, but it was to change the nature of current affairs on radio; already it had become required listening on the Home Service at lunchtime. Its main presenters William Hardcastle and Andrew Boyle ran their little empire from a series of small rooms on the third floor of Broadcasting House. Working on the programme was, as Bill was to say later, 'a real adventure in broadcasting'. It owed a great deal to a far-sighted controller of the Home Service, Gerard Mansell, who felt that lunchtime audiences would be happy to listen on after the end of the traditional one o'clock news bulletin. He backed the new idea and found money in the budget to fund it. *The World At One* was immediately a success; listeners took to its freewheeling agenda and its serious but often irreverent look at the events of the day. There had been nothing like it on radio before. By 1967 it had well over two million listeners, and ambitious young journalists were keen to work on it. Like many a successful radio programme it had an enviable *esprit de corps* if you were part of the team; but it could also be remarkably unfriendly to outsiders, as I was to discover.

Reporting for duty on my first morning at eight o'clock, as instructed, I hovered at the door for what seemed like ages before anyone acknowledged my presence. The office – or rather, offices, for three or four rooms had been knocked into one – seemed to be in a state of some confusion, with people rushing about in what was already a dense fug of cigarette smoke. Andrew, ruddy-faced, with locks of grey hair flopping over his forehead, sat at one end of the office; Bill, a big, rumpled balding man with beetling brows, took up most of one side of a table in the middle. The table itself was strewn with well-read piles of the morning's newspapers and dozens of reels of magnetic tape. Bill was in shirtsleeves and smoking hard – obviously, I thought, ex-Fleet Street: all that was missing was the green eyeshade. A clutch of what looked to me like distinctly middle-aged editors and studio producers were on the phone or furiously cutting tapes on portable editing machines. Reporters dashed in and out with progress bulletins on their morning assignments. With five hours to go before transmission, there was an air of concentrated chaos. Andrew eventually noticed the new arrival and rose to greet me. He introduced me to the team, but no one had much time to do more than give me a quick nod. The atmosphere of slightly panicky endeavour made me more than a little nervous. I was conscious of being relatively inexperienced in the world of hard news and current affairs. I was also about to take on a subtly different persona. For all of my five years in broadcasting in South Africa I had been known rather formally as Susan MacGregor. 'We can't have that,' said Bill Hardcastle a couple of days later. 'What do your friends call you? Sue? That's better. From now on you will be *Sue* MacGregor. Much easier to say.'

I was shown the reporters' den at the other end of the corridor. The small team I was to join consisted of three men – Jack Pizzey, Nick Barratt and Nick Woolley – and two women: Wendy

121

Jones, and a blonde Australian called Sandra Harris, who instantly welcomed another colonial with a camaraderie for which I was grateful. I admired her confidence and her infectious cackle, and we soon worked happily at adjoining desks. Sandra specialized in show business and popular culture; I tended to cover the broad human interest stories, as well as political interviews which had to be recorded away from base, and Wendy the 'social concern' items. But we were all expected to turn our hands to anything, and do what the BBC called 'vox pops' on a daily basis. In the late 1960s gathering *vox populi* – literally, the voice of the people – was a relatively novel journalistic device, but Bill Hardcastle was extremely keen on it, and the public usually came up with trenchant opinions on most things once the idea had been explained to them. Vox pops, though, were time-consuming and demanding for reporters in a hurry, for many yards of tape had to be cut and shaped into a neat sixty seconds as the studio clock ticked on. For this reason Oxford Circus and the Marylebone Road – a mere five minutes from Broadcasting House – were popular hunting grounds, though at least one supermarket got so fed up with my standing on its threshold talking to its customers that I was forbidden to return.

One of my early vox pop assignments was to garner opinions on sexual activity among the over-forties after a survey had revealed some new statistic about the sex lives of the middle-aged. I was a little uncertain of how I would be received if I accosted strangers on this topic outside Oxford Circus tube station, so I took my microphone instead to an office block in Knightsbridge where I knew a number of the young secretaries. They were all appalled by the idea of regular sexual activity in anyone over thirty-five: to them, mature lust was almost unimaginable. Their opinions, alongside the statistics of the survey and the comments of an agony aunt, were broadcast to the nation at lunchtime.

While – unlike at the SABC – there was no gender discrimination in the BBC pay packets, I discovered that not all the most interesting reporting jobs were evenly distributed. Foreign assignments and anything involving possible physical danger were handed out to the men in the team: rioting students at home or abroad, or industrial unrest, were not considered the province of women. Surprisingly, perhaps, with hindsight, we accepted this division of labour with little protest. In any event, there was always plenty going on in hard news to challenge all of us; I liked the media scrums, and having to elbow my way in to catch soundbites. Celebrity interviews and 'human interest' stories were deemed more appropriate for women. One of my first interviews for *The World At One* was both: a conversation with the conductor Sir Malcolm Sargent, just as the new summer season of Promenade Concerts began. Sir Malcolm lived in a sumptuous mansion flat close to his beloved Albert Hall. He was ill – indeed, dying – but he greeted me sitting up in bed immaculately wrapped in a pure silk dressing gown. We spoke about the postwar popularity of certain composers and of his fondness for the young prommers, vast numbers of whom were at that moment standing outside in queues snaking round the Albert Hall, waiting for second night tickets. It was an effort for him to talk at all, though he had managed a brief farewell appearance on the podium the night before. Though greatly tempted, I did not have the heart to press him for a long series of reminiscences. This I was to regret, for my interview was the last he gave: three weeks later Sir Malcolm was dead.

Sandra Harris was more in tune with the exploding pop and rock scene at the other end of the age spectrum. She had an enviable contacts book and discovered some sort of hotline to Mick Jagger, whom she persuaded, with his then girlfriend Marianne Faithfull, to reveal his thoughts on the direction popular music was taking. They both came across as rather sweet, wayward children; Sandra did not broach with them the current ribald rumours about what they got up to with Mars Bars. She did, though, reveal to *World At One* listeners something of the lifestyle of the Playboy bunny. Hugh Hefner had just opened the London Playboy Club in Park Lane, which was to become so successful, thanks to the suitcases of dollars brought to the club by Gulf Arabs, that it could underwrite the entire Hefner empire. Sandra became a bunny for a day, squeezing into the costume – tail, ears, fishnet tights and all – to learn the finer points, such as serving drinks while bending with a 'bunny dip', so that the well-placed cleavage dazzled a customer into ordering a generous second round. There was a strict 'no touching' rule: bunnies were respectable. Bunny-dipping even became a career option for one or two who went on to embrace the women's movement, including its glamorous American high priestess in the seventies, Gloria Steinem.

As I had surmised on first setting eyes on him, for almost all his life up to the mid-1960s William Hardcastle had been a newspaper journalist. He had worked for Reuters, and went on to be Washington correspondent for the *Daily Mail* and then briefly its editor, only to be sacked: he had little interest in the administrative work that editorship involved. He was not a natural broadcaster, but was picked for *The World At One* because Gerard Mansell and Andrew Boyle admired his urgent and pugnacious style – he had already contributed successfully to other current affairs programmes on the Home Service. Andrew Boyle, in contrast, was a much cooler and more contained character: a Roman Catholic and a well-regarded modern historian, he wrote a distinguished biography of Lord Reith, and some years later unmasked the art historian Anthony Blunt as the 'fourth man' and a former spy in his book *The Climate of Treason*. Andrew was a more intellectual man than Bill Hardcastle, but he shared Bill's delight in pricking pomposity and annoying the staider members of BBC management. Together they made a formidable team. Bill had the good journalist's nose for a story, and Andrew had the broader vision, rapier judgements and a dry wit. I got on well with them both, and genuinely admired them. Andrew, in particular, went out of his way to employ equal numbers of men and women reporters – an even-handedness unprecedented at the time, and a far cry from the prevailing ethos within the BBC.

They were tough men to work for, and Andrew's briefings to reporters were famously opaque. Few of us were any clearer about what was expected of us after he had explained the purpose of the piece than we had been beforehand; it was usually necessary to ask one of the other editors what he really wanted. And quite often by the time the piece was complete Andrew had changed his mind, or Bill had decided that something else was more interesting; the final running order for the programme bore little resemblance to the one set out at eight in the morning. As a reporter for the companion programme *The World This Weekend*, which went out on Sunday lunchtime, you could work for days on a project that, in Andrew's words, simply 'dropped off the end'. This was to be my first broadcasting experience of being 'spiked'. If Bill didn't think a story 'had legs', then it didn't make it on air. 'WGAS', Bill would mutter as a doubtful story was explained to him. These were the initials one of his Washington stringers used to put at the end of a particularly boring wire story. They stood for 'Who Gives a Shit?'

After *PM* began in 1970 most of us were working on three programmes. The frantic pace seemed to energize Bill and Andrew. When Julian Holland joined the programme from the *Daily Mail* as an assistant editor in the early seventies, he was told to spend the first three days simply observing how things were done. At the end of three days he was so exhausted that he lay down on a bench at the back of the studio and fell asleep. Gordon Clough was similarly taken aback by the intensity of the work when he joined the team from the Russian Service at Bush House. He recovered, adjusted and went on to be a highly effective presenter of *The World This Weekend*.

With my change of name came a change of broadcasting style. My South African training by Dewar McCormack in the sixties had concentrated on clear speaking and breathing in the right places. Now that I was working on a fast-moving current affairs programme, I had to learn to take a rather different approach, with a more colloquial style and a more rapid delivery. I think many of us began to copy Bill – however unconsciously – though in some ways he may not have been the best model. No one had trained him to read aloud a written script convincingly, and he was impatient with other people's words. The programme's pace and his own excitement at being involved in it often got the better of him: sometimes his urgent delivery deteriorated into a flustered jumble. Bill always claimed to be totally calm once the programme began, though he seldom sounded it. He had a permanent difficulty with foreign names, especially the more challenging Russian ones. Occasionally he tangled up the name of the newsreader at the beginning of the programme: Pauline Bushnell once became, to her intense annoyance, Pauline Cracknell. Bill even got his own name wrong, telling astonished listeners one lunchtime that 'This is William *Whitelaw* with *The World At One*.' But he loved the speed, the immediacy and the flexibility with which radio tackled the news, and his unmistakable authority made him difficult to resist.

The audience for the programme began to approach the astonishing figure of three million, and in the autumn of 1967 *The World This Weekend* came into being, also presented by William Hardcastle. It became required listening, especially for fellow journalists, though on slow news weekends, especially in the summer, it was not always easy to drum up exciting items with which to fill it. One Saturday evening in July 1969 the editorial team, which included – unusually for the time – a woman, Eleanor Ransome, were sitting about scratching their heads over the agenda for the next day's programme. It was the beginning of the 'silly season'; parliament was winding down. 'We were', as Eleanor put it later, 'working quite hard but larking about a bit too.' The newsroom rang: there was a story coming through from the American press agencies about an accident on the island of Chappaquiddick off

Cape Cod. There was a possible drowning, and it seemed Senator Edward Kennedy's car had been involved. They were waiting to find out more. *The World This Weekend* team was galvanized – but unsure exactly how to cover the story. Bill Hardcastle suddenly had a brilliant idea: why not ring the local police chief and see what he knew? Direct dialling to the States was newly possible, and directory enquiries were helpful. Within minutes Dominic J. Arena, the local chief of police, was on the line, and he gave the programme what turned out to be its biggest scoop in a decade. He told Bill everything he knew about the discovery of the Kennedy car and of the body inside: that of 28-year-old Mary Jo Kopechne, one of the senator's staff. He was prepared to hint that she and the senator had been alone together in his car for some time. It became the most controversial car accident in modern American history, starting off months of speculation about what Teddy Kennedy had really been up to and whether he had lied about it. Why was the accident unreported for nearly ten hours? If Kennedy had called the police immediately, could Mary Jo Kopechne's life have been saved? Eventually Senator Kennedy was found guilty only of leaving the scene of an accident; but the event dogged him for years, and ended his presidential ambitions – though not the string of extraordinary controversies and tragedies to hit the Kennedy family.

Much of the domestic news of the late sixties centred on industrial relations, a pattern which would continue well into the next decade. Halfway through the Wilson administration, battles were being fought on several fronts: in the docks, on the railways, in the Post Office and in the motor industry. Powerful union bosses came in to the studio to argue their case – Clive Jenkins of the white-collar ASTMS union regularly got the better of gentlemanly Tory ministers. Abroad there was the Biafran War, the Middle East's Six Day War, and above all the war in Vietnam. Anti-Vietnam War demonstrations took place regularly throughout the United States and were spreading to Europe.

There were plenty of new opportunities for vivid on-the-spot radio reporting, and Andrew Boyle and Bill Hardcastle were keen to go beyond the familiar voices of the BBC correspondents for accounts of these events. The established correspondents sounded a cautious lot: generally they did not go in for speculation, nor were they prepared to convey breaking news to the nation. Every story had to be heavily authenticated before it became a formal despatch. Newspaper journalists were more willing to take risks, even if it meant being wrong, and this, both Andrew and Bill believed, made for more exciting radio. Anthony Howard, then the *Observer*'s man in Washington, was a regular contributor to the programme: because of the time difference he was often still in bed when he was rung at home in the US capital, and I was constantly impressed by his ability to sound alert and coherent from a horizontal position. Anthony Lewis of the *New York Times* was frequently used for American political analysis – more often, indeed, than the BBC's own Charles Wheeler or Gerald Priestland, though I suspect neither of them objected to having his heavy workload lightened. Newspaper editors in Rhodesia, South Africa and Jerusalem were interviewed down the telephone line. *The World At One* was the first radio news programme regularly to make use of the spontaneous and unscripted telephone interview, and though the sound quality was often poor, the general effect was powerful and immediate.

Print journalists were sometimes used as programme presenters, too. William Davis, the financial editor of the *Guardian* at the time, often stood in for Bill Hardcastle. Dr Donald Gould, the editor of the *New Scientist*, was a frequent commentator on medical issues. He had strong views on Dr Christiaan Barnard's famous first heart transplant operation in Cape Town in December 1967. In a memorable tussle with Barnard on one of the early editions of *The World This Weekend*, Gould accused him not only of leaping into dangerous medical territory – the problems of rejection of a new organ had not yet been solved – but also of being an outrageous self-publicist. This line was supported on the programme by Dr William Thompson, the editor of *The Practitioner*, who deeply disapproved of doctors talking to journalists about their work in the operating theatre. My own sympathies were largely with Barnard. I had known of him for some years; my father was a colleague of his at the Groote Schuur hospital in Cape Town, and thought highly of his surgical skills. Barnard was certainly well pleased with himself, and enjoyed talking to the media whenever he could, but he was also a brilliant and pioneering heart surgeon. His fame followed him to the end of his life; his death from a heart attack thirty-four years later, next to a swimming pool in Cyprus, was worldwide front-page news.

Its rising audience figures made *The World At One* the radio programme on which the politicians preferred to be heard. They knew they could expect robust questioning from Bill – his forensic style was equalled only by Robin Day on BBC television – but most of them believed he was fair, and he rather enjoyed their company. Others disliked Bill's style and resented being edited in any way, or even, as happened occasionally, not being used at all. Iain Macleod, as Tory shadow Chancellor, stormed out of Broadcasting House the morning after the pound was devalued when he learned that his interview for *The World This Weekend* would not be used after all; he swore he would never appear on the programme again. Even a personal visit from the chief assistant to the director-general could not pacify him. But Macleod was not typical; the Labour minister Richard Crossman once said he would rather have five minutes on *The World At One* than on any television broadcast. Jim Callaghan, Denis Healey and Barbara Castle were all regular visitors to the studio, as were Sir Alec Douglas-Home and Quintin Hogg (later Lord Hailsham) for the Tories. Quintin Hogg usually arrived on his bicycle and entered the studio wearing his cycle clips and bowler hat; Sir Alec, immaculately dressed, frequently had to suffer Bill tripping over himself and introducing him as 'Sir Alice'.

The young reporting team generally watched these political exchanges from the wings; it was only when an MP could not or would not come in to the studio that we got our chance. I was sent several times to Westminster to interview the Tories' new spokesperson on educational matters, the member for Finchley, Margaret Thatcher. She was usually well briefed and willing to keep to our strict time limits. Some of her male colleagues were unstoppable and had to be fiercely edited back at Broadcasting House. One of them was the interviewee we most dreaded: such was the force of his halitosis that one had to hold the microphone at arm's length, and breathe in cautiously.

Andrew Boyle was careful not to make *The World At One* top-heavy with serving politicians: there was usually a good helping of light relief, and during the parliamentary dog days of August and early September the reporting team had to work harder than usual. One scorching summer's day I was despatched to Piccadilly Circus to see if the pavement was indeed, as the old tabloid cliché claimed, hot enough to fry an egg on. It was the sort of jokey item that we reporters were meant to produce regularly and at high speed. I bought a dozen eggs at British Home Stores and took along a box of matches, but having broken the eggs on the pavement I failed completely to persuade the gloopy mess to sizzle. As I was unwilling to return to the studio unsuccessful, I popped into Boots and bought some methylated spirits. With its help and several matches I eventually managed to fry the egg – indeed, several eggs. The frying noises were very satisfactory, and afterwards the eggs were scooped up and eaten by a couple of hippies who had observed my attempts with interest. I took the recording triumphantly back to the office, just in time to get it on to the programme – but when Bill discovered that I had cheated with the methylated spirits he was furious. I had misled, he said, not just him but the listeners.

We also had our regular comic turns. Bill Hardcastle had a soft spot for the romantic novelist Barbara Cartland, the self-appointed

Queen of Health, who brought in various potions and pills to preserve, she said, his youthful virility. Two hours after her departure
from the studios a telegram would arrive for Bill thanking him
profusely for allowing her to be on 'your lovely programme'. She
was then at the height of her success as a writer – she claimed
that her 620 books had sold over 700 million copies. She was a
busy woman: they were dictated from her comfortable *chaise-longue*
to a team of secretaries at a rate of many thousands of words a
day. I was once invited to lunch at her extremely grand house
near Hatfield in Hertfordshire. I was warned by a previous guest:
a quarter to one meant a quarter to one precisely. It was all very
regal, with butlers serving, and a preprandial tour of a room with
walls entirely covered by the framed originals of her book jackets.
After lunch, at exactly two-thirty, we were shown the door. Each
of her guests was given a signed copy of one of her novels and a
small jar of royal jelly.

Barbara Cartland was considered a great expert on one of
Andrew Boyle's obsessional interests, the British class system.
Sandra Harris, with her colonial background, was thought to be a
suitable interviewer, and was despatched to the Cartland mansion.
Miss Cartland waxed lyrical about her youngest son's easy affinity
with anyone from a duke to a dustman. 'So, Miss Cartland,' said
Sandra, 'you're saying that in modern Britain class doesn't matter
any more?'

'Of course it doesn't, darling,' came the answer, 'or I wouldn't
be talking to you!'

The question of political balance within programmes was always
a sensitive one, and one which caused uneasy stirrings in news
and current affairs management. Sir Hugh Carleton Greene, as
director-general of the BBC until 1969, made it clear that he
believed political balance within each programme – matching
every Tory with a Labour member or vice versa – was too restrictive
an imposition on editors; to him, it was perfectly acceptable to
match opposing views on a programme over a matter of two or

three days. But over Northern Ireland the deputy director-general Oliver Whitley won an exception: each time the Ulster situation was discussed there must be balance within individual programmes. It was a stricture which was not always observed – sometimes simply because speakers were not available. Andrew Boyle preferred to display political balance in a much more entertaining way: get two experienced journalists from the right and the left to discuss an issue of the day and have what he called a 'punch-up' between Alan Watkins of the *Observer*, for instance, and T. E. Utley or Peregrine Worsthorne of the *Telegraph*. They became regular star turns.

This was a time when the laws governing sexual behaviour and personal choice were rapidly changing. The Wolfenden report in the 1950s had led to the decriminalization of adult male homosexuality in 1967. Female homosexuality had never been a criminal offence, but in 1965 Frank Marcus' play *The Killing of Sister George* had caused a *frisson* with its portrayal of the star of a fictional BBC radio soap opera as a lesbian, and when the film, starring Beryl Reid and Susannah York, went on release two years later, I was dispatched to the Gateways, a gay women's club off the King's Road in Chelsea, to see if I could rustle up some opinions on the merits of both play and the film. For once the vox pop was virtually silent: most of the club's members were far too suspicious of a reporter with a tape-recorder to talk to me.

That same year the young Liberal MP David Steel, the 'baby' of the Commons when he arrived there at the age of twenty-seven, steered through his private member's bill liberalizing the abortion laws. By the autumn of 1967 the Abortion Act was law, for the first time making one of the criteria for ending a pregnancy the mental health of a woman and her unborn child. One of the key 'social' clauses took into account a woman's likely capacity to be a good mother. The medical profession largely supported the reforms, but there were many reservations on religious and moral grounds, and in the run-up to the parliamentary vote all the most prominent pro- and anti-abortionists came into Studio 3B to talk on *The World At One*. One woman, a doctor and a convinced 'pro-lifer', startled us all by whipping from her handbag a small dried human foetus just before going on air. Bill managed to conduct the interview without once glancing at the strange object in her hand.

Once the law was passed one of London's largest abortion clinics, the Langham Clinic, opened up just behind Broadcasting House. Frequently young girls from Ireland or the continent, mistaking the address, tried to check in at the BBC's front desk and had to be gently steered round the corner.

The arts were not entirely ignored. *PM* had a regular slot for interviews with authors of new books. These were usually marked down for Bill to record at the beginning of the afternoon, but sometimes, after a briefly relaxing lunch and also having failed to read the book, Bill ducked out of the assignment just as the writer was on his way to the studio. In these cases a hapless young reporter, quite often me, was handed the book as its author emerged from the lift. There was just time to read the flyleaf before the author sat down in front of the microphone, after which it was usually possible to bluff one's way through the interview. But when Sir Oswald Mosley, the leader of the British fascists in the thirties, came over from his exile in Paris to promote his memoirs, Bill chose to do the interview himself – even though he could hardly bear to greet Mosley. He conducted an icily efficient conversation in the studio, making clear his contempt for Sir Oswald: it was one of the few occasions on which I remember him revealing his own political views. 'Everybody who's now writing history or judging that situation believes that I was right in the thirties,' said Sir Oswald. 'I don't,' retorted Bill curtly.

If *The World At One* was a success with its listeners, BBC management was not entirely convinced by its editorial judgements, and continual sniping emanated from those who were unhappy with Bill's interviewing manner and Andrew's news agenda. *WATO* did some pioneering reporting of the deepening troubles in Northern Ireland and, to the dismay of the BBC's Northern Ireland office, bypassed BBC correspondents in favour of newspaper journalists with good access to the Catholic community – among them Mary Holland of the *Observer*, one of the few writing with sympathy in the mainland British press about the Catholics. In the early years of the troubles the young nationalist politician John Hume of the SDLP was interviewed by Bill about the tarring and feathering of a girl from the Bogside area of Londonderry because she had been seen with a British soldier. When John Hume condemned the punishment on the programme, Bill asked him why he had not said as much on the streets of the Bogside. 'I live in the Bogside, Mr Hardcastle,' said Hume. A week later, someone tapped on Hume's door. It was Bill. He had come to spend the weekend in the Bogside so that he could familiarize himself with life in a community of which most people on the mainland knew little. John Hume was mightily impressed with Bill's professionalism.

Thoughts of returning to South Africa continued to dwindle, although I kept in close touch with political events there through letters from my parents. My mother wrote twice a week: long, warm and delightfully unpunctuated letters. My father was an assiduous correspondent too, typing each Sunday a witty account of his week and of the latest South African political concerns. The domestic news was usually deeply depressing. Dr Verwoerd's successor John Vorster continued with grim efficiency to strengthen all the apartheid policies; the laws that kept the races apart were supplemented by an all-powerful police force and a well-equipped army. Under the draconian ninety-day detention law, political offenders could be held without trial, and sometimes in solitary confinement, for three months. When they were released, detainees were frequently arrested and incarcerated all over again, as Albie Sachs was, in a hideous game of cat-and-mouse. The sole effective voice of opposition belonged to Helen Suzman, the Progressive

MP for the Johannesburg constituency of Houghton. Her energy and persistence in criticizing the government were formidable. In private she was a wonderfully warm and entertaining woman – I had met her in London a few years earlier at the wedding of her niece, the actress Janet Suzman. Not only was she subjected to constant personal attacks in the South African parliament, she also suffered from some less than subtle antisemitism – being referred to in the House as 'the lady from Lithuania' was one of its milder forms. I tried to return to the Cape to visit my parents every two years, and usually managed to have lunch with Helen in the parliamentary dining-room. She enjoyed pointing out some of the more notorious members of Vorster's government relaxing at tables nearby, happily chewing their way through large helpings of a popular Cape dish called *gesmoerde snoek* – curried fish, Malay style.

Around 1968 I moved from my tiny Cornwall Gardens flat into a much more spacious one, thanks to my old friend Nonie Crossman, who had bought a short lease on an apartment in Stafford Terrace, just off Kensington High Street. Here I stayed until 1972, when I bought my first – tiny, but very modern – flat, in Fulham, for £13,000. Nonie and I barely saw each other during the week, sometimes meeting over a rushed breakfast, and at weekends I usually had the flat to myself. In this I was very fortunate, for it was not the sort of accommodation I could possibly have afforded on my own. I was still close to my naval friend Richard, and it was now possible to have discreet meetings whenever he came to London, though I was steeling myself to bring matters to an end. Even if he had been free to marry me, I was not keen to make our relationship permanent. I decided I was enormously fond of him, but nothing more. There were other men who came into my life, and went out of it. Marriage and babies – the sort of 'normal' life which so many of my contemporaries had embarked upon – seemed no closer for me. But I enjoyed my single state. Indeed, by the age of about thirty I began to admit to myself that marriage might not be on the cards at all, though I kept an open mind about meeting 'the right man' eventually. One day I was disconcerted when a South African lawyer friend told me I should 'settle down' before I was forty, as 'no one wants to spend old age alone'. I conceded there was something in his argument, but long-term planning has never been my strong suit – I have always rather preferred to let things happen, or not happen. It wouldn't have occurred to me to marry simply to avoid solitude. My work was stimulating and highly satisfying; I had friends, men and women, whom I cared for very much; and I had no huge longing for children. Sometimes I even actively sought my own company rather than be in a crowd. Odd, maybe; but it suited me.

In the late sixties the pill was still a relatively novel form of con-traception, though it had been available in Britain since 1961. Its convenience and efficacy made it hugely appealing to an enormous number of women, though there was still a fierce debate about its possible health risks. When the pill's safety became a matter of parliamentary debate, the Labour peer Lady Gaitskell declared her support for it despite the risks. 'In the controversy about the contraceptive pill,' she said '. . . it is just conceivable that some women would opt for a short life and a merry one.' Most pill users did not see it in quite such stark terms: what they welcomed was the control it gave them over their own fertility, and the possibility for the first time of enjoying sex without fear of pregnancy. Arguably, it was the most important breakthrough for women of the twentieth century. But for those who were not in a long-term or permanent relationship other forms of contraception were still an option, including the unwieldy Dutch cap. I can remember smiling in recognition as I read the passage in Mary McCarthy's novel of Catholic girlhood, *The Group*, which described the frustrations of a cap user as she tried to insert a device so springy and unmanageable that it popped out and bounced clear across the room. Pill or cap, the family planning centre close to Broadcasting House was there to provide sympathetic and discreet advice.

*   *   *

Over time the team of young reporters on *The World At One* changed. Sandra Harris left to join Thames Television, and was replaced by Margaret Howard, who went on to present *Pick Of The Week* on Radio Four for many years. Jack Pizzey and Nick Woolley were also lost to television, and were replaced by Jonathan Dimbleby and a bright young Oxford graduate called David Jessel. The team was further augmented by two New Zealanders, Nancy Wise and Roger Cook: Andrew called the three of us his 'colonial contingent'. Roger, with whom I shared an office, was an imposing figure, almost as large as Bill. His direct approach and fearless foot-in-the-door technique went down well with the editors, and led eventually to his own programmes, *Checkpoint* on BBC radio and *The Cook Report* on television, but he did his earliest investigative journalism on *The World At One*. His first target was a mortgage company, who persuaded those who were least able to pay to take out large loans. When they almost inevitably defaulted, they were roughed up by 'heavies' sent by the man who ran the company. Roger got wind of this and confronted the company's owner at the door of his office. 'What are your qualifications for running a company like this, apart from being a former heavyweight wrestler?' he asked. The former heavyweight wrestler flew into a rage and pushed Roger hard down the stairs. His tape-recorder, which was still working until it hit the ground, burst open, leaving precious tape unwinding into the street. Roger picked himself up, retrieved the tape safely, and returned to our office bruised but triumphant.

David Jessel was one of the team to benefit from the assumption that potentially dangerous assignments should go to the men. He quickly became a protégé of Bill's, and got a plum job in May 1968: he was sent to Paris to give his impressions of *les événements* – the student protests against the French educational establishment which led to violent clashes with the police. David's reports were exceptionally vivid. We could hear the shouts of the students, the

137

klaxons of the riot police and the smashing of uprooted cobbles. We could feel the full impact of a tear-gas attack, as both the students and the journalists covering the story coughed and retched. That sort of reporting from the middle of an angry crowd was not considered women's work: the nearest I got to the rioters of Grosvenor Square in London was an interview the following year with one of the veterans of the occasion, the actress Vanessa Redgrave.

Interview with Vanessa Redgrave, broadcast 2.3.69

SM: You have a reputation as a taker-up of causes. A lot of people might accuse you of showing off, certainly of a lot of self-advertisement.

VR: Well, I think it's very understandable. People are rightly a little bit wary and suspicious of actors and actresses talking on subjects outside their field, because I suppose some instinct tells them – what is our profession? It's being very good at pretending things. I shall have to prove by what I do that their suspicions aren't in fact justified.

SM: You have appeared in anti-American demonstrations, recently the one in Grosvenor Square; and yet a lot of your films are financed by American money, aren't they?

VR: I draw a very clear distinction. I identify myself with particular Americans of which there are a great many which I admire. I'm anti-capitalism and anti-exploitation, neo-colonialistic exploitation.

SM: But if you're anti-capitalism the big million-dollar films you're making are surely all financed by capitalist money, British or American?

VR: I do make money out of that, and it is up to me to see how usefully I can use it. However, I will put the onus on them to give me the sack. If they say that I've gone too far, then that's up to them.

SM: What are you proudest of doing in your life?

VR: The only thing that I really do feel proud of without one single complication was giving birth to my two children. That was the most special thing that ever happened.

SM: Are you ashamed of anything you've done?

VR: Oh yes, a great many things. I'm very ashamed of having been a prefect at school. It make me blush every time I think of it [laughs]. I was a very bad one.

SM: Anything in adulthood?

VR: Well, I'm really rather ashamed of having accepted the CBE.

SM: Why – because it makes you feel part of the establishment?

VR: It's not so much that it makes me feel part of the establishment. But it is a proof to myself of the attraction of the establishment for me. I kidded myself when I accepted it that it would show people abroad that when I got involved in things, that it is conceivable that somebody who's been given an honour still carries on and does things which it's supposed you don't do when you have an honour, but that wasn't really truthful.

SM: Have you thought of giving it back?

VR: No, I haven't, because I don't know quite how to do it.

Disarmingly honest and direct in her responses, she requested that her interview fee should be paid directly to the Workers' Revolutionary Party. BBC rules, I explained, meant she would have to make that particular payment herself.

By the summer of 1968 my sister had left her South African school and was in Britain to spend a year, like me, at Miss Neville-Rolfe's House of Citizenship. Kirsty was now just eighteen and suddenly no longer my baby sister: we were simply siblings a few years apart, friends who could laugh at the same things. Both of us could put on strong Cape accents for telling the sort of jokes that are only funny to fellow South Africans, and fall about at our wit. (We still do.) She followed the secretarial course at Hartwell House, learning to type under the fierce tutelage of Miss Adler, accompanied by the same scratchy old marches that I remembered hearing played over and over again on the ancient gramophone. She, like me, was to return to South Africa for a while before settling in England for good.

Our parents returned to Europe for the first time in a decade, and we organized a family holiday in the Italian hilltop town of Ravello, on the Amalfi coast south of Naples. Here we rented a simple and charming apartment in a large medieval building close to the cathedral. There were three bedrooms and a challenging hot water system; best of all, when the massive shutters were thrown open in the morning, we had a ravishing view of the twin hilltop town of Scala, across a deep ravine. Each day we explored the Amalfi coast and scrambled down to the sea to swim off the rocks. It was a good time to be a family together again – to sit in the piazza as dusk fell, and talk. My mother was intrigued by my job in 'real journalism' and loved to hear every detail of what it involved. In the evenings after dinner we tuned into the BBC World Service to keep in touch with what was happening in the world outside. My mother must have wondered when I was going to 'settle down', but she never even hinted that she would prefer it if I did. She was delighted that I seemed to have found a niche at the BBC, an entirely respectable place in which to earn a living. If working as a girl reporter was not quite as prestigious as presenting your own programme, she was confident that I would move on, and possibly up.

On 20 August 1968 we heard the astonishing news that the Red Army had marched into Czechoslovakia. By the following day it was clear that a full-scale invasion had begun, with the aim of crushing Dubček's liberal regime in Prague. *The World At One* managed to organize some memorable reports on the crisis. An enterprising reporter on the team found a Czech radio journalist in Prague who was prepared to send despatches to the BBC, and at one point, to emphasize the reality of the crisis, he hung his microphone out of a hotel window in Wenceslas Square so that his listeners in Britain could clearly hear the rumble of the Russian tanks. The BBC monitoring service at Caversham near Reading picked up several Czech-language radio stations run by students; some of their transmissions were rebroadcast by *WATO*. As the last of these *samizdat* stations was closed down, a despatch in English was picked up by BBC monitoring and passed on: 'The Russians are at the door. This will be our last broadcast. Remember Czechoslovakia when it is no longer a news item.' By the time I returned to London it was plain from every news bulletin that the temperature of the Cold War had plunged to freezing point.

If 'abroad' was off limits for me as a woman reporter, I certainly had some eye-opening professional assignments even in London. Coming as I did from a relatively protected middle-class background, I had never visited a British housing estate, nor seen real poverty among white people. The foreign media might concentrate on 'swinging London' – *Time* magazine devoted almost a whole edition to Britain's new stylishness – but in the country as a whole the number of unemployed was already half a million and rising, and there were still massive gaps in the provisions of the welfare state. Andrew Boyle wanted us to examine social deprivation by talking directly to the people most affected. This was something few radio programmes had tackled before. For a story about the inadequacies of unemployment benefit, we needed to find a family scraping by on a pitifully inadequate weekly payment. It was not difficult to track one down, and I was astonished by their willingness to answer all our questions about how they fed and clothed themselves. I learned to probe to find just how far they were prepared to go in revealing the details of their lives. This did not come easily to me at first; but I found most people 'opened up' if questions were reasonably put.

At the time there was little state help for disabled people, and I spent a day with a determined campaigner for disability rights, Megan du Boisson, who was in a wheelchair herself. I could see that it was simply impossible for her to travel beyond her own front door without physical help from other people. It was some years before the laws about access for the disabled made life in a wheelchair a little less daunting; despite her best efforts, Megan did not live to see the changes.

Quite a number of what we called our 'problem' stories came to us directly from listeners' tip-offs. Nancy Wise followed up a letter which had come in to the office from a young man painfully disabled with spina bifida. He too was in a wheelchair and unable to type for himself; he had dictated his letter. Nancy went to visit him in Darlington and recorded a moving account of his daily struggle to cope. Listeners were touched and sent in donations which amounted to well over two and a half thousand pounds – a large sum at that time. It went towards purchasing one of the early computerized typewriters for the disabled, which allowed the young man to type and print out his own letters and eventually to write full essays. He obtained a number of A-levels and went on to get a good law degree at Reading University.

As well as honing my interview technique, I was learning how to use the material recorded to make an effective sound picture, cutting and splicing the tapes to weave together the different strands of a story. It meant sitting for hours bent over a large portable editing machine, strands of tape draped round my neck, reducing reels of recorded material into something which would last less than five minutes. Sometimes the deadlines were terrifyingly close: I would still be shaving off the excess seconds minutes before the package was due to be broadcast. The pressure was made worse when a duty producer breathed impatiently down one's neck.

After *The World At One* came off the air there was little time to unwind before the *PM* programme started. But as the chimes of Big Ben announced the six o'clock news, the team gathered in Andrew's office and a large, well-loaded drinks trolley was wheeled into position. I was never quite sure if the 'hospitality trolley' was meant for us or perhaps for visiting members of parliament recovering from a Hardcastle grilling, but we certainly made full use of it. Several bottles of cheap red wine – what Andrew called the 'red infuriator' – were opened and an increasingly lively programme post-mortem was conducted until the hospitality ran dry. Andrew and Bill expected the highest of standards, and if a report or an interview hadn't come up to scratch, the reporter or producer responsible was very publicly made aware of it. Occasionally this ended in tears, and they were not shed only by the female members of staff. All of us on short-term contracts knew that they could be terminated at any time.

Fortunately most of the rows blew over quickly. Only two members of the programme team never really came to any sort of mutual understanding, and they were Bill and Steve Race. Steve, who was well known as the questionmaster and pianist on the *My Music* programme, had a regular slot on *PM*. He was a meticulous worker but not a natural news man, nor much of an office drinker. He was also considered a bit of a prude; Bill spotted this at once, and would deliberately provoke him. Steve sat with an unmistakable air of disapproval at the riper language and smuttier jokes. In the end Steve Race left the programme; his experience of current affairs had not been a happy one.

Around this time one of my future radio partners and I made a brief appearance together, though we were not actually to meet for many years. On *The World At One* programme of 23 October 1969, I talked to the distinguished psychiatrist Dr William Sargent about the beneficial effect of nightmares; they were nature's way, he said, of sorting out one's worst fears. This interview was immediately followed by a news report from outside the Vauxhall factory at Ellesmere Port on Merseyside, where the workers were on strike. The young northern industrial reporter, struggling to make himself heard above the furious shouting of the wildcat strikers, but telling the story clearly in the best Home Service manner, was John Humphrys. We were not to set eyes on each other for eighteen years. In the interim he was to become a fully fledged foreign correspondent and a familiar face on television.

On general election day in June 1970 no overtly political items were allowed on to the programme: a polling day rule which still obtains. To fill one of the gaps, Bill got a whiff of something happening at the famous Fleet Street watering hole El Vino's. Some real trouble was expected, but though it involved women one of the male reporters, Nick Woolley, was despatched to cover the story. This seems remarkably odd now; at the time we simply accepted it. El Vino's had what seemed even then an extraordinarily old-fashioned attitude to female drinkers. They were allowed in, but on sufferance: they had to go into the back of the pub, and then only if there was a seat for them; all standing female drinkers were banned. Most of the women journalists now had equal pay with their male colleagues, and that election day a group of them, including Jill Evans of the *Mirror* and Unity Hall of the *Sun*, decided to stage a revolt. They stormed into El Vino's and demanded to be allowed to drink standing at the bar. All hell broke loose. Soda siphons were squirted and glasses smashed, and, as other women joined the rebellion, one of them, Alice Barstow, was knocked to the ground and kicked hard by one of the male drinkers. Nick Woolley had his tape-recorder ripped out of his hands by one of the staff and was manhandled out of the pub by a couple of bouncers. Considering the appalling way in which they were treated, the women reacted with an extraordinary calm. No police were called; in the end they simply went back to their desks. But El Vino's was never quite the same – especially after the big newspapers deserted Fleet Street. Its regime was to be challenged some years later in the courts by Tess Gill and Anna Coote, but by then most women had found more congenial places to drink.

At least twice a year *The World At One* team gave good parties, to which politicians and journalists were regularly invited. One of our regular commentators on Russian affairs, Vitaly Kobych of *Izvestia*, returned Andrew's hospitality one evening by inviting a small group of us back to his flat in Swiss Cottage. Most Russians on temporary work permits in London at this time lived in one of the large 1950s Swiss Cottage apartment blocks close to the underground station. Vitaly was a generous host. There was Beatles music on an old-fashioned gramophone, a lot of noise and copious amounts of vodka. Our fellow guests were Russians, vaguely introduced as working in the London embassy. Few of them admitted to speaking English. It all seemed rather daring, being at a party with Russians, especially when one of them, a handsome man in his forties who spoke excellent American-accented English, asked if he could give me a lift home to Kensington. His card told me he was one of the embassy's scientific counsellors. I accepted and climbed into the black Moskva, but I was conscious of deep disapproval from two women and a man in the back seat to whom I was not introduced.

The following day the handsome Russian telephoned from a public phone box: could we meet for a drink? Russian security arrangements made things a little awkward, he said; perhaps I wouldn't mind if we met somewhere not too close to the embassy? I invited him round to the apartment in Stafford Terrace. He was amusing company and I was intrigued, and over the next few weeks we enjoyed a not very serious affair. He was a helpful visitor: one evening, as if to prove his scientific credentials, he did a good repair job on some doubtful-looking fuses in the flat's fusebox, and marked them up in Russian. When I mentioned my new acquaintance to my naval friend Richard, he warned me that my Russian was almost certainly up to no good: he was probably keen to make use either of my BBC connections or of my South African ones. I assured him that I was careful in my conversations with the Russian not to give him any information that might conceivably have been politically useful.

A few weeks later – on 25 September 1971 – what came to be called 'one of the biggest spy scandals of all time' broke in all the news bulletins. The foreign secretary Sir Alec Douglas-Home expelled from Britain 105 Soviet officials for espionage activities. They came not just from the embassy but from all the Russian trade organizations based in London: it was assumed most of them had been engaged in industrial counter-intelligence. Moscow, it was made clear, would be permitted no replacements. Some of the spies were named – and there heading the list, to my astonishment, was my friend the scientific counsellor, identified as the top KGB man in London. He disappeared back to the Soviet Union and I never heard from him again. But I often wondered how many future owners of that flat were puzzled by all the Russian markings in the fusebox.

Played back over thirty years later, Bill Hardcastle's interviews and his linking commentaries on *The World At One* still seem astonishingly fresh. He could make the daily stuff of politics seem vital, and give the politicians and the powerful union bosses an entertainingly uncomfortable ride. Conscious of the rising numbers of listeners and the growing power of the broadcast media, MPs and ministers lined up to appear on the programme. As Bill pointed out in an article in the *Listener* in the early 1970s, although there was by that time 'an increased wariness between broadcaster and politician, the politician who does not try to "use" the media is not worth the votes that elected him'. He noted with regret that the then prime minister was not often heard. 'Mr Heath', he said, 'may be a reluctant performer, but his ministers have never been so freely available to the airwaves.' Enoch Powell, whom Bill admired not at all for his politics but greatly for his broadcasting skills, knew the value of an appearance on *The World At One*; he made sure his speeches were available to the programme well in advance. The combination of Bill's strong news sense and Andrew's searching intellect had made radio important again; by turning a lunchtime news programme into essential listening, they had rejuvenated the medium. At a time when there was still no live broadcasting from parliament, they helped shift the political centre of gravity from the debating chamber of the Commons to the broadcasting studio.

By the spring of 1972 I had been with *The World At One* for almost five years. One morning, as I sat at my editing machine slicing away at some tape, the phone rang. It was the editor of *Woman's Hour*, Wyn Knowles. She was thinking of making a few changes, and having one or two fresh voices introducing the programme. They had a number of people in mind; would I like to be considered? It would mean an audition in their studio. I was intrigued. This was potentially an enormous opportunity. If it worked out for me, it would be a huge step up the BBC ladder, from being one of a reporting team to fronting my own programme again. I arranged to attend an audition the following week; there, as

I read a linking script and interviewed people on issues important to women, I realized I felt immediately at home. This was not rushing about recording three-minute interviews with people in the news, or pulling together yards of edited tape to make a short feature. It was sitting down in a studio as the main presenter of the programme, as I had done in South Africa, feeling 'in charge', and talking to people – really discussing things with them, examining arguments – with far fewer time pressures. A decade and a half later I was to have to change again, and re-adapt to the hurly-burly of news.

Ten days after the audition I was offered a contract, initially to share the presenting with Marjorie Anderson; if everything worked out, I was to replace her six months on as the full-time voice of *Woman's Hour*. But Marjorie was not herself quite ready to go, and there would be some difficult negotiations ahead.

CHAPTER SIX

Hours with Women

MT: Will our voices sound rather similar?

SM: Well, there might be a similarity of *timbre*, but I expect the listeners will be able to tell the difference.

Exchange between the author and Margaret Thatcher prior to the Conservative leader's appearance on *Woman's Hour* in 1975.

Woman's Hour has been described as 'a clever mixture of Women's Institute and Women's Lib'. It is certainly an institution: the longest-running daily programme on BBC radio. By the early 1970s it had a hard core of loyal followers, some of them women who had inherited the habit of tuning in just after lunch from their mothers. Listening made them feel, as their mothers had felt, like members of a friendly women's club.

Woman's Hour began life in 1946 when rationing and postwar blues still enveloped Britain. It was a programme aimed unashamedly at housewives, dreamed up, it was said, to encourage women back into the home after all the vital war work which had taken them out of it – into factories, into the services and on to farms. The emphasis was on cooking, childcare, medical problems and making-do-and-mending. One producer claimed, only half jokingly, that the practical postwar advice included tips on how to de-slime your face flannel and on knitting a brand new stair carpet. The home hints sat side by side with humorous talks, celebrity interviews and listeners' letters. After a slightly rocky start with a male presenter, Alan Ivieson, *Woman's Hour* flourished under his successor, Jean Metcalfe, who occupied the presenter's chair from 1947 to 1958: the programme soon had an audience of over four million, roughly one in five of the adult female population.

The programme had always been run by a clutch of devoted producers and a handful of formidable editors – the humorous writer Basil Boothroyd once called the trio of editor, deputy editor and presenter a 'triumvirago'. Some of the producers were men – never more than one at a time – but editorial control remained firmly in female hands. Rather like *The World At One, Woman's Hour* was confident it knew its audience well. It had famously taken up 'taboo' subjects from an early stage. In 1948 a respected obstetrician, Dr (later Dame) Josephine Barnes, gave a carefully crafted talk on 'The Older Woman', with some good advice on coping with the effects of the menopause. It caused a tremendous flutter in the managerial dovecotes, few of whose inhabitants could believe that such intimate matters had been freely discussed on a radio programme. A memo went flying from the Head of the Home Service to the Controller of the Spoken Word: 'I do believe the inclusion of such a talk represents a lowering of broadcasting standards. It is acutely embarrassing to hear about Hot Flushes, Diseases of the Ovary and the Possibility of Womb Removal transmitted on 376 kilowatts at two o'clock in the afternoon. This view is shared by the female staff in our department.' But the *Woman's Hour* audience had already been fascinated by discussion of a subject no other programme would have touched – and, presumably, grateful for it: there is no record of a single objection from any listener.

By the time I joined the programme in the autumn of 1972, hot flushes would not have caused the slightest raising of an eyebrow, not even in BBC management. They were part of the rich tapestry of being female, picked out in some detail by a programme used to informing and reassuring. Most of the programme team believed management hardly ever listened to the programme anyway: at two o'clock they were probably still at lunch. Gynaecological talks were now joined by regular discussions on abortion, the pill, homosexuality, piles and incontinence. The programme's format had not changed markedly over the preceding twenty-five years, and much of the content was very kind and cosy; but there was also a decent helping of topical and current issues, particularly explanations of the changes in the law affecting women, of which there were a number in the early 1970s.

Divorce, single parenthood, physical and mental handicap – anything could be considered as long as it was well done, interesting and relevant to the audience. In the past, 'storm warnings' had been issued at the beginning of the programme to women who might be listening in the company of children: anything sexually explicit, for example, was preceded by an alert, in case embarrassing questions were asked at home. No doubt this heavily increased the attention span of the under-twelves. There were few storm warnings by the time I arrived, though a 'different' audience at half-term and during the longer school holidays was still taken into account. There had been a brief flurry of concern in 1971, just after Wyn Knowles took over from Mollie Lee as editor, when the f-word cropped up. It was incorporated in a recorded feature about current attitudes to sex; the word was used by a teenager, speaking rather disapprovingly of its ubiquity in popular 'alternative' publications of the time like *Oz* and *International Times*. Its use had to be cleared with Stephen Bonarjee, the man who ran radio current affairs. Bonarjee decided that if the programme team weren't offended by it, then it was fine by him. But the tabloid papers picked it up on the broadcast, and two days later, much to the derision of some members of the team, the managing director of BBC radio, Ian Trethowan, deemed it necessary to appear on air and make a personal apology in case anyone had been offended.

I presented my first *Woman's Hour* on 4 September 1972, from

Studio B9, deep beneath the surface of Portland Place in the bowels of Broadcasting House. I had been warned not to be disturbed by odd noises: the London Underground's Bakerloo line was close by, and every few minutes its faint rumblings penetrated the studio's soundproofing. *Woman's Hour* went out in those days on the old Light Programme, just after *Listen with Mother* and the two o'clock news bulletin. It was live but carefully rehearsed. The editor listened to the rehearsal from her office several floors above, and I was warned that it was as well to remember that unguarded comments about anything were usually overheard. Over five years had passed since my last live *Woman's World* in Cape Town, so I felt both nervous and a bit unpractised as I sat down in front of the microphone. But the rehearsal and transmission went smoothly enough, and I remembered not to rustle my script.

Most of the contributors were female, including, on that first afternoon, the managing director of a new publishing company called Octopus Books that specialized in 'leisure publications'; she was confident that within a few years all women would be working a four-day week and have plenty of time for new hobbies. The 1967 Plowden Report on primary education had described gypsy or traveller children as among the most deprived in the country; June Rose, a regular freelance reporter, talked to gypsy families and those trying to help them about the problems of educating children who seemed so far outside the normal school system. Roy Strong – then in charge of the National Portrait Gallery in London – and the journalist Anne Sharpley wondered whether, as Oscar Wilde had it, wearing 'far too much rouge and not quite enough clothes' is 'always a sign of despair in a woman'. Anne Sharpley was a writer for the London *Evening Standard* who had recently discovered a sympathy with feminism. She referred that afternoon to 'profound and interesting social changes' taking place in Britain's social fabric. She thought that women would soon have less a need to cover despair with make-up than an urgent requirement to find themselves satisfying lives. 'If you have the divorce laws changed as we have just seen them changed,' she said, 'women can no longer count on marriage as a bed ticket. They know that they now have to bustle about and make themselves a career, because their marriage may not last five years whether they want it or not.' Bustling about and making themselves a career was a more novel idea at the time than one might have supposed. The divorce laws to which she referred had three years earlier shifted the emphasis from the behaviour of one or both of the parties to the state of the marriage as a whole. The idea of 'no fault' divorce was introduced for the first time, along with the possibility of divorcing after five years' separation if one party objected. The numbers of couples divorcing had trebled in a decade in England and Wales: it was to double again in the following ten years.

I was conscious, as I returned to the office after my first pro-gramme without having dropped too many stitches, that I was in a rather delicate situation. I was presenting *Woman's Hour*; but I was not yet *the* presenter. Wyn Knowles had arranged that for the first six months I should alternate with the established presenter, Marjorie Anderson. Marjorie was approaching her sixtieth birthday and was not in the best of health, but showed no inclination to move aside. In the event she did retire at the end of those six months; she was by then very frail, and I felt sorry for her. She was popular with listeners – so popular that one of them had left her ten thousand pounds in her will 'because she always replied so nicely to my letters'. She had a gentle personality and a beautiful voice, and had been fronting the programme for fourteen years. She also had a devoted friend in Pat Tottman, the office manager, who generally looked after Marjorie and answered all her letters. With this rather stern redhead I had to share an office; and when I returned after my debut, in a state of some apprehension, Pat did not look up from her typewriter. It was clear I was to get no comments or encouragement from her. Wyn Knowles was a little more forthcoming and seemed satisfied with the way things had gone, if a little cautious about expressing any real approval. I was to learn that this was Wyn's way: she kept her enthusiasms, as well as her strong dislikes, to herself. But I knew that she had pushed hard to get me the job over several other well-qualified rivals, so I was grateful to her. I had now made a significant shift up the ladder, from being part of a team of reporters to presenting one of BBC radio's best-known programmes. As well as seeking other people's views, I would be asked to reveal my own when from time to time the press took an interest in me. It was exciting, but also a little disconcerting.

Woman's Hour, I quickly discovered, had its own special way of doing everything. There was the carefully chosen team of producers, each with her own area of special interest, from cookery, current affairs and childcare to the serial reading at the end of the programme. There was one man on the permanent staff: Anthony Derville, a charming and diffident soul who had been there for years and whose areas of expertise were fashion, make-up and celebrity guests. The programme's contents were arranged several weeks in advance so that details could be put in *Radio Times*: there was little flexibility. Each day's rehearsal took place between eleven and half-past twelve. The editor, listening in from her office, would make suggestions – cut something here, add a little there – before everyone paused for lunch. This was rather a formal affair, known officially in the programme's daily diary as Luncheon. Its lavishness astonished me after the snatched sandwiches of *The World At One*. A table was laid with a fine white cloth, and there was a hot and cold buffet. The programme's cast and its producers sat down and enjoyed all this for an hour or so before it was time to put the show on the air; sometimes it seemed almost a shame to leave the table. After the frantic rush and last-minute nature of news and current affairs all this struck me as just a little unspontaneous as well as being enormously time-consuming.

On my second day, after he had handed me my list of twenty questions for the week's special guest, I asked Anthony Derville if I could think up my own questions in future. I put the question tentatively; I knew he had spent hours preparing the list. A look of enormous relief crossed his face. 'My dear! Of *course* you can ask your own questions. Nothing could be better.' I decided I could get bolder still. I asked Wyn Knowles if she thought the programme as a whole might benefit from living more dangerously: could the rehearsals perhaps be done away with altogether? She beamed; Wyn, unlike some of her predecessors, was always happy to consider new ideas. It was the scripted talk which required most rehearsal, and this was on the wane throughout the BBC. From then on, although the lavish lunches lasted for a few more years, *Woman's Hour* began to be a lot more topical.

We still observed the ground rules which took into account the very different kinds of women who might be listening. During the week the audience was assumed to be women at home not in paid employment. Therefore cookery items on *Woman's Hour* should never advise putting something 'in the fridge': many lower-income households might not have one. It was better to recommend leaving food 'in a cool place'. The audience for the omnibus *Weekend Woman's Hour* on a Saturday was assumed to be different: most of the women who listened then would have been out at work during the week, so their household incomes might well be higher. Therefore mentioning fridges or even freezers at weekends was quite permissible. All the same, we had to be careful about referring to women earning money outside the home as 'working women': this might offend those who toiled away at home all day. 'Women who went out to work' was the acceptable phrase. There should also be no assumption that the women who listened could afford to take holidays abroad. The cheap package holiday had only been invented in the previous decade – as I well knew: *The World At One* had sent me to cover one of the first inexpensive all-in trips to Majorca: ten pounds for a long weekend in Palma – and in the early seventies it was assumed that most people holidayed in the United Kingdom. One practical tip offered on *Woman's Hour* to listeners holidaying in a damp British resort was: 'Take your library ticket along. You'll never be bored for a moment.'

155

The women's movement had begun to disturb the old certainties. A book by the American feminist Betty Friedan, *The Feminine Mystique*, had begun what was called 'consciousness-raising' in the sixties, but it had nothing like the impact in Britain of Germaine Greer's *The Female Eunuch* in 1970, with its cover showing a pair of breasts which could be worn or discarded. I remember reading it in a week, sitting up in my narrow bed in my shared Kensington flat. It was a trumpet blast of defiance. Women, it said, should fight back against male hierarchies and be proud of themselves, and it was fine to forget about marriage. Indeed, said Greer, if a woman is interested in a better deal, she must positively refuse to marry. Suddenly, for me, it felt quite normal to be single; and I was entranced by Greer's wit and outrageous logic. The book became an instant best-seller, though some married women said they had to read it at home disguised in a plain wrapping. It transformed Germaine Greer from an academic and occasional television performer into a national figure. I went along to a massive gathering of women in Trafalgar Square which she addressed – in much the same state of excitement I had experienced when I had tried to hear Bobby Kennedy's speech in Cape Town. Greer stood at the base of Nelson's Column, her long cloak flapping in the breeze, looking from a distance like a Victorian statue of Boadicea. There were banners all around, held aloft by women with long hair and middle partings, calling for equal pay, equal rights, and free abortion on demand.

This was heady stuff: but there was a good measure of political sympathy for much of it. David Steel's bill to legalize abortion under certain clearly defined criteria had been passed in 1967, but it was still by no means easy to arrange to terminate an unwanted pregnancy. Avoiding it in the first place was easier; the pill had been available in Britain since the early sixties, and by the end of the decade it was usually a straightforward matter to have it prescribed whether or not one was married, though it was not free on the NHS until 1974. Despite regular scare stories about possible side-effects, including an increased risk of breast cancer, it was widely accepted and popular. One survey in 1971 showed that almost 20 per cent of women of childbearing age preferred the pill to any other kind of contraceptive.

Strangely, although there were regular discussions on contraception, there was not much on *Woman's Hour* about the early manifestations of women's lib. There had been reports on conferences on women's rights, and advice for women who wanted to return to work after a break to have babies; Barbara Castle was interviewed on her equal pay bill in 1970; and there were occasional accounts of what the women's liberation movement in the United States was doing. But young grassroots feminists in Britain were virtually ignored. This may have been due to an innate conservatism among the programme's editorial staff: many of them were older, full-time professional career women who hadn't had to juggle the demands of home and office. It was also quite likely that they found the more radical members of the women's movement extremely wary of talking to journalists.

While I was still working on *The World At One* in 1971, Frances Donnelly and I were commissioned by Radio Four to make a five-part series with the rather serious title 'Militant women: an examination of the current women's liberation movement'. Frances was a passionate supporter of women's lib. Her sensitivities to traditional male attitudes had no doubt been honed by her experience as a 'sub' in the radio newsroom, where women were heavily outnumbered. She was later to join the *Woman's Hour* production team, where she adorned her office walls with popular women's lib posters of the time. Two of them, bearing the exhortations 'Women Unite – Liberation Now!' and 'Women of England Say Go!' (a reference to a First World War recruiting poster) so upset Stephen Bonarjee that he demanded their removal. Frances complied, to her everlasting regret. As Frances and I prepared our series for Radio Four we had enormous difficulty persuading the members of the women's movement to talk to us. Many of them operated in Marxist feminist cells in cities like Liverpool and Manchester, and were highly suspicious of the media. The Bristol Women's Liberation Group initially agreed to talk to us only if all twelve of them could participate, considering the concept of a single voice a masculine perversion of the way society should work: it was the collective view of the sisterhood which mattered. We had to explain patiently that twelve versions of their message might confuse even the most sympathetic listener. They reluctantly agreed to select one or two representatives. We spent a morning with them as they handed out leaflets demanding free contraception for all to some slightly surprised women shoppers. One woman told them firmly that her husband 'didn't believe in it', though whether this was sex or contraception was not entirely clear. We made five programmes on Militant Women, but they were safely tucked away on Radio Four's schedules at ten-thirty at night.

Germaine Greer, who appeared in our series, had no problems with sharing her ideas with the media – she thoroughly enjoyed the limelight. She and her fellow writer Eva Figes, who had just brought out her own book, *Patriarchal Attitudes*, discussed marriage. Greer reiterated the views expressed in *The Female Eunuch*. She told me that living with a man in a permanent relationship, married or not, crushed a woman. Of the two, marriage was the worse option, for the law as it stood then put her under her husband's financial control. 'As it stands, the institution of marriage does not recognize a woman's existence as a separate entity. To the extent of cloaking her name, absorbing her income in her husband's income, insisting on mutual domicile and so on . . . you have no right in a legal situation to anything. In a marriage, the marriage itself becomes an abstract for which you have to be prepared to suffer in order for it to succeed.' All sorts of avenues would open up to women once they had a choice about their relationship with men.

Eva Figes, a divorcee, approved of the general tone of Greer's message but said she had no faith that 'the ordinary girl' would reject marriage for a freer life. 'I have talked to young sixth formers at comprehensive schools and they are absolutely horrified at the suggestion. And I have said in my own book that as long as marriage is there, people will [get married]. This is true of even fairly sophisticated people who have lived together for years. Marriage is a final challenge and at some stage in their relationship they feel they have to go through with it.' So would marriage be with us for ever? 'I hope not. We now have the situation where a woman can be divorced without her consent and without having committed any fault in the eyes of the law. I hope we will eventually get to the situation where it is legally unnecessary for a woman to be protected by the marriage laws, because the trouble with the marriage laws is that they provide [a woman] and her children with no protection and no security. I hope people will be able to love each other more effectively when they don't feel they are tied down legally.'

Nothing of this kind was heard on *Woman's Hour* at the time. Wyn Knowles has been described as a facilitator rather than an innovator: she was more interested in social than in political issues. Wyn was in her late forties, unmarried, small, neat and pretty. She was keenly aware that her audience consisted largely of home-bodies: women who did not go out to work, whether because they chose not to, or were retired, or were young mothers at home with small offspring. Some of them would undoubtedly be fascinated by discussions about all-women communes and whether men were unnecessary; but the majority of the audience, she decided, found such concepts threatening. In a world where equal pay and equal opportunities were coming closer, she thought it best not to alienate those women who were perfectly content to be housewives. The programme would highlight other, less revolutionary movers and shakers.

Each Wednesday on *Woman's Hour*, in the slot called 'Guest of the Week', famous or important people were invited to come in and talk about themselves in a non-confrontational way. It was an invitation not many could resist, though some guests were a great deal better at it than others. Artists and designers were often curiously inarticulate, unable to describe clearly the wonderful things they did. Mary Quant, for instance, still ravishing in her mid-forties in her trademark geometric Sassoon haircut and tailored grey shorts, was virtually paralysed with nerves when she came into the studio; her answers to my questions got shorter and shorter. One of my colleagues tried to tidy up the interview for the Sunday omnibus edition of the programme and removed over a hundred 'ums' and 'ers', which she kept on a long spool of tape. My attempt to interview the artist John Bratby RA was even less successful. He arrived at Broadcasting House with his new fiancée, Patty, whom he had recently met through the Lonely Hearts columns of *Time Out*. Throughout the interview he gazed lovingly at Patty through the studio glass, answering my increasingly desperate questions with distracted monosyllables.

A few months later I had an invitation to visit John and Patty, who were now married, at John's studio in a converted watchtower in Hastings. Patty promised that John would paint my portrait. Despite our earlier encounter, I was highly flattered: a Bratby, with its unmistakably thick layers of vivid oil paint, could command many thousands of pounds, and at the very least my portrait would be a unique record of our broadcast. As I made myself comfortable in his studio I noticed what looked like several dozen portraits of recognizable people stacked against the walls. It dawned on me then that I was merely one of many Bratby sitters lured down to Hastings by the charming Patty; few of them appeared to have taken their portraits away. Bratby painted assiduously all morning, and I sat as still as I could. Patty came in from time to time, gazed at the canvas and exclaimed at the excellence of its likeness. Eventually I was allowed to see the result. It was rather startling: a portrait of a wild-looking woman with bright red hair. It was, I supposed, just recognizably me, so I forked out my four hundred pounds and was allowed to take it home with me. I have it still, though since few of my friends admire it as much as Patty did, it has been consigned to a small upstairs room.

A number of our Wednesday guests were Hollywood actresses visiting London to appear on the stage. Jean Simmons took the lead in the first West End production of Sondheim's A Little Night Music, but her reviews had been lukewarm and she was not in a good mood when she arrived in our studio. She wore a huge floppy hat and dark glasses, both of which she kept on throughout lunch and the interview: I could see only the lower third of her face. Without eye contact or a willing subject it was almost impossible to extract anything of interest, and we were both relieved when she departed. Angela Lansbury, who was in London for Gypsy, was the complete professional. Crossed wires over the arrangements resulted in a live appointment with us just an hour before her matinée performance. To save time she had to come in wearing full stage make-up. But she was relaxed, charming and co-operative, and talked of her uncle George Lansbury, one of the founders of the Labour party. Ingrid Bergman, who was in London to appear in Shaw's Heartbreak House, arrived modestly at the reception desk in a plastic rainhat and carrying a Selfridges bag. Perhaps for her radio was a pleasant change, requiring none of television's time-consuming preparations. Barbara Cartland, who always arrived in her white Rolls-Royce, heavily bejewelled, her hair like spun sugar and make-up to match, certainly felt that way. 'Such a relief, darling, when it's only the wireless and not to have to take trouble!'

Occasionally the big stars could not come in for live interviews and it was necessary to go to them with a tape-recorder. In the early seventies Julie Andrews experienced a slight lull in her career and turned to writing children's books. I went to her London hotel with a Uher tape-recorder, of the kind I had used probably thousands of times over the years. Ten years after its première, the film version of The Sound of Music was still a phenomenal success, and Miss Andrews was happy to talk about it. For the famous swooping opening shot as Maria bursts into song on a hilltop, filming took place on a freezing cold day with the cast wrapped up as warmly as they could manage. Each time the sun emerged for a few minutes, layers of clothing had to be cast aside as a jet helicopter zoomed in, cameraman hanging outside. The shot, Miss Andrews told me, was repeated at least half a dozen times. 'There was a tremendous downdraught from the helicopter as it swept round me and went back to do the shot again. Each time I was knocked absolutely flat. Eight times, maybe more, I was knocked right on my back.' She ended up raising her fist at the helicopter pilot in mock fury. It was a nice story – except that when I checked the tape at the end it was completely blank: nothing at all had been recorded. This was the interviewer's nightmare. I asked her nervously if we might do the whole thing again. But she was quite up to it. 'That's fine,' she said in her best Mary Poppins voice; 'it's often better the second time.' It was, and I could have hugged her.

Bette Davis came to England in the late seventies for a 'character' appearance in a children's film, and she agreed to talk to me one afternoon after her day's work was over. We had been given sufficient notice for her name to be printed in advance in the *Radio Times*, and hundreds of fan letters had already arrived in the *Woman's Hour* office: more than for any other special guest I could remember. Miss Davis was staying at a discreet hotel in Ascot; we were bidden for five o'clock, and warned by her publicity people to be in good time. My producer and I thought it best to use a professional driver, someone who would be sure to pick the quickest way to Ascot from central London. We settled in the back of the car and chatted away without taking much notice of the route. After an hour on the road we arrived inexplicably in Wimbledon. The driver was undoubtedly lost. Eventually, long after the appointed time, we arrived nervously in the lobby of Miss Davis's Ascot hotel. There, poised at the top of the stairs, stood a familiar figure. 'You're LATE!' she screeched. Just for a second she looked terrifyingly like the character she played in *Whatever Happened to Baby Jane?* It took several minutes of abject apology to calm her down, but in the end the interview went well; she was an articulate and intelligent woman, and gave an honest assessment of her career strengths and weaknesses.

Interview with Bette Davis, broadcast 12.9.79

SM: Are you critical of your own work?

BD: Oh, I don't like it very much. I never have liked myself very much, no. When I see it many many years later I am able to separate myself from it. I have never been terribly enamoured of myself, totally satisfied with anything I did. Which is good. You better stay that way. My favourite experience with that, and I learned it very early, was one night after the theatre I came home to my mother and I said, 'Tonight I really gave the greatest performance of my life. I was magnificent tonight.' And my mother said, 'I was there. That was the worst performance you have ever given, because you were having too much fun doing it.' In other words, I had lost control. You mustn't have that much fun. I never forgot that.

SM: Does not being satisfied with what you do mean that you are an absolute perfectionist?

BD: Oh, all Aries people are. It's the real curse of our lives, you know. If I cook a dinner – I had a friend say to me once, 'Why must that dinner be the best dinner in the world?' I said, 'Well, that's the way I'm made. If it isn't, I'm heartbroken.'

SM: Does that make you difficult to live with, do you think?

BD: I don't think I'm very difficult to live with. I think I'm basically difficult with stupid people. The only time I'm

difficult in my own business is when somebody's just dumb
– whether it's a director or whatever – and then it becomes
self-preservation, professionally. I asked my oldest daughter
once 'What would be the one really difficult quality I had as
a mother?' And she said I was always unpredictable. I think
I am very unpredictable, very quick, and probably too much
so. But you know people get very tangled up with parts I've
played. And I'm not an Actors Studio woman. If I'm playing
Mildred in *Human Bondage* I certainly don't go home and
act like Mildred. Or if I'm doing *Little Foxes*. And I've played
quite as many other kinds of women, like in *Dark Victory* or
Voyager. But people are most attracted by evil, aren't they?
How else do you fill newspapers, or gossip columns? People
are fascinated by evil. We certainly know that from the films
they're making these days, don't we? But then it started way
back with Shakespeare, didn't it?

Once the tape machine was turned off she invited us to stay on
and have a drink with her. For almost two hours over several gins
she regaled us with wonderful behind-the-scenes tales of Hollywood.
We were enchanted; we felt we had been forgiven. I could boast to
my friends that I'd spent the evening with a legend, and survived.

Margaret Thatcher appeared as a *Woman's Hour* special guest in
1975, the year she was elected leader of the Conservative party.
She was surprisingly tentative and ill at ease in a radio studio: her
shoulders were hunched as she sat down in front of the microphone.
All too obviously out of her natural element, she confessed to being
a little unnerved at the thought of talking about herself rather than
hard politics. 'Will our voices sound rather similar?' she asked me.
'Well,' I said, not quite sure what the required answer was, 'there
might be a similarity of *timbre*, but I expect the listeners will be able
to tell the difference.' I expect they were.

Ten years on a very different Margaret Thatcher swept into the same studio as our guest. As Prime Minister she was there to talk of the pound (it was dropping close to parity with the dollar), the miners' strike and the necessity to raise interest rates. She was completely at ease, and even answered my questions about her relationship with her husband Denis. 'Do his views sometimes differ from yours politically, and do you argue at home?' I asked her. 'I think he sometimes is more forthright than I am or would dare to be,' she said. 'I sometimes have to exercise a little bit more tact than he might do. But isn't it *nice* to hear it coming straight from the shoulder sometimes?'

All decent interviews are the product of some good research and advance collaboration between producer and interviewer, and though I have always asked my own questions, some of the more cautious producers on *Woman's Hour* occasionally suggested a more careful line than one's instinct dictated. Kate Adie once stood in for me as presenter in the mid-seventies. She recalls that when Cliff Richard came in for a *Woman's Hour* interview she was asked by her producer not to broach the subject of his alleged homosexuality, though it had been the stuff of tabloid speculation for weeks. She cornered him outside the loo just before they went on air. Would he mind a query on all the rumours at the beginning of the interview, just to set the record straight? Not at all, he said; 'Ask away.' Although he fended off the subject with an answer along the lines of 'People can think what they like, but I'm entitled to a private life,' the question had been asked, and he was not at all offended.

In the early seventies Stephen Bonarjee noticed that very few people working on *Woman's Hour* had offspring of their own, and determined that new appointments to the production team should have more direct personal experience of family life. Mary Redcliffe was a freelance journalist and local radio broadcaster in the north of England: she was the mother of two healthy teenagers and of a handicapped child. Soon after she joined the team as a producer, childcare became a regular topic. Mary signed up Dr Penelope

Leach and Dr Hugh Jolly from *The Times* for their own series within the programme. I learned a lot about the delights and frustrations of motherhood, useful for my future role as an aunt, simply by listening to the advice of the gurus. As part of the programme's thirtieth anniversary celebrations in 1976 we followed through a year the progress of a number of babies born on a single day at Queen Charlotte's Hospital in London. The net was swept wide. One new mother we talked to lived in a gypsy encampment and told Mary Redcliffe how perplexed she had been when the midwife had asked her to call her 'when the contractions come every five minutes': she had no watch because no one, she said, had ever told her how to tell the time. So it was that when my sister Kirsty produced her twin girls that same year I felt rather better equipped to know what to do than if I had relied on my own last experience of nappy-changing – almost twenty-five years earlier, with Kirsty herself wearing the nappies.

When Kirsty's twins were four she came on to the programme herself, along with a health visitor, also the mother of twins, to discuss the challenges of caring for two babies at once. For Kirsty, the textbook advice about the breastfeeding of two – simply hold one in the crook of each arm – didn't begin to work. After unsuccessful attempts at some alternative methods – including, she told us, 'kneeling above them like a cow' – she gave up and resorted to bottles. She remarked that the twins, Susanna and Emily, were so closely bonded to each other that she once found them lying in adjoining cots picking each other's nose. When their younger sister Isabel came along she quickly learned to use the twins as her role models, though fortunately not in that respect.

I also learned quite a bit about cooking. My culinary repertoire had never been very large, though my friend Nonie and I had once attended an evening course run by the Cordon Bleu school in London. It was supervised by stern Miss Beverley, who brooked no backchat. We learned how to whisk egg whites the hard way – by hand, in a warmed copper bowl – and how two people could cook a reasonably sophisticated three-course meal in two hours. I soon

'Will we sound alike?' I reassure Margaret Thatcher: *Woman's Hour,* 1976. (BBC Picture Archives)

Royal Wedding commentary team, July 1981: Terry Wogan, Susannah Simons,
Lorraine Chase, me (hatless!), Wynford Vaughan-Thomas. (BBC Picture Archives)

Receiving Sony Award for 'Female Radio Personality of the Year', 1983 (left) and getting to grips with Olympic gold medallist Daley Thompson (above). (BBC Picture Archives)

Sir Robin Day with the *Woman's Hour* team, 1985. Left to right: Kay Evans, Jane Houghton, Robin Day, Sandra Chalmers and me. Note the bow ties. (BBC Picture Archives)

My father (then seventy-two) and me climbing the Madrisa in
Gargellen, Austria, 1983.

Princess Anne adding her name to the BBC's VIP book:
Broadcasting House, 1985. What could have been so funny?
(BBC Picture Archives)

Zandra Rhodes' amazing
creation! One critic likened me
to a 'gold-plated armadillo'.
(Victor Watts)

Getting organized in the
Woman's Hour office, 1986.
(BBC Picture Archives)

With the audience queue for the final *Woman's Hour*, in September 1987: an emotional day.
(N.I. Syndication)

The *Today* Quartet, 1987: (clockwise) me,
John Humphrys, Brian Redhead, Peter Hobday. (BBC Picture Archives)

A friendly word with Diana, Princess of Wales, at the Floral lunch, 1988.
(The Press Association)

Getting close to Walter Matthau: Hollywood, 1988.
(BBC Picture Archives)

Observer cartoon reflecting
prime minister Margaret Thatcher's
concerns of the day. (Trog/Observer)

CAUGHT OFF GUARD

John Humphrys about to destroy *Today's* last
typewriter: Broadcasting House, 1988.

James Naughtie, my partner
for the Millennium morning at the
Dome, in the early hours of
1 January 2000.

discovered that elaborate French cooking against the clock was not one of my talents, and although I use some of Miss Beverley's tips for a smooth white sauce to this day, I picked up more basic skills through the favourite cooks of *Woman's Hour*. Marguerite Patten and, later, Delia Smith, Mary Berry and John Tovey were among our experts, though weightwatching listeners always complained about the amount of double cream John used. Someone installed a Baby Belling in the studio so that cooking could be done 'live' on the spot – much to the consternation of the BBC's fire officers. The only real mishap I can remember was when an aubergine exploded loudly just as we went on the air.

Marika Hanbury Tenison, who wrote on food for the *Daily Telegraph*, was a regular and popular performer for us, and she did not confine her contributions to cookery. In 1982 she knew she was dying of cancer, and she discussed openly with Andrea Adams her attitude to death. She admitted that she had three times contemplated suicide when surgeons had suggested radical surgery on her legs and her lungs, but had decided against it with the help of what she called 'talking to God'. After she was told she had just a few months to live, Marika said she spent 'three weeks when I turned my face to the wall. I just couldn't cope. It seemed such a terribly short time when I had so much to do. I don't know what happened, but one day I woke up and suddenly it was totally different. And I didn't mind about the timing. I just wanted to have as much fulfilment as I could and give as much to other people – as much enjoyment as I could. I wasn't worried about dying. I'm totally unconcerned about the whole thing now.' Her bravery and honesty brought in a huge postbag of appreciation and sympathy. When the news of her death was announced a few weeks later the response was massive and touching.

My sister had married her long-term boyfriend Tristram Cary – known as Chippy to all his friends – in 1974. He came from a family with strong South African connections: his mother Isabel was the sister of my mother's closest friend in Cape Town, Jean McGregor

– indeed, Kirsty and I had first met Chippy when we were infants. They had met again when he was studying at Shrivenham Military College of Science. We were all pleased that they were to marry, though as Chippy was a lieutenant in the Royal Navy – they were to be based near Plymouth – it was possible he would be away at sea for long periods. Our parents came over to England for the wedding in Henley-on-Thames, and Aunts Mona and Sheila arrived from Scotland and the United States. The three sisters had not met since just after the war, and they circled around each other rather warily. Mona, always a plain speaker, caused deep offence with over-critical assessments of the wedding outfits of the other two. There was so much bristling going on that I found it hard to imagine the close and loving sisterly relationship my mother said she remembered. In the end, fortunately, all three of them seemed to part fond friends. The trio were not to see each other together ever again.

As the bride's elder, unmarried sister with no obvious man in tow I was doubtless expected to feel rather uncomfortable at the wedding celebrations. But I did not. It was a happy family occasion, I was delighted to see my parents again – and I had an interesting dinner date that evening back in London. I had first met John Hemming in Cape Town several years earlier. He was good-looking and clever, a businessman who was also a considerable historian: his highly regarded book about the conquest of the Incas was about to be published. I stayed with him the following April in his cottage near Sintra in Portugal as he completed the Inca book. Conditions were spartan: there was no telephone and only a modicum of hot water. There were also some rather disconcerting signs that one of the local hens had used the place as her home before John arrived. The hen turned out to be called Marilyn, and I got to know her quite well as John typed away in another room. She was not allowed back in the house after I arrived, but she regularly obliged us by laying eggs for breakfast outside the back door. John and I saw a great deal of each other once he returned to London, and his family welcomed me almost as a second daughter. His mother Alice, a Canadian, was a strong feminist and a regular fund-raiser for educational scholarships for Commonwealth students; she was a delightful woman, and I was as fond of her as I was of John. Eventually, though, John and I had to face the fact that we had different ends in mind: his thoughts were gravitating towards marriage (not necessarily to me!) and mine were not. Inevitably we parted company – but I stayed close to the whole family after John married Sukie Babington-Smith, and they asked me to be godmother to their daughter Beatrice.

In the early seventies women were beginning to flex their industrial muscles, and the old disputes about wages and job demarcation in the male-dominated industries were joined by strikes by women demanding equal pay for equal work. The first of these was at the Ford factory in Dagenham in Essex, where women sewing-machinists downed tools to demand the same pay as the men. They wanted equality with their male colleagues for doing, in the words of the Equal Pay Act of 1974, 'broadly similar' work. The Dagenham women were followed by women at Ford's Halewood plant in Liverpool and at the Electrolux factory. The trades unions naturally encouraged the new demands, and began to appoint women officers who specialized in the equal pay issue, though not all the male rank-and-file members supported the idea. The Equal Pay Act was supposed to be fully effective by 1975, but despite backing from the new Equal Opportunities Commission the fight for parity was a hard one.

Woman's Hour began to take a cool look at some of these struggles with the help of Tess Gill, a specialist solicitor who was given her own series on the programme, 'Women and the Law'. In 1975 she and a group of women journalists returned to El Vino's in Fleet Street to test the validity of that year's Sex Discrimination Act by demanding to be served standing at the bar. The licensee refused them, as he had done five years previously, and claimed he had every right to do so because they were becoming 'rowdy'. Once again the women were thrown out. Later, in the 1980s, Tess Gill and the journalist Anna Coote challenged this practice, taking their case to the Court of Appeal. They succeeded, and were proud that they had done especially as one of the judges was an El Vino's regular.

Another piece of mid-seventies legislation that was of great importance to women was the Domestic Violence Act of 1976. This made it easier for a woman who was a victim of a violent partner to find somewhere safe to live, and also to get an injunction to prevent him from entering her household. Erin Pizzey, whose husband Jack had been one of my reporter colleagues on *The World At One* and who now had a young family of her own, ran a campaign absolutely crucial to achieving a change in the law. She had opened the first women's refuge in Hounslow in London in 1971; later it moved to larger premises in Chiswick, where I talked to her in 1973 about her pioneering work. What she dealt with there, she told me in the crowded house, were not victims of the odd slap: these women had suffered really vicious punching and kicking. Her description of a typical experience was shocking. A woman might well have 'a husband who when he gets drunk comes home, batters her head against the wall, beats her unconscious, puts her head under the cold tap, and then does it again'. The establishment Erin Pizzey had founded in Chiswick was a genuine refuge: no man could enter unless he was invited to do so by his former partner. Until the change in the law, the police were reluctant to intervene. Many of them might have been individually sympathetic when a complaint was made, but violence in the home was considered to be just that – a 'domestic'. Social service departments were also unable to help with rehousing a victim: if the woman had left home 'voluntarily' there was nothing they could do. I remember Erin Pizzey's stark statement: 'If a man beats his dog the RSPCA is after him; if he attacks his children it's the NSPCC; but if he beats his wife there's no one to help.' Another three years passed before legislation to improve matters was passed; and even twenty-five years on, only around a third of the number of refuges recommended in that 1976 Act have been set up.

I found I liked working with women. I had enjoyed my years on *The World At One*, but after the highly competitive and sometimes abrasive atmosphere of a daily news programme it was a relief to spend time in a less hectic atmosphere. In the early seventies news and current affairs programmes were run by and largely staffed by men: Andrew Boyle was the exception in employing equal numbers of male and female reporters. And once I joined *Woman's Hour* I learned an enormous amount about a political world we had hardly touched on *WATO*.

In February 1976, as the United States celebrated its bicentennial, I introduced a series of interviews recorded by Pat Rowe with a number of black American women in New York who felt that they had yet to see their share of the American dream. The women's movement was of scant relevance, they said, to the majority of black women in the United States. Over a century after the abolition of slavery, they were still struggling to be accepted as ordinary middle-class Americans. Eleanor Holmes Norton, now a member of Congress but then working with the Human Rights Commission in New York, pointed out that only fifty years earlier a black woman had but two occupations open to her: teaching, if she was educated, or domestic work if she was not. In the mid-seventies the struggle for a better place in society was still a protracted and difficult one. White women who claimed to be oppressed seemed to have little in common with black women on the bottom rung of the ladder. Ms Holmes Norton advised Britain to copy the new American race discrimination laws, and go for tough legislation from the start: there was little point, she said, in a gradual tightening of controls. Florence Kennedy remembered moving into what had been an all-white area and her father standing on his new front porch with a shotgun when white neighbours objected to her family's presence. 'My parents were very much into not taking shit,'

171

she told us. 'He dared anyone who objected to put his foot on the first step up to the front door.' They heard no more complaints.

It was a kind of black defiance unthinkable in the South Africa I knew. During one of my trips back to Cape Town to see my parents, it suddenly occurred to me that much of the misery inflicted upon individual black people in South Africa by the apartheid system could be sharply conveyed by a look at the life of an ordinary black domestic worker. The relatively affluent white society which was my own background was strongly underpinned by a world of 'maids and madams'; most middle-class white households still employed at least one black servant, often several, who lived on the premises but in their own quarters. At the time around 800,000 black women were in domestic service in South Africa, adding up to a sizeable section of the economy. Sometimes, but not always, there was a close bond between employer and employee, but even then it was an utterly unequal relationship, and the black women who cooked, cleaned and babysat earned very little. Few employers knew the surnames of their maids, or much else about their private lives; few of them cared to know, as long as the servant worked satisfactorily, there wasn't a string of 'boyfriends' in their room at night, and the dreaded pass book was in order. In rural areas there was more likely to be exploitation of black servants, and often back-breaking work was expected for a pittance.

For Radio Four's *Profile* programme I presented a picture of the life of Pauline Mzantsi, who was employed by an old schoolfriend of mine, a social worker called Anne Templeton. Anne and her husband Peter, a former Roman Catholic priest, had three children; they both went out to work and needed a highly reliable woman at home to take responsibility for the children during the day. They were model employers in the South African context: they paid decent wages (at the time ninety rand – forty-five pounds – a month was considered a decent wage) and they treated Pauline well. The Templetons were interested in Pauline's family and her background, and both Anne and Pauline herself were happy to talk to me about their relationship.

Pauline's life was utterly constrained by the apartheid laws. As a black woman from the Transkei area of the Eastern Cape, she could not automatically follow her husband to Cape Town, live with him and find work. The law stated that 'the African migrant labour force must not be burdened by *superfluous appendages* like wives and children and dependants' (my italics). Life in the Transkei was hard: poor farming practices made self-sufficiency difficult, and there were almost no jobs. So Pauline had arrived in Cape Town as an 'illegal' with no pass. As a result she was constantly being arrested in the daily sweeps by the police on any gathering of black people, and without her pass she automatically spent the night in gaol. Anne and Peter were willing to employ her as an illegal even though it meant a fine for them of five hundred rand if this was discovered. Any job in a city was better, Pauline told me, than hunger back home, but she felt especially lucky to have found the Templetons. She stayed with them for thirteen years; without her, as Anne told me years later, they would have found it impossible to do the community work they did in the nearby black townships, or, as she put it, to 'get our hands dirty in the struggle'.

If *Woman's Hour* throughout the seventies covered the changing lives of women from vastly differing backgrounds, one section of the programme was utterly constant: the fifteen-minute serial slot at the end. This was run with huge devotion and fiercely high standards by Pat McLoughlin, a former Wren officer and BBC studio manager. I took to Pat instantly: she was tall and slightly craggy, with a huge smile and a very loud laugh. As a skilful abridger and producer, she was held in immensely high regard by all the actors she worked with. Alan Bennett recorded his memoirs for her, and so did Dame Edna Everage; Martin Jarvis, Hannah Gordon, Janet Suzman and Juliet Stevenson all regularly read *Woman's Hour* serials, as did Patricia Hodge, Diana Rigg, Harriet Walter and Nigel Hawthorne. Pat sometimes did the abridging herself, and she told me that it was not uncommon for a book to be reduced to an eighth of its original size. The authors, if they were alive, never complained, and even devoted Jane Austen fans happily accepted Pat's versions. One book became a best-seller after it was serialized on *Woman's Hour*: *Diana's Story* (1989), Deric Longden's moving and even humorous account of looking after his dying wife.

Pat sat in an office slightly removed from everyone else's, from which she would emerge to attend the post-programme meetings and offer her sharp opinions of each day's offerings. She and the deputy editor Kay Evans, another former Wren officer, could reduce the team to wild waves of laughter, but she took her role very seriously indeed. Like almost all devoted *Woman's Hour* fans both inside and outside the BBC – including myself – Pat was furious when in 1991 Michael Green, the Controller of Radio Four, considered changing the programme's name. He thought it sounded old-fashioned and wanted something less specific to women, but had no real idea of what that should be. Pat crept unseen into the BBC's Council Chamber one evening and stuck badges bearing the legend 'I'm a *Woman's Hour* man' on the portraits of all the director-generals. When two years later she retired at the age of sixty, she confessed at her farewell party that it was she who had done it. *Woman's Hour* did keep its name, but not its time: it was moved to ten-thirty in the morning, and has been a morning programme ever since. I remain unconvinced that this was a good idea; for mothers of young children especially, the afternoon slot fitted in well with the daily routine, giving them a chance to listen while their offspring had a nap.

Although formal written 'talks' began to be used less frequently, when the New York writer Helene Hanff was persuaded in the mid-1970s to become a regular correspondent for *Woman's Hour* she rapidly became one of our most popular contributors. Her 'Letters from New York', delivered in her unmistakably gravelly gin-and-cigarettes voice, were delightful. Her quirky and touching postwar correspondence with Marks & Co., the London secondhand booksellers, had turned into a best-selling book called *84 Charing Cross Road*, making her much more famous in Britain than she was in her native land. The correspondence with Frank Doel was adapted into a play, and then a film starring Anne Bancroft and Anthony Hopkins. The play became a standard favourite with regional repertory theatres. It brought in regular royalties for Helene for the first time in her life, and gave her some financial independence. This meant she could have badly needed cataract operations in New York. The results were startling. She told me that when she looked in the mirror and saw herself clearly for the first time in over twenty years she was appalled. 'Oh my GAHD!' she'd yelled. 'It's a GARgoyle!'

Helene encapsulated for us the sensation of living in New York – 'It's like being shot out of a cannon each morning as the alarm goes off!' – but her monthly accounts of daily life as seen by a modest East Side apartment dweller generally involved her neighbour Bentley the English sheepdog, her well-off friend Arlene, and local events like the replanting of the Shakespeare Garden in Central Park. I looked up Helene whenever I was in New York, and we lunched at the Oyster Bar in Grand Central Station. She was always ruthlessly honest. Once I brought her a new recording of a Mozart symphony in the mistaken belief that she might enjoy listening to it. 'Oh, but I LOATHE Mozart!' she informed me. After she died in 1997, just before her eightieth birthday, the actors' church of St Paul's in Covent Garden gave her a magnificent memorial service, and it was packed with her fans.

In 1977, two years after I had first interviewed Mrs Thatcher for *Woman's Hour*, I had a chance for a more extended encounter with her as Conservative leader. She was invited to visit China, and a small selection of British journalists was allowed to accompany her. They were a rather distinguished bunch of columnists and feature-writers, including Katharine Whitehorn of the *Observer*, Ann Leslie of the *Daily Mail* and George Gale of the *Express*. Rather to my surprise, *Woman's Hour* was offered two places – one for Wyn Knowles and one for me. It was a time when it was difficult for foreign journalists to get visas to enter China, and although everyone was ostensibly covering the Thatcher visit, we were determined to try to paint as broad a picture as we could of modern China only a year or two after Mao's death.

We flew to Peking via Karachi on a China Airways plane that turned out, to the loud dismay of most of the party of hacks, to be entirely dry: not a drop of alcohol was available to anyone in economy class, though we noticed that this did not apply to the VIPs in first class. Mrs Thatcher took pity on us and sent through some small bottles of a fierce Chinese firewater that she had been given in advance by her hosts. She was accompanied on the trip by her daughter Carol, who was rather nice, and by Douglas Hurd, who had served in Peking as a diplomat in the 1950s and eventually became her foreign secretary. While we journalists worked our way through our briefing papers and newspaper cuttings, I imagined Mrs Thatcher grilling him on what he knew of modern Chinese life.

Several days into the trip we paid a visit to the People's Evergreen Commune outside the city of Suchow. It was obviously a showpiece place, with lush acres of flowers – grown for scented tea – and fields of well-fed pigs. As usual, the morning began with a harangue from party officials about the misdemeanours of the Gang of Four – Mao's widow Chiang Ching and her three cronies, who had recently been arrested. We were to understand that they were responsible for any failings we might observe in their country. We were taken on a tour of the Commune's hospital and pharmacy, and I asked some questions about family planning in view of China's strict 'one child' policy. I learned that family planning lessons according to the precepts of Chairman Mao began even in the kindergarten. If a woman became pregnant with a second child she generally opted for abortion and then sterilization – or was encouraged to. At the end of the morning we repaired to the village hall for a question-and-answer session with the village elders and our translators. There was much discussion about the role in the Commune of the famous 'barefoot doctors' – medical auxiliaries who specialized in working in remote and impoverished areas. The idea had been dreamed up by the Chinese as an efficient way of bringing modern medicine to the rural poor, and by now had spread to other areas of the Third World. It had been particularly successful in Julius Nyerere's Tanzania. As proceedings drew to a close Mrs Thatcher raised her hand. 'What exactly', she asked, 'is a barefoot doctor?' Whatever she and Douglas Hurd had spoken about in the front of that plane, it was not about the way Chinese society was run.

It was spring in Peking, but the city was a vast and dusty place: the beauty of the Forbidden City and the greenery of the parks were in sharp contrast to the bleak, wide streets and acres of unattractive Soviet-style buildings. The main roads were wide and crammed with cyclists, most of them, like nearly all Chinese, still dressed in severe blue or grey Mao-style suits. Only the children were permitted to wear brightly coloured clothes. Our hotel was one of the few high-rise buildings in central Peking: a massive place with shabby rooms, all too obviously inspired by its gargantuan equivalents in Moscow. The early morning call consisted of the telephone operator ringing the room and shouting 'Get UP!' No doubt our rooms were bugged; we were certainly carefully monitored by our guides and translators, and it would have been almost impossible for us to get any sort of picture of Chinese domestic life had it not been for Gladys Yang.

Gladys was born in China of English missionary parents and had lived there since 1940; she and her husband Yang Xianyi, who was a graduate of Oxford University, worked for the Foreign Language Press. Back in the 1950s Gladys was a regular correspondent for *Woman's Hour* from Peking, and Wyn had kept in touch with her. She welcomed us cheerfully into the crowded apartment which went with the job, and which they shared with four generations of Yangs. Gladys and her husband were highly regarded translators, but because of their professional and family connections with the West had gone through severe hardships during the Cultural Revolution. They were imprisoned for four years, during which time Gladys had also spent many months in solitary confinement. In Mao's maddest times, any foreign connection meant public vilification as a class traitor. During this time, too, the Yangs' son died tragically. Yet by the mid-1970s Gladys and her husband were fully rehabilitated and remarkably unbitter about their experience of political disgrace; they never once referred to it in front of us. She was not in the least ground down by what seemed to us the extreme poverty of her surroundings and the dirty and insanitary apartment building in which she lived. The Yangs' daughter Pug had got married the week before. There had not yet been a wedding party, as Gladys' husband Xianyi was having trouble with his false teeth; he was not ready for a celebration. We all smiled sympathetically. Suddenly the Chinese seemed just like the rest of us.

And yet, of course, they were not. The most populous nation on earth lived under one of the harshest and most intimidating regimes to be found anywhere. For an Honoured Foreign Guest like Mrs Thatcher this meant that any acceptable whim could be satisfied immediately. In Shanghai her hosts discovered that she had a liking for Chinese silk paintings; she had expressed an interest in seeing some modern examples and in perhaps making a purchase. At nine o'clock at night Shanghai's biggest department store was opened up and we were invited to accompany Mrs Thatcher on her visit. There were no shoppers other than our small entourage of perhaps thirty people. In case the Honoured Guest wished to buy some lipstick, or a satin slipper, or perhaps a book or two, hundreds of shop girls had been ordered from their homes back to work to stand behind the display counters. Every single sales counter on seven vast floors was fully staffed. We were guided quickly up to the top floor where the best of the silk paintings were on display. The Honoured Guest made her purchase, and we departed, sweeping past the rows of obedient employees standing to attention.

The constraints of Chinese life were brought forcefully to my attention again over fifteen years later, when I interviewed Jung Chang, who had left China the year after Mrs Thatcher's visit and whose novel *Wild Swans*, a long time in the writing, had become an acclaimed best-seller.

Interview with Jung Chang, broadcast 12.6.93

SM: You wrote [*Wild Swans*] a long time after you left China. There was a gap of about ten years or so. Was that because your life was so painful to relive?

JC: Yes, that was the reason. When I left China in 1978 I thought I should put all that behind me, I should never look back, I should start a new life. I had always wanted to be a writer in China, when I was working as a peasant barefoot doctor, or as an electrician, I composed long passages in my mind. But to write for publication was out of the question, because in those days China was consumed by political persecutions and writers were denounced or sent to prison camps – it was impossible for me to write. When I came to Britain it was another planet. I developed a kind of urge to write about my life in China. I wrote little bits now and then, but I couldn't dig deep into my memory because the past was really too painful. In 1988 my mother came to stay with me. This was her first trip outside China and I thought I should just take her sightseeing and give her a good time. But after a while I realized that she was restless: she was not having the time of her life and that something was on her mind. One day – I remember very clearly – my mother declined a shopping trip and said she wanted to talk to me. She started telling me some of the stories of her life. When she started she couldn't stop. She left me sixty hours of tape recordings. Now the book is published she's a completely different person – she's very much at peace with herself.

SM: It was 'another planet' when you came here?

JC: Yes, but I felt immediately at home. The thing I felt most strongly in British society [was that] I'm left alone. I'm Chinese, I don't have to be terribly British, I don't have to like football or pubs or cricket. I can be perfectly happy – I am left alone to be myself.

SM: But were you on your own when you came here?

JC: We came in a group of fourteen people: one of us was the political supervisor. When we first came we were not allowed to go out on our own. We had to go out in twos and threes. So the first year in London for me was absolute torment. To live in this free London and not to be allowed out was terrible for me, and so I developed all sorts of schemes and excuses to manage to go out. I also developed a paranoia, because when I was doing things secretly I was terribly afraid that I would be found out. I remember that I had an English boyfriend, and he once took me to the Empire discotheque in Leicester Square, and as there were several people staring at me I was convinced they were spies sent by the Embassy. So I insisted on leaving. He took a look at them and said, 'They are no more spies than I am – they're just men!' [laughs] Everything was a new experience, to see a film, to see a play, to go to a pub. I think I must be one of the first Chinese to have walked into a British pub, because the Chinese translation for the word 'pub' suggests somewhere indecent, with nude women gyrating. So no one was allowed to go. So on this day I just pushed the door open and marched in, and saw nothing of the sort. Only some men sitting there drinking beer. I was terribly disappointed!

The morning after the shopping trip I had an appointment to record an interview with Mrs Thatcher in our Shanghai hotel. The place was comfortably furnished. There were silk and mahogany in the public rooms, and upstairs good old-fashioned bathrooms with brass taps. More astonishing still, our evening baths were drawn for us by a silent valet in a white jacket: a hangover, perhaps, from Shanghai's prewar, pre-revolutionary days as a thriving international port. But of truly modern aids like electric hairdryers there was no sign. I was feeling, and must have looked, a little frazzled after nearly a week of Chinese travel. Mrs Thatcher was all solicitude. 'Would you like to borrow my heated rollers, dear?' she asked. Suddenly there was a possibility of looking well-groomed again.

This was not merely a matter of personal vanity; in the BBC of the seventies there was still a strong emphasis on decorum. Somewhere in the *Woman's Hour* office there was a musty old hat in case someone had to go to a funeral or got invited to a royal garden party. Trousers for women were frowned on, unless you were on night duty. Nancy Wise remembers, as editor of *Pick Of The Week*, being stopped by the controller of Radio Four, Clare Lawson-Dick, as she entered the front door of Broadcasting House. She was carrying her lunchtime purchases in two British Home Stores shopping bags. 'Where are you going with those?' asked Clare. 'It is not appropriate for someone of your status to be seen in the foyer with plastic bags.'

Part of the appeal of working in radio for me was that it allowed a good degree of anonymity: it was unlikely that anyone who appeared exclusively on what was still called the wireless would be recognized or stopped in the street. Desmond Wilcox, who was then in charge of *Man Alive* on BBC1, once offered me the chance to become a reporter on his programme, and was hugely astonished when I turned him down. Perhaps I lacked a certain courage; I knew that reporters in television often came and went with some speed, and the chance of working on a highly regarded documentary series was not enough to persuade me to give up the security of a daily radio programme. Towards the end of the seventies I did present a short series of mini-programmes on television called *My Kind of Movie*, in which celebrities were asked to choose a favourite film and talk about it; and later I made a rather curious series for the religious broadcasting department in which people talked about favourite hymns. One of them was Carla Lane, who had just had a huge success with *The Liver Birds*. I met her in Liverpool in front of the Adelphi Hotel, in whose main lounge she had written some of her first scripts for television. We did a 'walking shot', which involved chatting while strolling towards a camera some distance away. The sound recordist monitored our conversation and recorded it from tiny, almost invisible microphones pinned to our chests. Unfortunately, two local lads spotted Carla, an attractive blonde, and one of them propositioned her in forthright terms. 'Oooh, missus,' he growled, 'I'd loov to shag yer!' His suggestion was clearly heard by the camera team fifty yards away. So we had to go back and do our walking shot again. The local lad, unaware of the film crew, repeated his frank suggestion. Again, we had to go back and repeat the shot. Then Carla and I got the giggles – unstoppably. I think the poor technical team had to record more than twenty attempts before we managed an unblemished thirty seconds for them.

When *Woman's Hour* celebrated its thirtieth birthday in 1976, listeners were invited to send in their own favourite memories of past programmes. For one, it was the triumph of the couple who had completed their self-build house; for another, it was a mother talking about bringing up a Down's syndrome baby. Dr Kit Pedlar, a scientist, then made his predictions for the year 2006, thirty years on. There would be no cars and very little air transport; our overheated planet would be terribly polluted and the world's population diminished. Curiously, no one was asked about what women might have achieved. Perhaps, like Mrs Thatcher herself when she was quizzed about the possibility on *Blue Peter*, they would have taken some convincing that there would be a woman prime minister in their lifetime.

CHAPTER SEVEN

Women Around the World

A news announcer needs to have authority, consistency and reliability. Women may have one or two of these qualities, but not all three.

Jim Black, presentation editor for BBC Radio Four, in 1973, quoted by Mileva Ross in *Is This Your Life? Images of Women in the Media.*

By the beginning of the 1980s women in frontline jobs in radio news and current affairs – working as newsreaders, reporters, interviewers and correspondents – were beginning to tap on the glass ceiling just hard enough to crack it. Sheila Tracy, a former jazz trombonist in Ivy Benson's Band, became the first woman to read the news on Radio Four in 1974; the following year Angela Rippon did the same thing on BBC television, with confidence and perfect enunciation. Where they showed the way, others followed. I, on the other hand, had found that being a woman was a positive advantage at this point in my career, though arguments were soon to rage in the *Guardian* about whether it was a good idea, in the newspaper world at any rate, to have special sections set aside for women.

Woman's Hour was embedded in a department called Current Affairs Magazine Programmes, usually known by its acronym CAMP. This was run by Alan Rogers, a man in his thirties who enjoyed working with women and who was keen to promote them. He had no power over hard news programmes, but *You and Yours*, *Does He Take Sugar?* and the numerous Radio Four phone-ins were part of his empire, and the production staff of all of them was well populated by women. The hours were relatively civilized and family-friendly. The less predictable and more demanding world of hard news was more of a challenge for women. I was aware that there were one or two colleagues who appeared miraculously to combine bringing up children with rigorous toughness as a journalist and more than a touch of glamour. Julia Somerville was one of them. Our professional paths seldom crossed – programmes can be very isolated from one another, as can radio and television – but we became friends, and I knew something of her experience in the BBC.

Julia had started out in the newsroom as a sub-editor in the early 1970s, when it was a large open-plan office crammed with clacking typewriters and the paper detritus of news bulletins – and populated almost entirely by men. The tannoy system squawked out newsflashes and information about correspondents' despatches. The work went on in shifts virtually twenty-four hours a day. 'It was hard-drinking, but fun,' she told me. 'As a woman you were accepted if you accepted that, and did a decent job.' Julia worked her way up through the radio newsroom from sub – writing pieces for the news bulletins – to full-time reporter. By 1981 she was the first woman labour affairs correspondent on BBC radio. It was a huge brief. Industrial relations were in a permanently fractious state – Ray Buckton, the general secretary of the rail union ASLEF, was characterized in the press at one time as 'the most hated man in Britain' – so she was constantly on the air, talking to union leaders and employers, and covering strikes among health workers, car makers, civil servants and railwaymen. After this Julia moved on to television to present the BBC *Nine O'Clock News*.

Other women were working their way into correspondents' jobs through local radio. Kate Adie benefited from a new willingness to send women out on dangerous jobs. She became a national figure in 1980 after her live reporting for BBC television news of the London Iranian embassy siege. This quickly led to her promotion from general reporter to specialist television news correspondent and eventually, by the time of the Gulf War, to fully fledged war correspondent.

Kate had begun her career in BBC local radio in the seventies, at a time when it was expanding rapidly and needed as much young talent as it could get, which meant new opportunities for women to become reporters, newsreaders and even station managers. In 1976 Sandra Chalmers became the first woman to run a local radio station, Radio Stoke-on-Trent; from there she went on to succeed Wyn Knowles as editor of *Woman's Hour* in 1983. But for most women career advancement was still a struggle. More than a decade later Dr Rosalind Gill's research into employment practices in local radio stations showed that even in the late eighties there was still a whole raft of excuses for not promoting women, ranging from a lack of job applications and a lack of female technical expertise to a natural audience preference for male voices.

BBC local radio had done some pioneering work in another area of broadcasting which was to become immensely widespread. From the late 1960s phone-ins were a regular part of their daily programming. Phone-ins are a relatively cheap form of broadcasting, and they were a good way for any local radio station to prove it was closely in touch with its audience. BBC national radio was much slower to follow the trend, though back in 1965 there had been some experimental injections of listeners' own voices into a programme called *Light Night Extra* on the old Light Programme. This involved a great deal of negotiation with the Post Office. Before they gave the programme its own special telephone number – Langham 6666 – they insisted that lines be checked for 'noise and cross talk'. They were nervous not only in case 'private telephone conversations' were unwittingly broadcast via a crossed line but in case the Post Office was blamed on air when things went wrong; so some of the early phone-in conversations were delayed by a 'five-second loop'. The experiment was discontinued after three months. The BBC had found the Post Office far too anxious to impose its own conditions, even suggesting that calls should be restricted to 'people who were used to broadcasting', though who these people might be was not clear. The following year the BBC set out its own highly cautious rules for future phone-in programmes. 'Unintelligible' calls 'must be instantly abandoned', though a follow-up call should always be made to the listener 'to avoid complaints from him that he was cut off'. If a call actually made it on to a programme, 'speakers should be requested to speak clearly and not too quickly, without shouting, and to ensure that the mouthpiece is not allowed to fall under the chin'.

Radio Four took some tentative steps towards a more permanent phone-in format with *It's Your Line* in 1970, chaired by Robin Day, in which politicians and other national figures talked directly to the public. Nothing like it had ever been broadcast before, but as Robin Day was a skilled performer and something of an institution as a result of his television work, it was considered a winning format and ran once a week in the evenings for six years. *Election Call* started in early 1974, the year of the two general elections, in February and October. According to the psephologist David Butler, the election phone-in was considered the 'great success' of the BBC's entire campaign coverage.

The original idea for *Tuesday Call*, which had begun in the summer of 1973, was to invite listeners to phone in and talk to a celebrity. David Willey, the BBC's man in Rome, was asked to approach Sophia Loren to see if she might be the first willing victim. Walter Wallich, the producer, suggested she could talk to listeners about 'hobbies, diet, clothes and similar matters of wom anly interest'. Miss Loren, evidently to everyone's surprise, turned it down. Instead, with the deadline for the launch programme fast approaching, it was decided to ask *Woman's Hour* to take over the slot, every weekday morning from 9.05 to 10.00 a.m. If 'womanly interest' was what was wanted, then it could be stretched to cover a multitude of subjects.

Wyn Knowles initially decided that Judith Chalmers and I should take it in turns to chair the programmes, and I found myself presiding over telephonic seminars on anything from having a baby to alcoholism. Pets, wildlife, coping with exams, income tax, holidays abroad and do-it-yourself were all regular topics. These exchanges were utterly 'live'; there was no five-second delay mechanism or 'panic button' to cut off loquacity or rude words, though listeners did have to submit questions in advance to avoid the phone-in moderator getting landed with the frivolous, the inarticulate or the completely mad. This filter system also eliminated some of the drama, and occasionally our phone-ins could be excruciatingly dull: one Tuesday I had to declare that 'This is National Pot Plant Week'. Though the controller of Radio Four was almost persuaded by our critics (who thought it too 'cosy', and too 'practical') to take the series off the air, *Tuesday Call* survived for over twelve years.

There were many unintentionally diverting moments. Dr Robert Burchfield, the editor-in-chief of the Oxford English Dictionaries, joined the writer Marghanita Laski to answer questions one morning on correct spoken English. A young boy from Kent rang in to ask why we so often refer to 'the 'flu' and 'the measles' but not 'the gastroenteritis'. The experts were baffled. Then someone else rang in to point out that the same thing applied to the names of well-known streets: in London it is customary to refer to 'the Tottenham Court Road', 'the Marylebone Road' and 'the King's Road', but not 'the Oxford Street' or 'the Goodge Street'. On the question of 'the 'flu' Miss Laski could still throw no light; she said it might be 'a local or regional thing'. Dr Burchfield claimed to have heard callers use the expression 'the 'flu' only in Japan. A week later Miss Laski wrote a letter to the *Listener* saying there had been a dreadful misunderstanding: she had misheard the question, and by the time she realized her mistake the caller was off the line. But she still didn't come up with an answer. It wasn't very convincing. The experts, it seemed, were less familiar with some aspects of their subject than were their listeners.

Tuesday Call was also honoured by the woman the press called 'the first senior Royal' to take part in a phone-in. Early in 1985 I was despatched to Buckingham Palace to record an interview with Princess Anne about her latest trip to Africa for the Save the Children Fund. I asked her as casually as I could if she might consider taking part in a live telephone chat with the public. 'I might,' she said, 'but so far nobody's asked me.' An official approach was made, and she agreed to join us for a *Tuesday Call* in September. BBC radio went into furious Royal Visit Preparation mode: the lavatory near our basement studio, which hadn't been refurbished for years, was suddenly spotlessly modernized. The best china was brought out for the royal cup of coffee; even the studio carpet was replaced. On the morning the princess arrived, members of BBC management never before seen by any of us stepped forward to join the royal welcoming party. We all curtsied or bowed appropriately, and Princess Anne sat down in front of the microphone while we explained the procedure to her. She said she would prefer to avoid any questions about her children, but otherwise no prohibitions were made. All she needed for refreshment was a sip or two of water, so the best china stayed on its tray, and the newly sparkling retirement room received no royal baptism.

Out of the thousands of listeners who tried to get through to us that morning with their questions, a dozen or so were successful. Not one of their queries would have got them sent to the Tower, but the programme was in its own way remarkable: the Queen's daughter was submitting herself to a public interrogation. The princess handled the queries briskly and efficiently. Two of her questioners were children, and she was noticeably more relaxed with them. Eight-year-old Abigail brought up the subject that most intrigued the press the following day. 'When you were a little girl, did you know you were a princess and did you play at princesses?' To which the answer was: 'Well, you know, I am sorry to say this, but I think the one thing I never played at was being a princess. I am not sure why. I don't know when you know as a child what you are or, if you have a title, what that means. I don't think a princess is anything I ever played at being really. I have probably been playing at it ever since!'

Laura, aged twelve, from Wimbledon, got in two queries: 'Do you have any pets and do you have a policeman wherever you go?' HRH replied: 'I think perhaps the three dogs that seem to live in the house would qualify as pets. I have a rather strange black and tan dog, and also what is commonly known as a lurcher, which is a sort of poacher's dog. It's a cross between a greyhound and a collie and is very fast, and a thief. We don't trust it in the kitchen. And there is a corgi which is in fact a refugee from my mother's collection of dogs, because he is a dog and she only has bitches. The children are supposed to look after him, but it doesn't seem to happen very much.' As for the question about having policemen with her everywhere, the princess replied that it depended what she meant by 'everywhere'. 'When I am at home in Gloucestershire, around the farm, the answer is no, although there is one actually staying in the house and there are local policemen there. If I go out, either riding or walking, no, I don't have a policeman with me, but when I go driving anywhere else or to any public engagements, yes, there's always one there.'

The following day the press gave it all quite a splash. 'Anne's Red Hot Line!' screamed the *Daily Mail*. 'Five thousand jam the BBC's switchboard as the Princess talks about food, pets and privacy!'

The wedding of her brother the Prince of Wales to Lady Diana Spencer in July 1981 was the biggest outside broadcast the BBC had organized since the coronation of 1953. Although the vast majority of the audience would be watching television, the radio commentary still involved a prodigious feat of organization. It would also go out on the BBC World Service. A spectacularly good anchor would be needed. Much to everyone's surprise, the Welsh-born actor Richard Burton agreed to do the job. He was still a considerable star, and not someone who might normally have been approached, but the BBC had a hotline: Burton's brother Graham Jenkins was a senior member of the engineering staff. It was a risky choice. Richard possessed a beautiful speaking voice, but he had never done anything like this before. He also had a reputation as a man not unacquainted with prodigious quantities of alcohol. It was agreed that Richard would read from a carefully prepared script and remain deep in the basement of Broadcasting House. He would watch the events on a television monitor and take directions from a producer at his elbow. There would be a minimum of ad-libbing.

I was one of the eight BBC radio commentators chosen to line that part of the royal route between Trafalgar Square and St Paul's Cathedral. I was relieved to see the team also included the highly experienced Brian Johnston and Wynford Vaughan Thomas. Wynford was once a distinguished war correspondent and had been outside Buckingham Palace when Charles was born; Brian was the most famous cricket commentator on BBC radio. The amount of rehearsal for the job was minimal; big state occasions – Trooping the Colour apart – offer no chance for novice commentators to have a practice run the week before. Instead the whole team, which also included Rolf Harris, Terry Wogan and the actress Lorraine Chase, gathered the day before the wedding in the august surroundings of the BBC Council Chamber in Broadcasting House. Somebody thought it would be a good idea if we all sat down in the order in which we would be heard from the following morning. Beneath the stern portraits of Lord Reith and his successors, the team sat in a long row of chairs and practised handing over from one to the other. Remember, Wynford said, describe only what you can see, do your homework, and you'll be fine. We were then taken on a coach and dropped off at our real positions to have a look at the route; as I was placed in a window above Thomas Cook's offices in the Strand

I could see only about twenty yards on either side of me, but I did at least have a loo at my disposal, unlike several of my colleagues.

The next morning we were taken back to our posts at dawn: we had to be in position by seven o'clock. The pavements all along the route were already packed with people, many of whom had slept there. It was a fine day, and everything went quite smoothly. The procession passed each commentary position exactly on time and we remembered to describe only what was in front of us, which in my case was a blur of royals in shiny carriages, going first from right to left, and then from left to right. I managed to see most of the bits I had missed – including the wedding ceremony itself – on a small television monitor behind me. Richard Burton linked the whole broadcast in perfect sobriety and with mellifluous efficiency. Although some listeners evidently found Lorraine Chase and her characterization of two Yeomen of the Guard as 'a couple of geezers in red' not to their liking. 'Who is this cockney girl?' one woman rang in indignantly. 'Her description is not suitable for a royal occasion.' When we eventually arrived back at Broadcasting House via the London Underground we found that Burton had left each of us a bottle of champagne.

The following year I had an opportunity to meet the Queen at much closer quarters. A call came through to me one morning in the *Woman's Hour* office as I sifted through the running order for that day's programme. 'Would you hold on a moment please for the Master of the Household?' Naturally I thought it was a joke, but the voice assured me that he was the genuine article. Would I care to join the Queen for luncheon? He suggested a date about six weeks hence. This was of course a Royal Command, and after I'd caught my breath I said I would very much like to. I was intrigued. The Queen's luncheon parties are held several times a year when she is in residence at Buckingham Palace. The guests – usually eight of them – are chosen broadly to represent their professions or trades. At that time only one of the eight was a woman; since then the number has risen to two.

My seven fellow guests that day included the editor of the *Sunday Express*, Sir John Junor; Brian Bevan, the chief coxswain of the Humber lifeboat; and Mr Justice Bingham, a High Court judge. I decided to drive myself to the palace. This was a big mistake, for I had forgotten that in the week of the Chelsea Flower Show, Park Lane comes to a standstill: ten minutes before the appointed arrival time I was still almost a mile from my destination. I seriously contemplated flagging down a motorbike, waving a five pound note, and begging the rider to give me a lift. Then suddenly the traffic surged forward, and I managed to drive through the palace gates in a sweaty panic but just in time. 'Come for a spot of lunch?' asked the laconic policeman. The palace staff dusted me down and assured me that Her Majesty would not be arriving for another ten minutes. The other guests, two royal equerries and I stood clutching our drinks and making small talk in a drawing room which looked out on to the immaculate gardens.

At exactly ten past one there was an unmistakable noise of dog claws clipping along the passageway. Several corgis entered, followed by the Queen and Prince Philip. We were formally presented to them and tried unsuccessfully simultaneously to look relaxed, sip our drinks and keep our ankles a sensible distance from the dogs. How strange it seemed to be standing so close to this familiar little figure, slightly shy, with glossy brown hair, perfect skin, and the rigid black handbag over one arm. (Later, after lunch, the handbag was opened and from it the royal hand extracted several dog biscuits. These were fed to the corgis, who rolled over obediently before snapping them up.) Luncheon was served in a dining room across the passage; each of us had our own special uniformed flunkey behind our chair. Seated on Prince Philip's right, I was intrigued to see that he tucked into each dish long before his wife had been served. I was nervous and remember little about the meal itself, except that the exquisite china rested on large gold plates, and that the glass fingerbowls were the size of soup tureens. Prince Philip and I spoke about horse inoculations –

a subject on which I could not claim to be an expert – while the Queen on the other side of the table surreptitiously slipped titbits to the corgis beneath. Afterwards we returned to the drawing room for coffee, where we discussed the progress of the Falklands War. Prince Andrew was then on active duty as a helicopter pilot and I gathered from his mother that they were able to keep in touch by letter. 'Though Andrew doesn't write very much,' she said rather wistfully. By around a quarter to three it was all over; we drove away and returned, slightly dazed, to everyday life and the London traffic.

By the early 1980s, I worked out, I had probably interviewed in one radio studio or another around seven or eight thousand people. For important interviews I might have spent an hour or two preparing, learning as much as I could about the person who would be the object of my undivided attention the next day. But however much I might warm to any particular individual, or wish to continue our conversation, I knew it was unlikely I would see them again. Fortunately a number of people I first came across in the studio have become extremely good friends: journalists, musicians and actors among them, including Simon Jenkins, Jane Glover and Janet Suzman. I first met Simon Jenkins when he was a columnist with the London *Evening Standard*. He and his wife, the actress Gayle Hunnicutt, have been north London neighbours for more than two decades now, and the quality of Simon's journalism is still inspirational. My friendship with the conductor Jane Glover meant taking an unexpectedly deep pleasure in the world of serious music and early opera; she in turn has been persuaded to show some brave enthusiasm for skiing. I first met Janet Suzman when she was a leading lady with the Royal Shakespeare Company. Through the small charity I help her run, I have kept in touch with the arts scene in both the old and the new South Africa. With many others I have kept up what I can call a warm acquaintance.

I can recall only one man so utterly unpleasant that I couldn't wait to remove myself from his presence: the publisher and news-paper owner Robert Maxwell, who was later to drown in mysterious circumstances off his luxury yacht. He had cancelled an agreed live appearance on the morning of the broadcast, instead insisting I took my tape-recorder to his offices in the City – Maxwell House. The interview was conducted with the impatient and audible background rattle of Mr Maxwell's coffee cup in the background: he was evidently as anxious as I to get the whole thing over as quickly as possible. He was also overbearingly rude to his staff. In our interview he spoke grandly of hoping, as a former Czech refugee, to 'contribute to the halt in the decline of the nation', though he bridled when I reminded him that he had once been described by a judge as a man whose accounting methods had left him unfit to run a company. 'That's a lot of tosh and not even worthy of comment,' he snapped. No doubt the beneficiaries of the *Daily Mirror* pension fund would feel rather differently.

I did once develop a very close relationship with one of my *Woman's Hour* guests, and on this occasion it was against my better instincts. One Wednesday in 1979 the actor Leonard Rossiter came in to the studio for what we by then called 'a light lunch' and to be our Guest of the Week. He was a hugely successful actor, at the height of his popular fame as Reggie Perrin and as the landlord Rigsby in *Rising Damp*. The Cinzano ads with Joan Collins which ran throughout the late seventies had made his face more recognizable still. I was a fan, though rather more for his theatre than his television work. I had seen his wonderfully manic portrayal of the Adolf Hitler figure in Brecht's *The Resistible Rise of Arturo Ui*: it was a virtuoso performance and had made him a West End star. I've always, I suppose, been rather dazzled by theatre people, and when Leonard arrived in Broadcasting House for the pre-prandial drinks I talked to him enthusiastically about the play. He must have enjoyed the flattery, and he was relaxed and amusing company over lunch. The live interview went well: he was quick and articulate, and refreshingly did not take himself or his profession over-seriously. It turned out he had been set for a career in the insurance business before somebody spotted his talents in local amateur dramatics. Despite the scale of his television success, it was evident that the theatre gave him greater professional pleasure.

Although we had seemed to get on rather well I was completely taken by surprise when the next day he rang me in the office and suggested meeting for a drink. I was also intrigued. Could this be simply a postscript to our meeting of the day before, and end in an offer of tickets for his next appearance in the West End? Or was he interested in something more? I had no intention, I told myself, of beginning another relationship with a married man; rather the reverse. My naval friend Richard and I had parted amicably, and I wanted to enjoy less complicated liaisons in the future. But after Leonard and I had had a glass or two of wine at a hotel close to Broadcasting House, he took my telephone number and visited me at home, and I suppose with a certain inevitability we slipped into a more intimate relationship. Quite a large part of me was flattered. I was also intrigued by an opportunity to get to know better someone whose face was so familiar, but whose real persona, I quickly discovered, was quite different from the Rigsbys and Perrins he portrayed.

Obviously we could no longer go on meeting in public, so our rendezvous generally took place in my new apartment in Primrose Hill. I had found a tiny maisonette on the top of a Victorian building without much of a view, but only two minutes' walk from one of the prettiest small parks in London. It had a large picture window looking out from the top floor past the back of several terraced houses to a large block of flats. On my first evening in the flat someone – I assumed a small boy – shot an airgun pellet through the window as I gazed out at the surrounding buildings, and large shards of glass splintered past inches from my face and landed all over the floor. It seemed an inauspicious beginning to my Primrose Hill existence, but luckily the unseen sniper did not repeat the attack.

It was a quiet road, but so anxious was Leonard not to be recognized when he came to visit that he usually arrived with his face buried in a large white handkerchief; I often wondered what my neighbours made of my male visitor with the permanent head cold. From time to time he also popped in to my office in Broadcasting House for a chat, but if my colleagues on *Woman's Hour* wondered what exactly was going on between us they didn't mention it to me.

Leonard was quick, clever, funny and an enthusiastic *bon viveur*, knowledgeable about fine wines. I found him immensely attractive. He could also be brisk, moody and quite serious. We talked about everything from politics to sport, and I was amused by his tales of his colleagues, not all of whom came up to scratch; evidently he did not suffer fools. I also appreciated his honesty about the inevitable limitations to our relationship. From the start, he made it clear to me that there would never be any question of leaving his wife. I understood this, and assured him that I had always considered myself a determinedly single soul. I would be happy to see him whenever he was free; on the other hand, I would not become the lonely mistress sitting at home waiting for the phone call. I did see other men from time to time, but none of them seemed quite as attractive.

Inevitably, though, after a year or so of furtive meetings I began to chafe against the restricted and secretive nature of our relationship. One afternoon after we had exchanged some sharp words over this – I wanted to see him more often, and he had to reiterate the reasons why this was impossible – I fled in tears, snatching up some dark glasses, and took myself for some fresh air on to Primrose Hill. We had not argued about anything before, and both my sudden outburst and his rather cold reasoning took me by surprise. As I settled down into a little heap of misery under a tree with a book, not a word of which I read, I was hailed by a large group of picnickers nearby. It was the BBC's religious broadcasting department having their summer get-together *al fresco*. They invited me to join them. It was the last thing I wanted to do, but I sat down with them to help them finish off the red wine. If they were puzzled by my rather sober demeanour they were too tactful to comment, and I spent the rest of the afternoon sipping wine and trying hard to laugh at their jokes.

Leonard and I picked up our relationship again within a few days as if nothing had happened, and I continued to see him once a week or so. I confided in very few people about our attachment, but one of them, curiously enough, was my mother, who came over from South Africa to stay for a few weeks, first with me and then with my sister and her family. There was no disguising the fact that a man who did not announce himself rang me at roughly the same time each evening, and I told her who it was. She took the news pretty well, though I'm certain she would have preferred to be told of a more conventional relationship. As it turned out, I was soon glad that I had taken her into my confidence.

Leonard was then back in the West End starring in a revival of Joe Orton's black comedy *Loot*. It was a technically brilliant performance that I had seen more than once; he had told me that he survived long runs in fast, furious farces, which are very demanding, by trying to reproduce his performance in exactly the same way night after night. On the evening of 5 October 1984 his fellow actors were astonished when he missed an entrance after the interval, as he was a meticulously professional colleague. Leonard was found slumped in a chair in his dressing room, and was pronounced dead on arrival at the Middlesex Hospital. He had had a heart attack.

That evening my mother and I were both staying with Kirsty at her house near Camberley in Surrey, and I did not learn of Leonard's death until the following morning, when it was announced on the BBC's eight o'clock news. When my mother came into my bedroom to find out why I had not joined the family at breakfast she could see that something had shocked me deeply. I told her what had happened, and she was immediately a wonderfully calming influence, though I knew she must have thought my relationship with Leonard at the very least unwise.

Somehow she talked me into coming down to join the others for breakfast. No mention was made of the morning's news bulletin in front of my sister's children. Tactfully, Kirsty did not refer to what had happened for a long time; I'm certain she had no idea what had been going on, and I expect was rather surprised. Meanwhile my mother, as a sensible and kindly presence over the next few days, helped me deal with my shock and grief. I felt closer to her than ever. A few weeks later she returned to South Africa.

Around this time, and perhaps the events were connected, I began to suffer unexpected bouts of what seemed to me uncannily close to stage fright. Once or twice a week as I broadcast live in the studio I was overwhelmed by waves of nervousness. It was extremely strange. I felt disorientated and slightly dizzy, sometimes so strongly that I wondered if I could continue doing the programme. I gripped the studio table in front of me as hard as I could. When I felt able to remove my fingers I grabbed a glass of water with a shaking hand. The people I was interviewing must have thought I looked a little odd. Fortunately after a few months these panic attacks faded and then disappeared completely. They did not return, and gradually too my misery ebbed. And I did not again become involved with a married man.

By the time Margaret Thatcher had won her second term of office in 1983 she was convinced that a significant part of the BBC – particularly sections of news and current affairs – was of a dangerously leftist tendency. She was also quite certain that the whole corporation was badly and wastefully managed. There had been several squabbles between Number Ten and the BBC's news directorate over the way the Falklands War was reported. There was also the famous Thatcher tussle on *Nationwide* with a viewer, Diana Gould, over the sinking of the Argentinian battleship *Belgrano* – chaired admirably coolly by Sue Lawley. Mrs Gould had rung in to point out that the *Belgrano* had been sailing away from the exclusion zone when it was attacked, and that therefore it had been morally dubious for the British to sink it. The Prime Minister denied that the ship was where Mrs Gould said it was. But Mrs Gould backed up her claim with an impressive number of compass bearings. Mrs Thatcher was floored, and the exchange, which was considered something of a humiliation for her, has been played over to students of broadcast journalism ever since: an object lesson in the importance of knowing your facts and sticking to your guns when challenging a top politician.

Margaret Thatcher's conviction that much of the BBC was run with profligate carelessness was confirmed by an official visit she made to Television Centre, described to me later by George Howard, then the BBC's chairman. George was a large and rather flamboyant man with a fondness for wearing shiny gold kaftans in the evenings. He owned one of England's most beautiful houses, Castle Howard in north Yorkshire, where he occasionally invited me to stay. He was a widower with four sons whom he adored and shamelessly indulged; they tried their best when I was there to keep me abreast of the current music scene. I was taken one Saturday – rather reluctantly on my part, but I felt it would have been discourteous to refuse – on a shoot. It was a freezing day. The sleet blew horizontally into our faces – and George's sister Christian Howard provided large hip-flasks containing a reviving mixture of gin and cherry brandy. Afterwards, over tea, George told me about his afternoon as Mrs Thatcher's host.

It was arranged that on her visit to Television Centre she should see the lavish historical series *The Borgias* being filmed. She came to the BBC fresh from a visit to the set of ITV's *Brideshead Revisited*, much of which had been filmed at Castle Howard. She had been impressed by ITV's efficiency and its high production standards. But when she watched the making of *The Borgias* she was appalled by what she saw as overmanning and ludicrously expensive sets; nothing that any of the BBC's drama department said could convince her otherwise. Unfortunately for the BBC, *Brideshead* was a huge international success and *The Borgias*, despite all the money lavished upon it, turned out to be a turkey. Mrs Thatcher no doubt congratulated herself on her excellent judgement, and made it her business from then on to monitor the BBC very carefully indeed.

By the mid-eighties the Tuesday morning phone-ins were so well established that it was decided that something more elaborate might be contemplated. Sandra Chalmers, as editor of *Woman's Hour*, was keen to make the programme sound livelier and more responsive to current events, and decided that the phone-in would go international. She arranged to run a weekly experimental series in collaboration with the World Service; and so it was that *It's Your World*, a new programme for Sunday mornings, came into being.

The idea was to persuade as many English-speaking international figures as possible to answer questions directly put by listeners in Britain and around the world. The programme would be heard on both Radio Four and the World Service. The producer, Liz Mardall, fired off several dozen letters, and a number of positive responses came in. The first series, which was largely chaired by Michael Charlton, started off impressively with Casper Weinberger, Ronald Reagan's defence secretary, and King Hussein of Jordan. Calls came in from Tooting Bec to Tel Aviv. Technically it was quite complicated, but the programmes worked well and it was decided to commission a second series. This time I was asked to be the anchor. Although they were meant to be topical, the programmes had to be planned some weeks in advance, and their newsworthiness in the end depended on good luck. Occasionally we got some scoops.

China was beginning to shrug off the legacy of Mao. Capitalism could be explored, if only in a carefully controlled fashion, and dialogue with the West was permitted, up to a point. In 1985 Huan Xiang from the Chinese foreign ministry in Peking agreed to answer questions for us on current policy, as it happened on the very day that the pop group Wham! was to give a concert in the Chinese capital. Mr Huan's English was good: he was even planning to attend the Wham! concert, he told us. He was a former diplomat who had been chargé d'affaires in Britain in the 1950s and had then, in common with many intellectuals, spent six years doing hard labour in the countryside during Mao's Cultural Revolution. For the phone-in the Chinese made no advance stipulations about permitted or prohibited areas for questioning. To me, the technical logistics of successfully linking a speaker in Peking many thousands of miles away, and dozens of callers from around the world, with our little basement complex in Broadcasting House were impressive enough; it was even more remarkable that a representative of a highly repressive regime was willing to take uncensored questions from listeners in Britain and around the world.

A caller from Cape Town asked about China's 'one child one family' policy and about reports of compulsory sterilization and forced abortions, even of officially encouraged infanticide. A visiting American sociologist had recently reported that in some rural areas of China newborn girl babies were left out in the open to die. All Huan could do was dismiss the sociologist as someone who had been expelled from China for what he called 'ungracious activities': he could not absolutely deny that girl children sometimes died tragically. He sounded distinctly uncomfortable when asked by a British caller why the Roman Catholic bishop of Shanghai had been sentenced to thirty years in prison, and was unable to be specific about the crimes the bishop was alleged to have committed. On other matters he was more certain. To a caller who questioned China's cruel treatment of Tibet, he simply declared, 'Tibet is part of China.' But it was heady stuff for us, not least because the link with Peking had worked perfectly.

The following year Georgiy Arbatov in Moscow agreed to take questions. Mr Arbatov was a member of the central committee of the Communist party, and one of the Kremlin's specialists in East–West relations. It had taken weeks of negotiation to get him and his political bosses to agree to his appearance. At the time

Mikhail Gorbachev had been in power barely a year, and *glasnost* – openness – was in its infancy. We could only hope that Mr Arbatov would turn up in the Moscow studio on the right day at the right time. But then something extraordinary happened which gave us every reason to think that he would pull out of the programme altogether.

On 26 April 1986, only two weeks before our planned broadcast, the nuclear reactor at Chernobyl in Ukraine exploded. The world knew about it almost immediately. There were terrifying reports of radioactive clouds spreading across northern Europe, though little information was given out by the Kremlin. It was another four years before Gorbachev acknowledged the full extent of the tragedy and its effect on human lives. Two weeks after the explosion, not one Soviet official had spoken in any detail about the event. Our programme on 4 May was due to begin shortly after twelve noon London time; I remember well the sweaty minutes from eleven o'clock, as engineers in London battled with their colleagues in Moscow to make the link work. At last, at about ten to twelve, we were through to the right studio. The first reassuring sound I heard was the clear tinkle of a teaspoon on glass – the unmistakable sound of Russian tea being stirred. I could imagine the dollop of jam melting in the tall glass. 'Are you there, Mr Arbatov?' He was. We were ready to go.

The first caller, a man in the Netherlands, got straight to the point. What does the new 'openness' in the Soviet Union mean if there is so much reluctance to give out any information at all about what the Russians have admitted was a catastrophe? Arbatov, a practised broadcaster and usually a smooth operator on political matters, sounded terribly flustered. He was reduced to tit-for-tat accusations about delayed American reports on the Three Mile Island nuclear accident, and to testy references to NATO's 'first use' nuclear defence strategy. He denied that the people of Ukraine, let alone in other parts of eastern Europe like Poland and Hungary, were in any danger. 'Nobody has found anything,' he said.

Mr Arbatov's remarks made the *New York Times* the following day. Under the headline 'Soviet Official Faces World's Questions On The BBC', the full-page report pointed out that the 'sharp questioning' from listeners in western Europe on the Chernobyl explosion had made Mr Arbatov sound 'increasingly defensive', and that he had interrupted callers to 'interject hostile comments'. The American paper recorded that when a listener in Manchester had asked him to specify when the accident had taken place, he had replied that he had not expected to be asked the question and therefore did not know the answer. It all boiled down, he said, to the Western press looking for a pretext to discredit the Soviet Union. It was a programme wonderfully revealing of Soviet obfuscation, and we were thrilled with the press coverage it received, both in Britain and abroad. A *Woman's Hour* production had made an international splash.

As Mr Arbatov had shown, *glasnost* was only just beginning. At the time he spoke to us, the young Russian poet Irina Ratushinskaya, a practising Christian, was still in a labour camp; she spent 138 days in solitary confinement in a prison in Moldova for her dissident beliefs before being released in October 1986. Four months later, after she had arrived in Britain to settle, she talked to me about the conditions in the camp.

Interview with Irina Ratushinskaya, 17.2.87

IR: For some months I was alone and I had a lot of time to think about everything and to compose my rhymes. I cannot say to write my rhymes because it was impossible. I was searched all the time, so I tried to remember them by heart. It was awfully cold in this cell and I was not allowed to wear warm clothes.

SM: What were you given to eat daily?

IR: I don't know any English word to describe those meals. It was not a soup. I know only Russian slang word *volanda*. It was salt water with little cabbage leaves. And we had a pound of black bread, but it was not real bread. It was special bread for prisoners. So they were really hard conditions, but it helped me because under such conditions I could not believe the KGB when they said we have real democracy now in our country.

SM: You have left behind many friends, fellow women political prisoners, some of them Christians, some of them not. You must think of them a great deal now?

IR: Some of them are not in the labour camp now, they are in exile; some of them are free now. But I still don't know anything about two women fellow prisoners, Lydia Daronina – she's a Baptist and she's sixty years old, and she's very ill. As far as I know she's still in this camp. And Galina Barats. She is a Pentecostal Christian. Both of them refused to sign a paper asking the authorities for pardon, because they are not criminals. Our authorities should ask them for pardon!

SM: I can understand, terrible though your conditions were, how you survived through your faith in God. But what I think a lot of people can't understand is how the people who don't have a faith survive.

IR: Some of my friends were not believers. They were not atheists, but they did not know anything about God. I did not feel any difference between those persons and Christians. I think it is not very important to belong to a church. But I remember when Tatiana Osipova was on hunger strike – she was alone in a little cell – she kept a Bible with her. But Tatiana Osipova's guards decided that the Bible helped her to be strong, so they decided after two or three months of her hunger strike to take this Bible away. But she started a dry hunger strike, without any water. It is very dangerous, because after five days of a dry hunger strike people die. Tatiana Osipova kept up her dry hunger strike for four days, and on the fourth day her guards came and returned her Bible.

SM: What do you make of the new *glasnost*, the openness? Mr Gorbachev says we are now going to have a new approach to humanitarian issues.

IR: I will believe in this when it is fact. Because thirty-two years spent in the Soviet Union taught me not to believe in words, only in facts. I don't think this word *glasnost* means a real right for all our people to read and write what they want. Now even my letters to my mother are stolen. I know that [my husband Igor and my] parents have troubles for our behaviour here. I sent a lot of letters to her and she did not receive one. It is very painful for me.

With *Woman's Hour, It's Your World* and from 1979 my own interview series *Conversation Piece*, the early eighties were busy years for me on the network. The controller of Radio Four, David Hatch, sent me a handwritten note pointing out that I had recently made five different appearances on the network in the space of thirty hours. I should, he said, make sure 'we don't abuse your willingness'. It was tactfully put, but I could see that he was really suggesting that it was often difficult to avoid me on the airwaves. Like all freelancers – BBC presenters are nearly always on contract, not on the staff – I was chary of giving up any of my commitments: they might not, after all, ever come back to me. But despite David Hatch's concerns no one actually pulled me off any of the programmes. And on *Woman's Hour* there were new opportunities for getting out of the London studio.

This occasionally meant going to what some of the audience research people called the 'bald areas' – parts of Britain where Radio Four's audience was normally rather sparse. One afternoon we went to south Wales, to the Rhondda valley, and broadcast the entire programme from an electrical parts factory. I was joined on the platform by the actor Donald Houston, a son of the valleys on a nostalgic visit home. The audience was large and polite, and seemed to be listening with their full attention. As I chatted to Houston and a local newspaper editor I was aware of a kerfuffle in the fourth row, but ploughed on, imagining the disturbance was not loud enough to be audible to the audience at home. Out of the corner of my eye I could see that an elderly lady was receiving attention from a member of the St John Ambulance Brigade. It turned out that she had had a suspected heart attack; but her sister-in-law, sitting next to her, was determined not to leave her seat and waved away the stretcher-bearers. 'I think she's gone, but it would be a pity to spoil the programme,' she whispered fiercely. 'Leave her where she is.' Fortunately, the old lady made a full recovery when she was eventually taken outside for some fresh air. We may not have gained a huge number of listeners that day, but nor, to our relief, did we lose one.

In the spring of 1984 we planned to broadcast an edition of the programme from the BBC's studios in Paris. Our star guest was Christine Ockrent, the political interviewer on the French television channel Antenne Deux. Clever and glamorous, she was also, happily for us, impressively bilingual. She couldn't appear on our programme live, but agreed to record an interview the previous night in her office. Once it was completed my producers Clare Selerie, Pat Taylor and I asked Christine for a recommendation for somewhere to enjoy a good fish meal. She told us of an Alsatian restaurant nearby where the seafood was superb. At least five kinds of oyster were on offer, and several delicious breeds of langoustine. We went, and tucked in. But later that evening, back at our hotel, poor Clare was overcome with violent nausea. The following morning Pat fainted in the supermarket MonoPrix, and much to her embarrassment had to be delivered back to the hotel in a supermarket trolley. I managed to hold out until just before we went on air from the studios of the radio station Europe Numéro Un, and then the *maladie* struck me too. After the challenge of trying to type my script on a French non-qwerty machine, I had to link the programme live between horrible stomach pangs. Our surroundings were surreal: rows of French disc jockeys broadcasting their programmes inside glass-walled studios from a standing position, all wiggling their hips in ecstasy. I felt considerably less enthusiastic, but managed to get through the entire live broadcast without having to use the tin wastepaper basket strategically placed at my feet. Afterwards we wondered if Antenne Deux had been trying to sabotage the BBC. Sadly, I've never since been able to touch an oyster.

A couple of years later *Woman's Hour* sent me much further afield – back to South Africa, and this time on my own. The idea was to record interviews with three local women to mark the programme's fortieth birthday, which fell in October 1986. The editor Sandra Chalmers and I plumped for three political figures: Helen Suzman, the veteran opposition MP; Rina Venter, a social affairs minister in the Nationalist government; and Winnie Mandela. We had little difficulty pinning down the first two – Helen was an old friend, and the government was only too pleased that the BBC wanted to talk to Mrs Venter, the lone woman in the National party cabinet. Winnie Mandela proved more of a problem. She was probably the most famous black woman in South Africa. Her husband Nelson had been in prison for almost a quarter of a century, and Winnie had served time herself, some of it in solitary confinement, some of it in internal exile in a remote town in the Orange Free State. Now she was newly back in the township of Soweto, just outside Johannesburg, in the

Mandelas' first marital home. It was a simple brick house on a corner of a dusty street: the house in which she had expected to spend the first years of her married life. In the end she and her lawyer husband had managed less than four months together in almost twenty-five years. She might, we realized, be difficult to pin down. Technically she was still a banned person and forbidden to give interviews; the telephone line into her house was undoubtedly tapped. This hadn't prevented her from talking to the foreign press when it suited her, nor from addressing selected gatherings. Perhaps the South African authorities now felt it was better to allow her some freedom than to attract more international fury by locking her up again.

Winnie was a famously mercurial and unpredictable woman, and recently she had appalled many of her former admirers by appearing to endorse the lethal township practice of 'necklacing' – tying up a victim and placing a petrol-filled car tyre round his neck. When the tyre was set on fire the victim died in screaming agony. Winnie's words, uttered at a public meeting 'with our matchsticks and our necklaces we shall liberate this country', had been recorded by a television sound man a few weeks earlier. So I had no idea whether she would agree to meet me, or keep the appointment if she did. I asked Helen Suzman, long a supporter of Nelson and an old friend of Winnie, having visited them both in gaol many times, if she might put in a word for me. She said she thought the omens were reasonably good, and I set off on the overnight flight for Johannesburg.

Shortly after I'd checked into my room at the Carlton Hotel there was a knock at the door. A tall black man introduced himself as Peter Magubane, a well-known photographer who worked locally for *Time-Life*; I knew he was very close to Winnie. I invited him in and we chatted briefly – I imagined I was being sized up on her instructions. I said how much I was looking forward to seeing Mrs Mandela the following day, but he didn't offer any hint as to whether she might see me, or offer to accompany me into Soweto. So I would have to go there alone.

Next morning I hired a car, and on a whim I decided to ask the young bell-hop in the lobby if he might come with me. I didn't feel like tackling South Africa's largest township utterly on my own. Whites were not encouraged to go in unless on official business, and the young black 'comrades' had their own ways of running things on the ground which might not bode well for me. I told the bell-hop I was visiting Winnie Mandela and didn't know how to reach her house. Would he help me? His eyes opened wide. 'Mama Mandela!' She was obviously the local heroine. He would indeed accompany me, and would show me how to get into the township by a back route, avoiding the attentions of the roving police vans.

It took only a few minutes to reach Soweto, and once we were in we drove slowly towards our destination in Orlando West. My guide suddenly motioned me to stop, and suggested I reverse quickly round a corner. He had spotted an armoured police vehicle outside the Mandela house. As I had no permit either to be in Soweto or to interview Winnie it would be as well to avoid the attentions of the police. After twenty minutes of rather nervous waiting we peeped round the corner. The police had moved on. We approached the house and parked a few discreet yards away. As I rang the bell on the wall I noticed an internal security camera pointing at us. I was let in by a young man and, with my companion and my tape-recorder, I was shown into a neat front room. Winnie came forward to greet us. She was then in her early fifties, and still strikingly beautiful. Helen had warned me in advance. 'Winnie is a charmer,' she said, 'if she likes you. But there are two sides to her. She's like the girl in the story. When she is good she is very very good; but when she is bad she is horrid.' To my relief she seemed friendly enough, if a little wary. There was a lot of activity in a back room of the house, and my young guide joined whoever was there; later it occurred to me that they were probably Winnie's notorious 'football team' protectors. I was eager to start recording as soon as possible, and she agreed, but before we could begin there was a tremendous commotion outside. One of the armoured vehicles had come back: it was parked against the wall and several uniformed men with dogs on leads were heading towards Winnie's front door. I stuffed the tape-recorder under a bed and sat in a chair in the second room, my heart pounding. The men and dogs came into the house, but they were not interested in me; I think they thought I was some sort of social worker. Two minutes later they'd gone. Winnie came up to me and put her arms round me. 'I can see you're frightened,' she said. 'But this sort of raid means nothing to me. They do this to me almost every day. Don't worry. Let's sit outside and have our chat.' It was typically defiant Winnie. We sat in her tiny garden with mugs of tea, talking quietly. The police officers stared hard at us from the top of their armoured vehicle on the other side of the wall. Eventually they got bored and moved off, and we could go inside and begin recording.

I reassembled the equipment, and tried to marshal my thoughts. I asked Winnie as coolly as I could what effect she thought her long years of banning and internal exile had had on her. 'I am terribly brutalized inside,' she said. 'I know that my soul is scarred. I know the pain of my people suffering and the pain of having a husband behind bars for over twenty-five years, and the pain of bringing up children in this atmosphere.' (Her two daughters were then in their twenties.) She spoke in her famously soft sing-song voice, and it was a compelling and tragic story. 'If I hadn't been living here under very primitive conditions, I might have broken along the way. I was very young when I got married, and not politically mature, and I found it very difficult at first to deputize for the man I had hardly lived with. I had to fumble my way along and find a way of representing him fully, not only in the eyes of the public, but according to my own code of behaviour.'

I knew I must bring up the question of her 'necklacing' remark. When I asked her about it, Winnie's eyes flashed; for a moment I thought the interview was over. Then she used the old defence: the remarks had been taken out of context. 'The version you have quoted is the version of the state, with of course the obvious intention. I hate explaining it because I don't owe anyone an explanation. But our children have been reduced to the level of fighting Pretoria with the matchstick and the necklace. I explained to the gathering that we belong to a disciplined organization, the African National Congress, that has gone out of its way to train armies outside [South Africa] to fight Pretoria's violence, and that one day they shall be called upon to use those disciplined methods to bring down the might of Pretoria. Not the necklace and the matchstick.'

It was an unconvincing explanation. I had seen the bad side of Winnie. She clearly seemed to believe that any sort of means might justify their political ends. Once the interview was over, I thought it best not to linger but to drive back to the hotel as fast as possible. I shook Winnie's hand. My young guide rematerialized and guided me safely home. There were no more armoured vehicles.

I made a copy of the tape in a private recording studio and posted it back to myself in London; the master I kept carefully in my briefcase. It accompanied me safely back to England a week later, and *Woman's Hour* broadcast my trio of South African interviews as part of their fortieth anniversary sequence. It emerged that just before I met her Winnie Mandela had for the second time been nominated for the Nobel Peace Prize. The small brick house in Soweto is now – much to Nelson's disapproval – a museum.

At the end of the assignment I took a quick trip down to Cape Town to see my parents. I tried to spend at least ten days with them once a year, if possible during the depressing dark days towards the end of a British winter. The Cape in March and April is stunningly beautiful, and strolling along the cliff top in the fishing village of Hermanus as the sun goes down is one of life's great pleasures.

Summer breaks in Europe have often meant trips to Italy – walking holidays in Umbria and Tuscany, a visit to the Amalfi coast, or going even further south where my old friend John Hemming's sister Louisa Service has a pretty whitewashed villa perched on a cliff above the Bay of Policastro. Here after dinner you can sit out under the stars, or lie lazily in hammocks talking till late. One night, unforgettably, after looking at the rings of Saturn through a powerful telescope, we lay dreamily listening to Jessye Norman's interpretation of Strauss's *Four Last Songs* while the black sea below shone with pinpricks of phosphorescence. It was a magical night.

In 1986 I paid my first visit to a brothel. It was in Herbertstrasse, just off the Reeperbahn in Hamburg. My producer colleagues and I decided that the main portion of the programme we were compiling about the city – a discussion on working mothers and local childcare facilities – was rather worthy, and that for a bit of colour it might be interesting to cover Hamburg's red light district near the old port. Here a quite different kind of female professional operated: Herbertstrasse contained at that point Germany's only legalized brothel, owned by a woman called Domenica Niehoff. Domenica was now middle-aged and had become a minor celebrity through her appearances on German television chat shows. She spoke a little English and was willing to talk to us – for a fee, as it turned out. After a great deal of negotiation involving the handing over of several hundred Deutschmarks from the programme's slim resources, she allowed us to 'sit in' with her in her reception area, while a series of male clients thumped up and down the stairs behind her. Domenica had a staff of five girls and business was brisk, though the English clients, she said looking meaningfully at our almost empty handbags, were the poorest payers. Hardboiled though she undoubtedly was, Domenica was in her own way quite impressive. She had made it to the top of her profession, and with an official licence to trade was presumably considered by the Hamburg authorities to be rendering some sort of public service. Recently I tried to find out what had happened to her. It seemed that in the 1990s she went through several transformations: for a while she became a champion of Hamburg's street children, and then landlady of a raunchy pub close to her own haunts, which was not a success. When last heard of, Domenica was running a telephone sex service offering 'Kein Vorspiel' – No Foreplay – at just over three Deutschmarks a time.

By 1987 I had begun to feel that *Woman's Hour* fitted me like a comfortable old glove. It meant it was time to move. It was a huge wrench to leave the programme after fifteen years – *Woman's Hour* had been an important part of my life, and I had made many good friends there – but I was in my mid-forties, and when the opportunity to transfer to another programme cropped up there was only one way the decision could go. *Woman's Hour* would benefit from a fresh voice once I had gone, I was sure.

On 10 September 1987 they gave me a wonderful send-off. The auditorium of the Royal Academy of Music in central London was hired, and listeners were invited to come along and watch my last edition go out 'live'. Over five hundred of them turned up, including Nel Romano, a studio manager on my first edition fifteen years earlier. Clare Selerie as deputy editor had marshalled an impressive line-up on the platform, representing important *Woman's Hour* themes. The American feminist writer Erica Jong, whose new novel was set in the Venetian ghetto and was a long way from her famous *Fear of Flying*, was there; so was Sheila Kitzinger, the campaigner for natural childbirth, whose loud imitations of birth noises in the studio some years before – 'Come on, PUSH!' – had startled some listeners. The philosopher and chair of the Human Fertility and Embryology Authority Mary Warnock joined us, as did the Foreign Office minister Lynda Chalker, one of the few women promoted to high office by Margaret Thatcher. Two musicians completed the line-up: the young composer Judith Weir, and the soul singer Ruby Turner, belting out 'Only Women Bleed'.

Sheila Kitzinger warmed once again to her thesis that modern childbirth needed fewer doctors and more midwives, and a more controlling influence from mothers. One not inconsiderable triumph for mothers in the eighties, she said, was that women did have more choice over how and where they gave birth. This was a subject dear to the heart of Dame Josephine Barnes, former President of the Royal College of Obstetricians and Gynaecologists, who told me on *Conversation Piece* the following year about her experiences of prewar maternity care.

Interview with Dame Josephine Barnes, broadcast 1.10.88

SM: You began in your junior posts – war was approaching – well before the days of the National Health Service. You must have seen some fairly deprived conditions.

JB: I did see the most appalling poverty because I worked as a medical student and then as a house officer on the district of University College Hospital which was all around King's Cross, St Pancras, up into Islington. All of that is now being, you might say, gentrified and the houses are now selling at enormous sums but in those days you'd have one of these tall houses on the Caledonian Road, six floors, a family on each floor, a cold-water tap half way up the stairs and a privy in the garden. And those were the conditions in which people lived and gave birth. It really was appalling.

I remember going up one Sunday night to a family and there was some problem with the birth – the midwives called me out – it wasn't very serious. They lived in two rooms. The bedclothes had been pawned so we were delivering on newspapers and sitting in the next room were six red-headed daughters eating chips. Father appeared – he was a corporal in the army – to his enormous disgust I produced a seventh red-headed daughter! So that was quite an experience. And that was an experience of poverty such as I had never seen.

I was in a way accustomed to poverty because my father was a parson and we used to go around visiting people, and burying people and so on, so I did understand what it was

about, but the deprivation was unbelievable. I mean not, at
the end of the week, to have the money to buy anything but
a few chips for your children with everything pawned . . .
and the baby of course always went in the bottom drawer of
the chest of drawers. There was no cot or pram or anything
like that.

SM: The coming of the war made a difference to a great
number of women in terms of what work they were able to do
in Britain. Did it make a difference to women in the medical
profession?

JB: I think perhaps the most interesting thing that happened
in obstetrics during the war was this. I was at Queen
Charlotte's and then in Oxford and then at University
College Hospital and of course there were air raids and there
were fire bombs. And we had to have our women mobile, so
we got them out of bed so they could carry themselves and
their babies out of the building if it caught fire. And this was
the beginning of people getting up after childbirth . . . and
we found they did much better when they got up so we got
everybody up.

SM: You were of course part of the Lane Committee which
looked into the possibility of liberalizing the abortion laws.
Controversial, very much in its time, and still controversial.

JB: Well, the Lane Committee was set up in 1971. The
Abortion Act was actually set up in sixty-seven and came
into effect in sixty-eight. And there was a great deal of
concern, and I think rightly, at the beginning. But we did
conclude that the Abortion Act was working well and in
relation to recent events we did recommend that the upper
limit for abortion should be reduced from twenty-eight to

twenty-four weeks. And of course the main purpose of the Act was to do away with back-street abortions and I had seen the most appalling results of back-street abortions when I was dealing with these people in extreme poverty. I'd seen two deaths – or more than that. So I think that from that point of view it has proved a success, it's virtually abolished the back-street abortion and there are no prosecutions for abortions now. There used to be before – even doctors were being sent to prison for doing abortions. I think the minus side is of course that the number of abortions doesn't get less, it remains steady or increases.

On that afternoon in 1987 we all – panel and audience – discussed other ways in which life had altered for women since the early seventies. Mary Warnock castigated girls' magazines for continuing to suggest that the most important thing in life was to catch a man. Erica Jong reminded us of what Ibsen had said in the nineteenth century: men would have to change before women could be liberated. Fifteen years of twentieth-century radical feminism, she said, had done little to alter women's lives. There were murmurs of approval from the audience, though I doubted there were many radical feminists among them. Peggy Makins, who had been the *Woman's Own* agony aunt Evelyn Home for decades, pointed out that most women probably couldn't care less about feminism. 'If her children turn out all right and her man is OK, she's happy,' she said, which brought a louder burst of applause from the audience.

It was a programme sufficiently live and unrehearsed for me to have to concentrate hard on keeping the show bubbling along nicely. There was no time to shed tears. I had to keep my eye on the clock, and make sure we reached our conclusions before I handed back to the continuity studio in Broadcasting House. But as I did so a huge chapter of my life closed. It was months before I could bear to switch on *Woman's Hour* again.

CHAPTER EIGHT

A New Voice

Dear Ms MacGregor,

For a number of years my wife and I have greatly admired your broadcasting style. However, when you moved over to *Today* a new edge, a slight steeliness entered your deliverance at times. Maybe this was required in a fast-moving pugnacious programme. But on Monday morning you interviewed some hapless chap about privatisation of public service contracts. At one point when he was trying to explain a point of view you seemed to us entirely to shout him down. It was difficult to believe the cacophony which flowed from the set, more (in my opinion) like an old fashioned screech owl than the measured tones of a distinguished broadcaster.

Letter to the author from a listener in Lincolnshire

*T*oday and *Woman's Hour* were very different, as I soon discovered. I had to adapt quickly to the world of hard news and hard pressure. It was a significant switch for me; but the opportunity to make the move away from *Woman's Hour* had surfaced much earlier than many people knew.

In 1979 two of the most important people in BBC radio, Aubrey Singer, its managing director, and the editor of news and current affairs Peter Woon, decided that *Today* needed a more permanent woman's voice. Brian Redhead and John Timpson had established themselves as the top team, and were a brilliantly contrasting pair, a perfect match – Brian the cheery, gritty, voice of the north, left of centre; John the smooth, sardonic southerner, probably a bit to the right. There was some natural rivalry between them when it came to who did what on the programme: John Timpson's wife was known to do an 'interview count' at home to make sure the slots were evenly handed out. Peter Hobday was a reliable third man, but Brian had a demanding weekly schedule of travel between his home in Macclesfield and his flat in London, and wanted to cut down on the number of days he worked on the programme. It seemed sensible, indeed essential, to find a fourth voice, and a female one.

Women's voices were thought to give added 'texture' to the programme, though there were still those who claimed that women sounded a great deal less authoritative than the men. Several had been tried out in the past on a temporary basis – including Gillian Reynolds, the highly respected radio critic of the *Daily Telegraph* and before that of the *Guardian*. But the right individual for the role remained elusive. Either the voice wasn't right, or they sounded uncomfortable with the format, or family commitments meant that regular rising before dawn was not feasible. Brian wanted to reduce his appearances to three mornings a week as quickly as possible. Aubrey Singer decided to approach both Ken Goudie, then editor of *Today*, and Wyn Knowles, to see if they might come to some arrangement about sharing me; it was thought that I might do one or two sessions a week on *Today*. I was at the time quite ignorant of all this: the early negotiations went on entirely behind my back, a state of affairs not uncommon in the BBC.

Wyn was on holiday in Greece at the time and Singer had to deal with her deputy, Teresa McGonagle, a tall, imposing woman with firm views. She was not at all keen on the idea of losing an experienced presenter several times a week, and told him she wouldn't let me go. Singer and Woon were keen to promote women, and were taken aback by this blocking move. Singer, too, was used to getting his own way, and a great shouting match ensued. 'I'm going to knock that fucking woman's block off!' was clearly heard along the corridors of the fifth floor after McGonagle left him, to shrieks of amusement when it was repeated in the *Woman's Hour* office.

Singer also found opposition down at *Today*, where Ken Goudie too was reluctant to agree to this new proposal, for rather different reasons. Ken was a veteran of the newsroom and possibly not immune from some of its prejudices about women in senior positions. He was also suspicious of someone from the world of magazine programmes who hadn't earned her spurs in hard news. He would be an unenthusiastic participant to the deal. When I eventually heard about all the plans involving me, I went to see Ken, and I could tell immediately that none of this was his idea. He shuffled papers on his desk, talked around the point, and made no attempt to persuade me that *Today* could be my new home. Years later he admitted to me, when I asked him why, that he thought at the time I was 'not quite right', although he did add that he'd subsequently changed his mind.

I had my own doubts about the move. The hours on *Woman's Hour* were civilized; those on *Today* were not. If its present editor was not keen to have me, then I would simply bide my time. So Aubrey Singer had to look elsewhere. At very short notice Libby Purves, then a bright young reporter on *Today*, was offered the job and accepted, though she resisted a long-term contract. She stayed with the programme as a presenter for another two years.

By 1984 things were rather different. Libby had left to start a family and do wider work in journalism, and *Today* had a new editor, Julian Holland, who had been a colleague of mine on *The World At One*; he revived the idea of my joining the team of presenters, initially part-time. Julian, with his background in newspapers, had already brought more rigour to what was essentially a news-driven programme. Out went some of the lighter stuff, and in came more political jousting. He also managed to get 'Prayer for the Day' moved from its rather awkward slot just after the programme began at half-past six to a more suitable place just before it started; eventually it was dropped altogether. And if some of what Ken Goudie called 'the fun' had gone from *Today*, it was compensated for by the sharper editorial tone. In any case Timpson and Redhead were well able to juggle the light with the serious: John enjoyed what he called his 'ho ho' stories, most of them culled from the morning press, and Brian could think up a merry quip about almost anything.

I discussed the move with people close to me outside the BBC. Some friends thought I was crazy to commit myself to so many regular early starts; others said I'd be equally mad to turn down such an offer a second time. In the end what seemed a workable compromise was agreed – I would keep my links with *Woman's Hour*, staying with it three days a week, and each Monday and Friday I would appear on *Today*. I could also retain the Tuesday morning phone-in, and my Radio Four interview series *Conversation Piece*. If it seemed rather a lot of radio work to have on my plate, I was happy to be in full employment. But it was an arrangement which would sorely test my biorhythms: getting up in the middle of the night two mornings a week, with normal working days in between, was going to be hard work.

This time the move went smoothly. In Sandra Chalmers *Woman's Hour* had a more flexible editor, happy that I should do a couple of days a week on another programme. And I was ready for a change; I'd been on one programme full time for twelve years, and *Today*, should I want to make the move more permanent, had a far higher profile than *Woman's Hour*. It was required listening for politicians and journalists as well as the so-called chattering classes, but its audience was a great deal wider than that. A substantial cross-section of the nation listened in most mornings. It would be a demanding job, and I knew it would stretch me and stimulate me.

I would also have to get used to a culture where women were essentially still second-class citizens. The radio newsroom just up the corridor was, in the words of a future editor of the programme, Jenny Abramsky, 'the last bastion of misogyny'. In 1984, though there were more women on the team than there had been, the *Today* programme still bore a heavy mantle of male supremacy. I think most of the women who worked there felt they were tolerated by some of their male colleagues rather than well-regarded and important members of the team. The supportive and proto-feminist culture of *Woman's Hour* would be left a very long way behind me.

Peter Hobday was to be my *Today* partner on Mondays and Fridays. He was a large, genial and clever man whose size was the object of quite a bit of teasing on air: the regular motorway traffic reports with their references to 'slow moving heavy loads on the M6' were usually linked to rather unsubtle references to his girth. Peter was the only member of the presenting team who could consume a full fry-up breakfast in the Broadcasting House canteen at 4.30 a.m. Before our first broadcast together, he took me out to lunch at Odin's near Marylebone High Street to give me a general run-down on how the programme worked, and who did what. He explained that it was essentially a 24-hour operation, five days a week. This meant employing a day team and a night team, with people working intensively for short periods and then having a couple of days off. There were day editors, night editors, and senior and junior producers, as well as researchers and reporters and 'programme assistants' to do what used to be thought of as secretarial work, all of them responsible to the main editor of the programme. Some were very young, newly graduated from university; others had come into the BBC from local radio or regional journalism; quite a few of the more senior journalists had been with the Corporation for years. Everyone worked long hours in not very comfortable conditions. But it was professionally rewarding work, knowing that all the 'top people' either appeared on the programme or listened to it. Peter was keen from the beginning that the two of us should not be overshadowed by Timpson and Redhead, the star duo. I thought this a little ambitious.

The two of them took me out to breakfast in the hotel next to Broadcasting House and imparted some very specific tips about getting through the programme – and the whole day, after rising at such an unearthly hour. John had some sensible warnings about not taking in too much alcohol the night before, and preparing all your interviews as far as you could before you went into the studio, because there would be so little time to brush up once you'd started. Brian said it was important to pace yourself – he always went to bed, he told me, between three and five in the afternoons on programme days, pyjamas and all; that way, he said, you put some good reserves into the snooze bank, and you could lead a relatively normal life in the evenings.

I could see that my social life was to be heavily circumscribed and that I would be catching up on sleep at odd times. Seeing friends in the evenings over a meal on programme days would be almost impossible, and so would most of my visits to the theatre, as bedtime would now be around nine. This would be quite a sacrifice. Ever since coming to London I had been a keen theatregoer; in particular I'd seen a great deal of the Royal Shakespeare Company's work in the sixties and seventies; and I had a particular attachment to the National Theatre, which I'd followed from the days of Olivier's Old Vic productions on to the South Bank (and on whose board I was to sit from the late 1990s). I would simply have to try it out, and see how big a price it was to pay.

I asked Brian how much he liked to know about the programme in advance: did he ring the office the night before to find out what the likely stories were to be, or did he come in 'cold' in the mornings? 'I almost never ring in,' he said. This was at a time when the industrial relations in the coal-mining industry were at rock bottom. 'I mean, would *you* want to know that you were talking to Arthur Scargill first thing?' It was advice I was to follow pretty rigorously. 'Coming in cold' put one in the position of a reasonably well-informed listener, and it seemed to me a sensible position from which to start.

On my first morning on *Today*, 10 September 1984, I must have kept going on sheer adrenalin. I had had little sleep the night before, and had risen far too early, determined to stick to my old habit of fifteen minutes on the exercise bicycle. This meant getting up at 3.15, pedalling away furiously while listening to the BBC World Service, having a shower and a cup of coffee, and then driving myself in to Broadcasting House. I stuck to this exercise regime for only a few weeks before common sense took over and the bike went back into the cupboard.

The *Today* empire on the third floor of Broadcasting House was, like *The World At One* unit up the corridor, not in itself very impressive. There were untidy desks with typewriters and newspapers scattered everywhere, and a small annexe off the main area where programme guests waited their turn. CNN glowed away soundlessly on a screen suspended from the ceiling, and there was an ancient map of the world on the wall. Reference books and telephone directories lay drunkenly on dusty shelves. 'Oh, just sit anywhere,' they told me, and so on that first morning I moved aside the night detritus of coffee cups, old scripts and yesterday's papers to clear a tiny bit of territory for myself. An ancient typewriter was provided. I also discovered in one of the drawers next to me a bottle containing some strange-looking green liquid. I was told it was a mixture of gin and Night Nurse, and that one of the presenters had been known to take a sip from time to time to keep himself going. It looked utterly lethal.

The first real shock was how little space I had to myself. The next surprise – though I should have expected it – was how quickly I had to get cracking: I had only a couple of hours in which to read the papers, try to master the interview briefs, discuss them with the night editor and type my own linking script. After *Woman's Hour*, where I'd had a half-share of a secretary and a small office all to myself, with plenty of time to think and prepare, it was quite an adjustment. And, as I already knew, a presenter is in a far more exposed position than a reporter. The studio suite from which the programme was actually broadcast – Studio 4A – was a windowless rather gloomy soundproof area on the other side of the corridor. Here the technical team and the producer stared at the presenters through thick panels of glass. It took about fifteen seconds to reach from the office – more if you were balancing a cup of coffee. You had to keep your eye on the clock at all times: live programmes wait for no one.

In fact, I didn't have a great deal to do on that first morning. The programme was what we called a 'three-header': John Timpson and me in London, and Peter Hobday presenting nuggets from the Social Democratic Party conference in Buxton. Topic of the day: 'Where does the party go from here?' Far from 'breaking the mould', as they had hoped to do, the Gang of Four – Roy Jenkins, David Owen, Shirley Williams and Bill Rodgers – had done poorly in the general election of the previous year, and there were some doubts that they could survive as a separate entity. There was the latest on the miners' strike: a set-to between Ian McGregor of the National Coal Board and Mick McGahey, the militantly left-wing national president of the National Union of Mineworkers. There was the threat of a dockers' strike at Tilbury – we were never short of stories about industrial strife – and there was the Equal Opportunities Commission demanding more 'girl-friendly' teaching in mixed schools. All I had to do was read the headlines a couple of times, give out a travel warning about a contraflow on the M1, talk to Louis Blom-Cooper QC about changes afoot at the Old Bailey, and interview an expert at Loughborough University on the dangers of being addicted to your computer. But after not very much sleep, and highly conscious of a great number of critical ears listening in, both inside and outside the BBC, I found it demanding enough. By the end of the programme I felt as if I'd been auditioning for Hedda Gabler.

After each programme, presenters and production team returned to the office. On this first morning, when I came back to what I thought was my carefully preserved bit of *lebensraum*, I found that it had been taken over by a member of the new day's team. Evidently presenters came in, cleared a bit of space, did their job, and went home again shortly after 9 a.m. That was the way it was – a Broadcasting House version of submariners' hot-bunking. In retrospect, the spartan cubicle which was my *Woman's Hour* office began to look a lot more glamorous.

In my first week Timpson, Redhead, Hobday and Julian Holland were solicitous and encouraging, even if the rest of the team – the duty editor, the producers and the reporters – continued to look on me with some suspicion. There were still remarkably few women current affairs presenters about – and I was also working on another programme a long way from the world of hard news. They and I knew I had much to learn. Live broadcasting held few terrors for me, but permanent time pressures were new: squeezing the essence of a news story into four, three, or even two minutes live was a challenge. Compared to the more leisurely approach of *Woman's Hour*, I discovered there was little time to lead listeners into a story. The background must be concisely conveyed in the introduction; the interview itself should take the story further as quickly as possible. The editor is above all looking for a 'news line': something to be quoted in forthcoming bulletins or the next day's newspapers. The presenter should achieve this as speedily as possible. Nobody actually told me any of this; I had to discover it for myself. Watching the clock while listening to what your interviewee is saying and to your producer talking in your ear must become second nature. My old passion for 'shaping' an interview – giving it a beginning, a middle and an end, with something meaty emerging along the way – counted for far less than an ability to get to the point quickly.

I also had to learn to work with a daily on-air partner after years of operating on my own. This was more difficult than it might appear. Timpson and Redhead always sounded at ease with each other on the programme, as if they could read one another's minds. I had a feeling that that sort of partnership took years of practice to achieve; meanwhile any mistakes or misunderstandings were likely to be heard by several million people.

In 1986 Julian Holland bowed out as editor, to be replaced by Jenny Abramsky. Julian was a rewarding man to work for; he had fiercely high standards, but was generous in praise when things went well – and prepared to admit mistakes. His one big error was to drop in some rather inappropriate 'jingles'. Most people loathed them; he admitted defeat and removed them quickly. We all knew Jenny would be a very different kind of editor. She was in her own way pioneering, and she was certainly forceful: someone who stood no nonsense, used her charm sparingly, and was in a hurry to get things done.

I had first come across her when I was a reporter on *The World At One* in the early seventies and she was a new young studio manager: small, bright, passionate about radio, and hugely energetic – obviously a high-flyer. Studio managing, which involved recording and editing tapes as well as running the complicated technical consoles in the studio, was a route often taken by young graduates who had their eye on production or even managerial jobs. In 1978 she was made editor of *PM* – the first woman to edit a daily news programme on the BBC – and at that level she had to deal with the radio newsroom, where she met a great deal of male resentment. This occasionally resulted in a refusal to follow orders. One of the older hands, when asked to cover a farming story which was to lead her programme at five o'clock, was heard to announce that he 'wasn't taking any orders from *her*'. He made sure his story was filed too late to be broadcast, which lost her the credit for a good editorial idea. Jenny had also started to produce children. One well-regarded woman in radio management, childless herself, was concerned about how Jenny, who already had a small son, would juggle her responsibilities. 'You can do the job with one child,' she announced, 'but you won't be able to with two.' Jenny managed to keep her second pregnancy a secret for more than five months. Her personnel officer had never dealt with a pregnant woman in management before; he knew nothing about maternity leave, and she had to explain to him patiently that she was entitled to three months' paid break.

Jenny arrived as editor of *Today* just before John Timpson's decision to retire from the programme. John was soon to turn sixty, and as he was, unusually for a presenter, on the BBC staff, sixty probably seemed to him an appropriate time to step down. Jenny needed someone to replace him full-time. She was determined that *Today* would remain the premier radio news programme, and she wanted, as all programme editors do, to have a team of presenters entirely of her own choosing. So she began to make adjustments. She brought in Jenni Murray from television's *Newsnight*, but then Jenni started to do regular work on *Woman's Hour* too, so some shuffling about had to be done, for she wanted me or Jenni, but not both of us. I was asked to make up my mind, and I chose to work full-time on *Today*, while Jenni Murray went to *Woman's Hour* on a more permanent basis.

Jenny also had her eye on John Humphrys. John had been on the *Nine O'Clock News* for some time, first with his old friend John Simpson, then on his own, and subsequently with Julia Somerville. Theirs should have been a perfect match but it was not: John did not look comfortable as a television newsreader and was apparently not all that happy to be paired on screen with a woman, however attractive and however experienced. When he was offered a contract to come across to radio to present *Today* in early 1987 he leaped at it. Most television people thought of radio as the inferior medium, but John had worked in radio as a news reporter years before, and he knew the pulling power of *Today*. Bringing him on to the team was a risky proposition – he had no experience of fronting a radio programme – but Jenny was confident it would work, and so was John. And it did.

So *Today* now had a quartet of regular presenters: Brian Redhead, John Humphrys, Peter Hobday and me. It was a good team of contrasts; arguably one of the best in radio news. But there were some big egos involved, and I wasn't entirely certain what my own role in all this was to be. Was it to be permanent female sidekick, rather than a presenter accepted as the equal of her male colleagues? It was made plain to me by Jenny Abramsky that I was expected to work with each of the other presenters in turn; this meant I had to adjust to a split-shift system, which played havoc with my sleep patterns. Jenny was very obviously keen to encourage John Humphrys as much as she could, seeing him as a potential successor to Brian.

This, however, might be some years off: Brian spoke at the time of staying with the programme at least until the year 2000, by which time he would have been over seventy. There was no reason for him to go; he was seen by most listeners, and certainly saw himself, as the premier ingredient of *Today*. He was, as *The Times* said in a leader after his death, 'one of the most compelling figures in postwar radio', and he knew it. In many ways he was an ideal radio man – he had a good voice, he was articulate, clever, quick, and endlessly fascinated by people as well as by the political process. His enthusiasm was infectious; he clearly adored his job, and his merry humming as he entered the office at five in the morning was an absolutely genuine sign of enjoyment. He longed to get cracking and have, as he liked to say, 'a word in the ear of the nation'. He was also maddeningly cocksure, bumptious and a show-off, and could be infuriating to work with. On occasion he was quite frighteningly pugnacious, and there were times when he almost came to blows with his overnight editor. At the very least he called everyone with whom he had the slightest disagreement a 'prat'. There was an element of Walter Mitty fantasy to some of Brian's own tales of his past achievements. Many of them – including one about successfully defending himself in a court martial – did not accord with others' recollections of the same events. And yet he was often helpful to colleagues and genuinely pleased when good things happened to them. A determined northerner, and one who went home as often as possible, Brian invented a group called the 'Friends of the M6', and reported regularly on the number of times the motorway was bunged up with cones for repair work while the emergency telephones were out of order. Some Conservative sympathizers, convinced that he was an unreformed leftie, took these comments to be disapproving references to the coming privatization of British Telecom.

Brian was at first an utterly kind and helpful colleague to me; but as I grew in confidence he would hand out some devastating put-downs. Any stumble on my part would be noticed and marked with a grin. Once he thrust a piece of paper with the word 'FOOL!' written on it in front of me as I finished a live interview. Occasionally he brought me close to tears, though I don't suppose he meant to. He accused me of being a 'suburban fascist' if I teased him about some of his anti-Tory views; I was more amused by this than offended, retorting that I objected to the 'suburban' tag. And he could be spontaneously generous – once he sent a huge bunch of flowers when I was languishing in bed with laryngitis.

At his best, Brian Redhead was an unrivalled radio broadcaster. He had two priceless qualities for the *Today* programme: a long political memory and an almost unquenchable cheerfulness. Jenny Abramsky had her battles with him over his approach to some of his interviews, but she was fully aware that he was a matchless asset to the programme. The difficulty now was to try to create a new partnership that would match the old one with Timpson. Brian's early pairings on air with John Humphrys did not gel instantly. Listeners complained that they sounded too alike: John may well have unconsciously modelled himself on his broadcasting partner

229

before he found his own voice. But he was a ferociously quick learner, and it wasn't long before he was as tenacious and adept as Brian at tussling with the politicians. They settled into a team that sounded professional and confident.

John was also paired with me from the time he joined the programme, and at first I sensed that he was much less at ease with me than he was with Brian; we had never previously met, though we had both worked for the BBC for years. *Today* is a long programme, and it is obviously preferable, over a period of two and a half hours, later stretched to three, if both partners feel relaxed and comfortable with each other. But with John there were no getting-to-know-you lunches or leisurely breakfasts together after the show; he always had to dash off after the programme to some other pressing outside engagement. So in some ways I found him hard to settle in with. I was keen to get to know him better, but in the frantic period of pre-programme preparation he showed little inclination to indulge in friendly chat. I also noticed that as John's confidence as a programme presenter grew, so did the length of some of his live interviews. This had its knock-on effect on me. On a programme like *Today* there is a finite amount of time into which all the interviews must be squeezed. If one presenter's interview overruns, the other loses a bit of his or her space. As John was busy establishing himself, quite a number of my interviews began to feel the pinch.

With Peter Hobday I felt no such tensions: he was always a relaxed and sympathetic companion. Without him I think my first few months on *Today* would have been unremittingly hard work. I had heard that even Libby Purves, who is no shrinking violet, had had some problems with her broadcasting relationship with John Timpson: in the studio he virtually ignored her, and one colleague remarked later that he thought Timpson had treated her 'with some contempt'. Libby denies all this. 'Any problems I had with the men were more to do with my youth than my femaleness,' she told me, though she acknowledged that as she had 'come up through the ranks' on the programme they were all well used to each other by the time she was given a presenter's job. Coming in from outside was rather different.

In the event, some of the barriers came down along with a great deal else. One morning in October 1987 disaster struck large swathes of the south of England. Some time after midnight hurricane-force winds blew in from the Atlantic, despite the earlier reassurances of Michael Fish at the weather centre. By the time I got up at three-thirty to drive in to work, fallen branches or even whole trees had made some roads in central London impassable. I managed to navigate my car past the impediments, but as I drove into the underground car park next to Broadcasting House all the lights went out. At first I thought I must have tripped some switch in the parking area, but as I emerged I could see that the sudden power loss affected the whole area around Broadcasting House. Once inside the BBC building I got myself up the stairs to the office on the third floor more or less by feel. Parts of the building were powered by the emergency generator, but curiously these did not include the *Today* department; my colleagues were working by torchlight. John Humphrys arrived shortly after I did with tales of enormous trees blown flat in Hyde Park. We decided to decamp quickly to the unfamiliar territory of the radio sports department which had generator power. Luckily we were not yet reliant on computers for our word processing, so we simply took over as many spare typewriters as we could and got on with the business of preparing the programme. We certainly had no problem identifying the lead story.

The production staff struggled to get their tapes edited on time; because the telephone system was partially down, reporters found it difficult to cover fully the events of the night. Some of the BBC's regional newsrooms were working normally; others, like ours, were operating on emergency power. There was a strange smell of diesel oil everywhere. Nevertheless, at half-past six we were ready to go on the air, and though it seemed like a programme flung together we had an even bigger audience than usual. Much of the morning television service was off the air and people tuned in to us on their battery radios to find out what was going on.

It was in some curious way a turning point in my professional relationship with John. After that hurricane morning I sensed a relaxation. Perhaps it had something to do with the camaraderie of successfully surviving a challenge; possibly I had passed some sort of test. By coincidence, that morning a journalist from the *Daily Express* was there to observe the preparations for the broadcast minute by minute. If the hurricane had spoiled his idea of marking the birth of yet another well-planned edition of *Today*, he did get a 'How We Survived the Hurricane' story, complete with a full-colour picture of a rather battered-looking team.

Political interviews are the backbone of the *Today* programme, and there have always been complaints about them from the politicians themselves. In June 1987 the Conservatives were re-elected to government, giving Margaret Thatcher her record third term as Prime Minister with a majority of 101. The hostility between Mrs Thatcher's government and the BBC had begun some years before; it was especially strong during the Falklands campaign of 1982, when Downing Street was convinced that not all BBC reporters in the South Atlantic were 'on side'. John Cole, who was the BBC's new political editor at the time, has described being 'assailed, quite rudely' by six Tory MPs in the corridors of Westminster over a *Panorama* programme which had examined domestic opinion of the Falklands crisis. I can remember a similar experience at a drinks party I attended in central London, which seemed to be entirely populated by elderly Tories; I was taken aback by their vehement criticism of the BBC and its news reports, for which they apparently held me personally responsible. But the eventual success of the Falklands campaign transformed Mrs Thatcher's political fortunes, and from a position in the polls third behind Labour and the fledgling SDP, she raced ahead.

As to the opinion of the BBC held in the private apartments of Number Ten, a friend of mine was left in no doubt. She heard it first hand from the Prime Minister's husband Denis. My friend and her husband – a prominent company director – were invited to a reception at Number Ten. Denis sauntered up amiably and gazed at her name badge. As a freelance broadcaster she was there under her own name and not as her husband's wife. 'So what do *you* do?' asked Denis. 'I work some of the time for BBC radio,' she replied. Denis's face fell. 'Oh Lord – not another of those damn BBC pinkoes!' he cried – and wandered off quickly to find more congenial company.

The terrible IRA bombing of Brighton's Grand Hotel during the 1984 Tory conference consolidated Margaret Thatcher's post-Falklands supremacy. But this did not stop the accusations of bias against the BBC. Norman Tebbit, who had survived the explosion, though his wife sustained permanent injuries, became one of the lead attackers of *Today*. One morning he came into our green room during the eight o'clock news to await his interview with Brian at ten past. He looked sternly at everyone over his half-moon glasses, and then to everyone's astonishment pulled out a feather duster and swished it over the head of the editor, Julian Holland. 'Just cleaning up the BBC,' he said. Brian then bounced in from the studio in his usual cheeky-chappie way and, knowing nothing of the feather duster, advanced towards Mr Tebbit for a quick word before the interview. 'In a couple of minutes we'll creep into the studio,' he told him. '*You* may creep,' said Tebbit, '*I* will walk.'

Nigel Lawson, the Tory Chancellor, had long thought of *Today* as an 'opposition programme'; he had even said so during one of his interviews with us. He had a famous clash with Brian Redhead on the morning after the 1987 budget, when Brian challenged him on the government's job creation programme, saying that low-paid, part-time jobs 'aren't real jobs'. 'Well,' said Lawson, 'you've been a supporter of the Labour party all your life, Brian, so I expect you to say something like that.' Brian was livid. 'Do you think we should have a one-minute silence now in this interview, one for you to apologize for daring to suggest that you know how I vote, and secondly perhaps in memory of monetarism, which you've now discarded?' Their exchange went into broadcasting history.

Brian frequently claimed that he had voted Conservative in at least one election. Macclesfield, the Cheshire constituency in which he lived, had as its sitting member Nicholas Winterton, of whom Brian was very fond. Brian told us that after he had placed his 'X' in the square next to Mr Winterton's name on the ballot paper, he wrote: 'This vote is for the person and not the party.' When the ballot paper came to be counted, the additional instruction was spotted and there was some concern as to whether or not this rendered it invalid. The returning officer showed it to all the candidates. If they were happy with it, it would count as a vote for Nicholas Winterton. No one objected. It was some months before Mr Winterton discovered who had supported him with such enthusiasm.

Five years after I joined *Today* full-time it was still unusual for women to do major political interviews on nationally broadcast radio and television programmes. Quite a number had tried; few had lasted. Sue Lawley for *Nationwide* and Mary Goldring for *Analysis* on Radio Four were among the rare exceptions. It's probably true that most women interviewers lack the more aggressive approach of their male colleagues. They possess perhaps more subtle skills: an ability to fillet out the facts of a story and tease out the threads of an argument without too much obvious pushing. It's an approach that can be just as effective, but not necessarily one which works as instantly as a fast-moving programme demands. When I first applied for a job with the BBC back in 1967 I was told that women's voices lacked authority. It was an excuse used on *The World At One*, even under the comparatively enlightened editorship of Andrew Boyle, for not giving women reporters the tougher political interviews. One of the first decisions I had had to make on moving from *Woman's Hour* to *Today* was what sort of tone to adopt: it would have to be sharper, certainly, but are women expected to take exactly the same approach to interviewing as their male colleagues? And when women do sound 'sharp', why does it apparently irritate listeners – and sometimes the interviewee – in a way that it doesn't when men do the questioning? I think I managed to settle into my '*Today* voice' fairly quickly, but I discovered that the *Today* audience is not slow in letting you know what they think.

Women's voices are usually both softer and higher-pitched than men's, and there is an argument that this, plus their lack of real natural aggression, makes them less effective when it comes to interrupting a politician in full flow. There is perhaps something in this, but I would prefer to think that it is more a matter of self-confidence and plenty of practice. In 1992, for instance, I tried unsuccessfully to separate Labour's campaigns coordinator Jack Cunningham and Michael Howard, then Conservative employment secretary, during a fierce spat in Studio 4A just before the general election. The heated discussion between them degenerated into total cacophony, and it was several minutes before they calmed down.

'Absurd and a total misrepresentation!' yelled Mr Cunningham on Mr Howard's interpretation of Labour's tax and spend figures.

'That is exactly what would happen,' spluttered Mr Howard.

'It's a total misrepresentation of Labour's plans,' repeated Cunningham.

('Gentlemen . . .' said I.)

'No, no, Sue, I can't let this absurd nonsense go unchallenged.'

'All those things would happen.'

'No, they wouldn't happen.'

'Of course they would.'

'I'm going on your own figures.'

'No, no.'

'Come along, are you going to let me . . . ?'

('Gentlemen, let *me* . . .' I implored vainly.)

'Are you going to let me speak or are you going to shout me down?'

('Let *me* speak . . .' I urged them.)

'Ah, come on, we must have an answer to this.'

('Hang on!')

'I'm not going to have Mr Howard . . .'

('You can answer that in a moment . . .')

'. . . misrepresenting us, and that's what he's doing. And what's more . . .'

('Right, you can come to that in a moment Jack Cunningham, but let me ask . . .')

'. . . he's not going to get away with it.'

It went on like this for several minutes. Short of throwing a bucket of cold water over the pair of them, I said at the time, I didn't know how I could have ended the dogfight sooner than I did. I was probably over-conscious, too, of my early training which said that two voices shouting simultaneously on the radio were awful and three a disaster. I suppose it was quite entertaining and 'good radio', and it made the leader pages of several newspapers, but it wasn't the sort of political chairing of which I could be proud. Hundreds of listeners rang in to complain about Howard and Cunningham, and one or two about me. Jenny Abramsky was quizzed about the episode on *Feedback* on Radio Four at the end of the week: would a man have made a better fist of it, she was asked? She loyally defended my performance on air: it was live, it was unexpected, these things do happen, it certainly wasn't my fault. I was grateful for her public support, but I learned a lesson from my performance – I should have insisted on taking charge from the beginning, even if it meant shouting at them. It was worth noting that the two politicians, after their spat, cheerfully shared a taxi back to the Palace of Westminster.

Naturally, it is not the presenters themselves who choose which interviews they do. That is done by the editorial team, and especially by the editor responsible for the programme overnight. Each presenter gets roughly the same number of interviews, and in theory they are handed out evenly each day between the two on duty. Looking back over the programme's running orders I can see how much has depended on the views of the programme's overall editor.

Jenny Abramsky, for instance, in the mid-eighties, generally preferred that Brian Redhead be given the top political story of the day, or perhaps John Humphrys. Phil Harding, who followed her, was more even-handed, though Brian still expected the 'big' interview by right. According to Roger Mosey, who became editor in 1993, the decision on who did what was a matter of mood and not of gender. He maintained that if there was no particular news point to tease out of a Tory cabinet minister like Michael Heseltine, it was 'good theatre' to use John Humphrys. Certainly the regular Humphrys/Hezza jousts were entertaining, even if no earthshaking headline emerged. If the day's agenda meant a particular fact had to be drawn out of a cabinet minister, then, according to Mosey, he was perfectly happy for me to do the interview as I was considered to have a certain dogged determination. But overall under Mosey's editorship my share of the political interviews declined substantially. Just before he joined the programme as editor, an article appeared in the *Independent on Sunday* hinting that Mosey did not rate me highly. When he took over officially I asked him if this was true. 'Malicious gossip,' he said, which did not seem to me to be an absolute denial.

If domestic politics were not to be my speciality I had no complaints about the number of foreign stories I was given, and from time to time there were rewarding trips abroad. In the eighties BBC news spent a lot of attention and money in American presidential election years on the big political conventions, and in the summer of 1988 I was earmarked to report on the Democrats' convention in Atlanta, Georgia. Less than three months before the trip I discovered that I was suffering from fibroids – benign growths in the uterus. A specialist told me that it would be sensible to undergo a hysterectomy straight away. I knew that this was a major operation and that it would be sensible to take at least two months off to recuperate. I calculated that I could just about make it to Georgia in June.

Poor Phil Harding, as our editor, had had to deal with me and hysterectomies once before – and in doing so confirmed my suspicion that men are a great deal more squeamish than women. One morning on the programme I talked on the transatlantic telephone to an American doctor who had successfully performed a new and less surgically invasive form of hysterectomy. This new operation, recommended only when there were no underlying complications, involved a form of vacuum suction to extract the womb. Recovery time from the operation, instead of being a matter of weeks, could be reduced to days. When the doctor and I discussed the method in a little more detail the word 'vagina' was used. Phil was appalled, and asked me afterwards if it had been necessary to be quite so graphic. I confess I was rather taken aback, as after all my years on *Woman's Hour* a clear anatomical description seemed perfectly appropriate, but Phil thought the word unsuitable for a breakfast-time audience. A straw poll in the office indicated that the men agreed with him, and the women with me. I made a mental note to be more aware of male sensibilities in future.

Exactly two months after my own successful surgery I was in Atlanta to cover the confirmation of the governor of Massachusetts, Michael Dukakis, as the Democratic party's candidate for the presidency. The razzmatazz atmosphere was highly infectious, and my two producer colleagues and I had a lot of fun chasing up stories over several days. The convention opened with an exceedingly tedious speech of great length in which the relatively unknown governor of Arkansas, Bill Clinton, almost smothered his future presidential ambitions. The star of the show was the Reverend Jesse Jackson, with his whooping chants of 'Keep Hope Alive!' The five-hour time difference between Atlanta and London meant that we were regularly broadcasting live between one-thirty and four in the morning. In my rather frail post-operative state I was longing to flop into bed just as I had to perform, and had to take frequent breaks to lie on the floor and do stretching exercises, but I think I made it through to the end of our stint without my colleagues suspecting how delicate I felt. They then returned to London while I took off with friends on a magical trip to the north rim of the Grand Canyon. As for Mr Dukakis, he turned out to be a surprisingly lacklustre candidate, easily beaten on polling day by George Bush senior and his team-mate Dan Quayle.

When William Hardcastle died in 1975 he was a difficult man to replace, but he was eventually succeeded as presenter of *The World at One* by Robin Day. This was an odd choice in some respects, for although Robin had started his career in Broadcasting House as a radio producer, he was an archetypical television performer and was not naturally at his best on the radio. His appearances first on ITN, then on the BBC's *Panorama* and ultimately on *Question Time* had made him a nationally recognized figure, his trademark bow tie and what Frankie Howerd called his 'cruel glasses' regarded with affection by the public. He loved being noticed, and television suited him down to the ground. I don't think he ever felt entirely comfortable with a medium which concentrated so exclusively on the spoken word; the unforgiving nature of radio exposed Robin's breathlessness, and he shared with Bill Hardcastle an impatience with any script he had not written himself. But he had become one of the Grand Old Men of broadcasting, and he stayed with *The World At One* for eight years.

Robin was naturally on the guest list for all the important BBC parties in Broadcasting House, and it was at one of these that I first met him. As the party began to thin out and I decided it was time to go home, I found myself descending in one of the lifts with Robin. It was full and its progress downwards was slow. He turned to me. 'Isn't it about time', he enquired at the top of his voice, 'that you *fructified?*' I took this as an enquiry about my ability to produce children, and a suggestion that I might have left it too late. There were some startled looks from the lift's other occupants. I was furious, and once the lift reached ground level I tried to get away as fast as possible, but Robin was not to be put off. 'Come and have a glass of champagne with me!' he shouted. I was so startled that I could think of no suitable rejoinder – other than to accept the invitation.

There followed a hilarious evening in Robin's flat with a great deal of champagne, a lot of loud music, and the chance to view several videos of Robin collecting awards and appearing on the Des O'Connor show. He was enormously good company, and from then on we saw each other regularly – for visits to the theatre, or for dinner at his club, or occasionally for the weekend at a cottage he used down in Dorset. At one point Nigel Dempster's *Daily Mail* diary had us practically engaged, but there was no question of that – both of us preferred our single state. Robin, I think, enjoyed the chase more than the conquest, and in some ways he was curiously uncomfortable with women. He liked to tease, but his personal enquiries at top volume did not always go down well with those who happened to find themselves sitting next to him. One friend of mine, invited to a supper party I gave where she knew Robin would be present, begged me not to place her within his range. He was, though, as all his good friends knew, capable of acts of great generosity, and he was a good father to his two sons. He liked and admired most politicians and some lawyers – the sort of people who belonged, as he did, to the Garrick Club. But when the Garrick took a vote about admitting women as full members, Robin voted against.

Over important broadcasting matters he considered himself to be a man of high principle: he was appalled in the late 1970s when BBC television broadcast an interview with a member of the Irish National Liberation Army, the group which had blown up the Tory MP Airey Neave. He was equally dismayed about the BBC's conduct over the *Real Lives* affair. *Real Lives* was a programme which included an unprecedented interview with Sinn Fein's Martin McGuinness, widely thought at the time to be a former IRA chief of staff, a role McGuinness has since admitted. The interview was at first pulled from the BBC's schedules and then broadcast, and there was an enormous row. Robin shared Margaret Thatcher's view that people with terrorist links should be denied 'the oxygen of publicity'. He would have loved to run the BBC himself: indeed he applied, unsuccessfully, to be its director-general in 1976. He firmly believed, as he wrote in his memoirs, that 'the decline in the BBC's reputation since the sixties has been due to inadequate leadership at the top'. Brilliant political interviewer that he was, he thought politicians were much more important than journalists and had once stood unsuccessfully as a Liberal candidate for parliament.

After I got to know Robin quite well I talked to him for *Woman's Hour*. I think what he said then still encapsulates perfectly for me some of the challenges of live interviewing.

Interview with Sir Robin Day, broadcast 9.1.85

SM: Are you ever frightened these days, after all your experience, by people you have to interview? Do they ever make you nervous?

RD: I'm never frightened by the people but I'm often frightened by the problem of interviewing them, because the problem is usually one of time. The problem is how the hell I deal with a, b, c and d in ten minutes or fifteen minutes, and what am I to say if he or she refuses to answer the question when it is a perfectly reasonable question. It's not fear in the sense that people understand the word fear. It's fear in the sense of apprehension, it is worry, it is anxiety, but it is not nervousness.

241

SM: Is it an anxiety that you won't do the job as well as you possibly could do in other circumstances?

RD: It's anxiety that I am in a very difficult position and won't be able to cover the ground properly.

SM: Does it ever disturb you talking to a powerful woman? I'm thinking of course of the Prime Minister. She's never disconcerting?

RD: No, not in the least. It never makes the slightest difference. There aren't many women in that position. I mean there's been Barbara Castle and there's been Shirley Williams – I've interviewed them. But quite frankly it never crosses my mind when I'm interviewing them. If I was interviewing Barbara Castle about her 'In Place of Strife' legislation – I've just been reading her diaries – or Shirley Williams when she was a cabinet minister, the fact that they're women doesn't alter the fact that I'm dealing with policy. They wouldn't expect any different. It's the same with the Prime Minister.

SM: I think it's quite well known that you would have liked to have been an MP yourself.

RD: Yes, very much so. I regard being an MP as an infinitely higher occupation than being a television or radio journalist. And that's why I was very sorry when Brian Walden, whom I greatly admire, left parliament, where he was a brilliant backbencher, to go to being a television interviewer, which I thought was rather a step down.

SM: But do you not think that as a television journalist, when you can challenge people's statements and can point out that they're telling less than the truth, that you have more power?

RD: It never crossed my mind that I had more power. First of all there are plenty of people doing interviews like me: there weren't when I started, but there are now. And power – no. I interview the Prime Minister very rarely, once every two years perhaps; ministers more often but quite briefly. This is nothing to the influence that an MP can have on one of these new select committees or in the House of Commons with a well-placed question. But parliament doesn't sit all the year round. I think a television journalist or a radio journalist has a function to perform and I try to do it as well as possible. So I think it's useful, but I don't regard it as being as important a function in democracy as being an elected member of parliament.

Robin thought many broadcasters – most of all himself – were woefully underpaid: he was convinced that I wasn't getting enough money, and kept telling me so. I never discussed how much I earned with Robin, but the eventual revelations about the pay scales of *Today* presenters confirmed Robin in his view.

As he got older, he became increasingly frail and more than a little deaf, but he still adored parties. He had to cancel his own seventy-fifth birthday celebration because of ill-health. A few months later he was unable to make the keynote speech at the birthday party of his fellow journalist and great friend Keith Kyle. I left a message on his answerphone saying how much we had all missed him, but there was no response from Robin – he was on his way to hospital for another check-up on his heart. I never saw him again; three days later this Grand Old Man of the airwaves was dead.

A few months later Robin's memorial service was held at the

Temple Church off Fleet Street. It was meticulously planned, at Robin's request, not by the BBC but by his old friend Sir Ronald Waterhouse, a High Court judge. There was fine music, interspersed with readings from some of Robin's best Garrick Club companions, including Lord Rees-Mogg, Sir Donald Sinden, Sir Ludovic Kennedy and Lord Taverne. Finally, 'by special request', one of Robin's favourite recordings was played: Flanagan and Allen singing 'Underneath the Arches'. I think Robin would have loved that best of all.

As the long period of Conservative government wore on, the party's hostility towards the BBC continued. Early in 1990 the journalist and former Labour MP Woodrow Wyatt decided to concentrate his fire on *Today*. 'The Voice of Reason' in the *News of the World* had now joined *The Times* as a columnist and wished to prove his theory that *Today* was a constant source of anti-government propaganda on Radio Four. He used the services of what sounded like an important and well-staffed bureau, the Media Monitoring Unit, set up five years earlier by two Tories, Lord Chalfont and Dr Julian Lewis. By 1990, however, it appeared to be a one-man band, run by the former editor of a right-wing student newspaper at Aberdeen University and an unsuccessful applicant for the BBC's news trainee scheme, Simon Clark. He issued a document ambitiously entitled 'Political Impartiality and the *Today* Programme' which was based on twelve editions over two weeks in January 1990. He accused the programme of 'attacking government policy without the pro-government arguments being adequately aired', but admitted that his real target was Brian Redhead, who, he told a journalist, he found not only a 'cocky bugger' but overly sentimental towards causes to which he was sympathetic. There was some truth in both those characterizations of Brian, but the document's pretensions to investigative journalism made the MMU an object of ridicule both inside and outside the BBC.

John Birt, in his official response as deputy director of the BBC to the MMU's accusations about *Today*, said he had no doubt of the Corporation's aspirations to impartiality. He also firmly believed that 'over a period, all significant views receive a full airing'. Woodrow Wyatt then demanded to know the 'political predilections and voting habits' of all *Today*'s producers and presenters. This information was refused him. Had I been asked, I might have said that I had voted for all three main parties, including once for Mrs Thatcher – largely, as I suspect many other women voters at that time did, because she was a woman. I had little idea of how most of my colleagues on *Today* voted, though I was absolutely certain that all the main political parties were represented on the team; Peter Hobday rather grandly declared that as a presenter of *Today* he felt unable to vote at all. Eventually the Media Monitoring Unit went away, leaving the spin doctors to do their own daily checking.

Interviewing for news programmes is a matter of instant gratification – or frustration. For better or worse, the whole business is generally over in a matter of minutes. So I enjoyed being involved in a series of radio interviews which was utterly different. Throughout the 1980s and well into my time with *Today* I continued with *Conversation Piece*, produced from the BBC in Manchester by Gillian Hush. The idea was to talk at some length – the first interviews were forty-five minutes long – to people who were not over-familiar to the audience through endless appearances on the popular chat shows. Some were famous, others less well known; many of them had achieved success despite quite lengthy odds against them. When the series was first suggested I was not the first choice of David Hatch, the controller of Radio Four, who wanted Robert Kee, a distinguished television journalist; but Gillian Hush persuaded him to accept me. She made an ideal professional partner – meticulous, cheerful and immensely knowledgeable. Our first series of *Conversation Piece* included as interviewees the Welsh actor and writer Emlyn Williams, the broadcaster Alistair Cooke, the publisher George Weidenfeld, the conductor Sir Georg Solti, the playwright Arnold Wesker and the French winemaker Baron Philippe de Rothschild.

Philippe de Rothschild invited us to his elegant apartment in Paris, tucked away in one of the smarter *arrondissements*. As we settled into our chairs, a woolly-hatted female figure scuttled past the open door. The baron was by now twice widowed, the first time particularly cruelly: his wife, who was not Jewish, was arrested in occupied Paris while he was out of the country, and eventually died in Ravensbrück in 1944. He had recently lost his adored second wife Pauline, an American. The intriguing female figure in the woolly hat turned out to be the theatre director Joan Littlewood, with whom he had formed an unlikely but warm friendship; having left her theatrical home in London, Stratford East, she now spent much of her time in France. We were introduced, and she sat as a discreet presence in the background as the baron spoke of his memories of the postwar struggle to turn his beloved Château Mouton into a premier cru estate. When the great Bordeaux wines were first classified in 1855 Château Mouton was not considered worthy of the highest honour, and only after the Second World War did it achieve top status; antisemitism, he agreed, had probably had something to do with the reluctance to confer the accolade. His English was excellent – he was a professional translator of the English metaphysical poets – and he was a man of huge charm. It was a delight to record an entirely relaxed conversation with no instant time pressures.

The following year we pinned down an even more eclectic list, including the New York crime writer Ed McBain, the novelist Catherine Cookson and the soprano Jessye Norman. Miss Norman was then in her early thirties and approaching her finest years as a singer. She dealt honestly during our conversation with the prejudices still operating against black singers in the world of serious music: 'a fact of life', she called them. 'It bothers some that [we] should be proficient at singing German *lieder*. It is more than incongruous for some, looking at me and

Where's the Lemsip? Coping with a cold: Moscow, 1990.

A last picture together before
my mother became disabled:
Cape Town, 1991.

My father, the BBC's John Simpson
(on holiday in the Cape) and me,
on slopes of Table Mountain, 1991.

Showing off my OBE, 1992. (Herald Photography)

What does an archbishop wear under his cassock? Desmond Tutu, Archbishop of
Cape Town, Peter Burdin (BBC producer) and me, 1993.

With South African politician and campaigner Helen Suzman in London.
(The Independent on Sunday)

Skiing in Gargellen, Austria, 1990s, and
concentrating very hard indeed!

With President Nelson Mandela, Cape Town, 1995.

Waiting to broadcast for *Today*, Cape Town docks, 1995.

With Colin Powell, 1995, after he retired as Chairman of the US Joint Chiefs of Staff.
(BBC Picture Archives)

Kirsty and me photographed for the *Sunday Times* series 'Relative Values', 1997.
(N.I. Syndication)

The Anatomy Lesson:
my father Jim,
his twin granddaughters and
half a skull.

Kirsty and me on
Primrose Hill, North London.
(N.I. Syndication)

My 'family' – Isabel, Susanna,
Chippy, Emily, Kirsty.

The Crossman twins Nonie and Georgie with me, forty years on –
Singapore, 1999.

hearing French or German songs. But after all, all brains are the same colour.' This was in 1979 – only just over a decade since the bitter battles fought by the civil rights movement in the United States. But she was confident that she had moved the boundaries for black opera singers: she was off, just after we recorded our conversation, to sing Richard Strauss's *Ariadne* in Paris. Since then she has so firmly consolidated her position that her colour is no longer an issue.

In 1988 we took the series to Hollywood and talked to Mel Brooks, Angela Lansbury, Anthony Perkins, Stephen Spielberg – and the delightful Walter Matthau, who invited us to lunch at his club in Bel Air. With Groucho Marx's son whacking a tennis ball in the background, and his accountant hovering tactfully nearby, he talked about living in Tinseltown.

Interview with Walter Matthau, broadcast 26.12.88

SM: You were once reported as having said that Hollywood is a terrible place for a serious person. Do you still think that?

WM: Oh yes. For a serious actor, anyway. Because there really isn't any acting in Hollywood. You give exhibitions of your former skills. And you have to do it piecemeal. You shoot the end of the picture first. Then you shoot the middle of the picture three weeks later. You really don't know what's going on, and all emotion is fake, it's engendered. Whereas if you do a two-and-a-half hour play that you've studied for three or four months then it's a piece of art, or it should be. Movies and their attendant catastrophes, such as Hollywood producers and studio heads, are not really serious. It's a place where if you get lucky you can make a lot of money in a short period of time, and then

247

you can buy a house with it and a piece of ground to do a bit of gardening once in a while.

SM: Is that what brought you to Hollywood? You had a successful stage career on Broadway before you came here.

WM: Oh yes, I was absolutely entranced by the money. I mean I became a well-paid whore. It's hard to get a million dollars for four or five weeks' work and then go back to the theatre and work your head off for a tenth of that amount for an entire year.

SM: Do you miss the theatre?

WM: No, I don't, because I suppose I really am a whore. Though I have chosen not to do scripts. It's like how to play poker. You win more money by the hands you don't play than by the hands you do. Poker is a money management game. It's deception and counter-deception. It's a microcosm of capitalism. You're allowed to be nasty and mean and knavish without losing the respect of society, because that's the whole object of the game.

SM: You've been in this town that you affect to despise for about thirty years now. But New York is your home town, and you come – as many people in showbusiness do – from a Jewish immigrant background.

WM: My mother was Jewish, my father actually was a Greek Orthodox priest. Everyone thinks I'm kidding when I say that, but he was. He preached papal supremacy. He was kicked out of the Ukraine for preaching papal supremacy. His name was Metushansky. He fell madly in love with my mother, and who wouldn't, with these magnificent watermelons for breasts and this pretty face. He impregnated her twice – me and my brother Henry – and then he ran away.

SM: Was your mother proud of your success?

WM: No. My mother was never proud of me, she was always ashamed of me. She said, 'If you'd had a decent father you could have been a lawyer or a doctor. Something with some substance.'

SM: You acted with Streisand at a time when her career was burgeoning – I think is the right word. In *Hello Dolly*. What was that like?

WM: Well – we had a big fight. She said to the director at one point, 'Don't you think at this point he should do this?' And I said, 'Just a minute. Let this man direct. He's the director. His name is Gene Kelly – he's an actor and he was hired to direct this.' And she said, 'I'm just making a suggestion.' I lost my temper with her. It was a very hot day and Robert Kennedy had just been assassinated, and I thought it was silly for me hanging around playing a role in a stupid movie listening to this poor unlettered girl give instructions. But she was right. She was only making a suggestion. She didn't do it well, though.

SM: Do you sometimes feel about movie-making that it's a strange profession?

WM: Movies can be good; movies can enlighten as well as entertain. They can be a very powerful force for good or evil. All the behaviour of me and my friends was garnered from the movies. We learned how to kiss a girl, and also unfortunately we learned don't do anything else to a girl unless you marry her first. What a stupid idea. So movies can be a powerful force for education, for enlightenment, for decency, for good solid social structures. But here we have all these crappy little movies making a hundred million dollars with no redeeming merit. So that's why sometimes I get short-tempered with it.

Conversation Piece came to an end in 1993 – just short of its two-hundredth edition. Gillian Hush discovered that the series had reached its conclusion by examining the Radio Four schedules for the second half of the year. Suddenly it was not there. It was simply dropped without notice, as sometimes happens in the BBC. It had been one of the most satisfying broadcasting projects I had ever been involved with. Throughout the series I had met some remarkable people. One of the most memorable was a tiny Jewish woman who suddenly found herself famous at the age of eighty, when her first symphony was premièred at the Royal Albert Hall in the 1989 Proms season. She had given up composing part-time when she was quite young, but took it up again seriously when she was sixty.

Interview with Minna Keal, broadcast 31.8.89

SM: This symphony is 'New Music'. Can you explain what people should listen for in your symphony?

MK: Most of the music is very stormy, because I've had a stormy life. I think my symphony expresses the turmoil and stress of modern living. All the joy and unhappiness: everything you have to cope with. Although there *are* some tunes in it. I don't think a tune is a rude word, and I know that a lot of modern composers have felt that tunes no longer exist. But anything that has different pitches is really a tune. You may not be able to whistle it or sing it.

SM: Are you a slow worker?

MK: I am an extremely, excruciatingly slow worker. I cannot tell you how slow. My symphony took me five and a quarter years. I think the reason for that is that although I have got a knowledge of harmony and counterpoint and so on, that's of no use to me at all. I think of a sound in my head and I have to find it on the piano. I work at the piano. I always know when it's wrong. I'm very meticulous. I cannot leave a thing alone until I know that it's absolutely right.

SM: It's quite noisy, isn't it – your composing?

MK: I make a hell of a row when I'm composing. When Bill [her husband] retired he couldn't stand it. It was driving him mad. There's a violin teacher up the road. She said, 'I'm out all day' – I was in the middle of my string quintet – she said, 'You can come and compose in my house'. When Bill saw I started going up the road every morning just as though I was going to a job, he realized that it was important, it wasn't just a folly. He was building an extension to the garage. He realized that my need was even greater than his and he let me use that. So that's how I started composing in the garage. I can make as much noise as I like and nobody can hear me.

I've lived a very interesting life, but now I suddenly feel that all my dreams are coming true. I feel like a teenager feels. I know that my life is finite: I'm eighty, I'm a realist,

I might live till I'm ninety or even a hundred but it'll come to an end. But I never think of that. I feel as if all my life is in front of me, and it's a wonderful way to feel when you're old.

Somehow she made the prospect of retirement seem wonderfully exciting.

CHAPTER NINE

Changing Times

Interviews should be searching and to the point. They should always be well-mannered, not aggressive, hectoring or rude, even when the interviewee is. Questions which attempt to disorientate an interviewee – are you in this mess because you are stupid or just foolish? – are out of place on the BBC.

Guideline from John Birt, June 1990

One morning in the summer of 1990 I found a long memorandum entitled 'Interviewing on the BBC' sitting in my pigeonhole. It had been sent out to every journalist in the BBC, from the newest recruits on local radio to the presenters on national programmes, as well as to their bosses. I ripped open the envelope and looked through the document with some astonishment. 'An interview should have a clear and specific journalistic purpose,' it said. 'It should be particular to a given interviewee and to a point in time.' There were tips on doing careful preparation and how to keep an interview to the required length. There were reminders about testing politicians 'from all political sides', and on dealing with evasion. It contained some useful reminders, but I thought it was a strange guide to send to experienced broadcasters, and there was little acknowledgement of the real pressures of fast, live, reactive programmes like *Today*. But it was typical of John Birt's determination to control every facet of the BBC's news and current affairs.

John Birt arrived at Broadcasting House in 1987 as deputy director-general to Michael Checkland. It was difficult to match the rather stiff grey figure with a tight smile and shiny shoes with the man who had once been responsible for *Nice Time*, the anarchically funny Granada television programme I had enjoyed in the late sixties, starring Kenny Everett and the as yet unknown Germaine Greer. Birt had plenty of experience of programme-making, but none of it within the BBC, and none at all in radio. He had spent almost twenty years working for independent television, ending up as director of programmes for London Weekend Television. From the moment he arrived at the BBC it was clear that he considered it his mission to reorganize its journalism. He would concentrate on television current affairs; radio mattered only in that it was, as one former programme editor told me, 'a citadel which had pulled up the drawbridge and wouldn't let him in' – a part of the BBC typically far too resistant to change. On an early visit to the *Today* office he confessed that he didn't listen to radio much, which appalled its then editor Jenny Abramsky, though he was quick to encourage her talents and promote her to be head of all radio's news and current affairs programmes.

John Birt's own work in television current affairs had already given him a reputation as a meticulous planner, someone who knew in advance what a programme would contain long before the cameras got to work. Like Alfred Hitchcock, he could construct an entire project in his head shot for shot, and it was difficult to divert him from the blueprint. This was anathema to most BBC current affairs producers, who were prepared to work out the detailed message of a programme as it was being made. Birt did not approve of such a freewheeling approach to programme-making. His belief that the BBC's television current affairs department needed thorough reorganization had been reinforced by the squabbles with the Thatcher government over *Real Lives* and the BBC's coverage of the Libya bombing raids of April 1986, when there were complaints about too much sympathy with Colonel Gaddafi; Norman Tebbit had described some of Kate Adie's coverage of the American attack on Tripoli as 'uncritical carriage of Libyan propaganda'. Birt did not approve of *Newsnight* either; in his opinion, it often squandered its considerable resources. Instead, he would invest more money in correspondents and in specialist units. Unfortunately he neglected to consult the very people whose work he was so determined to reconstruct, and a great deal of ill-will was brewing.

Birt was meticulous in laying down a power base for all the change he was planning: important lieutenants were recruited from outside the BBC, particularly from his old television company LWT. Samir Shah, a relatively inexperienced television journalist, was given special responsibility for weekly current affairs programmes. Ian Hargreaves, a highly regarded print journalist but with limited experience of television or radio, was brought in as managing editor of news and current affairs. Birt appointed battalions of expensive management consultants to produce reports on implementing change. He made programmes and departments buy and sell facilities to each other. It turned trying to make programmes by the old and trusted methods into real battles over scarce resources. Suddenly we found it cheaper to buy a CD than to borrow it from the BBC's own record collection, and less expensive to buy a book than to get it from the in-house reference library. Consulting newspaper cuttings – something current affairs programmes have to do many times a day – became prohibitively expensive at ten pounds a time. Birt also had a disconcerting habit, even in front of the people who made them, of impersonally referring to radio and television programmes as 'product'. A number of senior and talented programme-makers, fed up with the new structures, left the BBC and set up their own production houses. They then proceeded to sell their programmes back to the BBC.

The first new *Today* editor of the Birt era was Phil Harding, who took over from Jenny Abramsky in 1987. He was a rather serious man, slightly stooped, with a worried frown and a disconcerting habit of rubbing his hands together when agitated, which was frequently. He was steeped in television current affairs – he had spent time on *Panorama* and *Newsnight* – but had little recent experience of radio, so he was given only a guarded welcome by the *Today* team. Undaunted, he threw himself into his new job with dedicated enthusiasm. He was determined to raise the profile of *Today* in the print media: on most mornings after we came off the air he and the production team would devote themselves to telephoning the papers' newsdesks with quotes from any of our interviews which they might have missed. Sometimes tapes were played back over the phone by Harding himself. It worked: the number of press mentions of *Today* rose, and he later claimed that the audience figures went up by 20 per cent. He made sure his team of presenters – Redhead, Hobday, Humphrys and me – were properly prepared in advance of our interviews, and invented a more rigorous system of briefings. These could run to several pages. Brian usually put his, good or bad, straight into the wastepaper basket.

Brian was often impatient with Harding, and once very publicly lost his temper with him. It was at the time of the conference of European heads of government which led to the 1992 Maastricht treaty. Harding had not thought it necessary to send a presenter to the Netherlands to cover the negotiations. Brian thought this was a serious mistake: our correspondents on the spot were all extremely well informed, but at crucial political moments he believed a presenter should be right in the middle of things. He shouted at Harding in the green room, calling him an incompetent fool in front of some of the programme's guests. Phil waited until the end of the programme before shouting back. It was a humiliating experience for him, and embarrassing for us. But Brian's fits of fury were soon over, and an arm would be flung over the victim's shoulder to show that all had been forgiven.

The late eighties was one of the most rewarding periods I can remember working on *Today*, for the world was changing fast.

Strange political shifts were taking place, not only through almost all of eastern Europe but also at home. By now the Thatcher government was beginning to unravel, and you could listen to the unravelling on *Today*. The programme's green room became an extraordinary place – a miniature forum where much of the British establishment met. Members of BBC management, including the director of radio David Hatch and Radio Four's controller Michael Green, though never John Birt, came in regularly to observe the panoply of celebrities. It was not unusual to see there the home secretary, the Aga Khan, the chairman of Guinness and the director of public prosecutions, all waiting to give an account of themselves in the studio. Rising Labour stars – Jack Straw, Gordon Brown and Tony Blair – took coffee there too. Kenneth Baker, as chairman of the Conservative party, seldom turned down a chance to come in. One morning, after some uncomfortable local election results, he was overheard rehearsing his lines for the interview at ten past eight: 'We *have* done well – we *have* done well – this is a *triumph* for the Conservative party . . .'

Occasionally political foes had to be kept apart. During the Iran–Iraq conflict ambassadors from the opposing sides waited their turn in separate areas; they also had to be interviewed in separate studios. The Iraqi ambassador in London at the time, Dr Al-Mashad, was particularly sensitive to criticism and unused to being questioned by independent journalists. One morning, sitting opposite him in the studio, I referred to the report in that day's edition of the *Daily Telegraph* that Saddam's army had used chemical weapons, specifically nerve gas, against members of the Iraq's Kurdish minority. It turned into an exhilarating encounter. Dr Al-Mashad was furious and began shouting, cutting across all my questions.

Interview with Dr Al-Mashad, broadcast 1.9.88

SM: Dr Al-Mashad, you've heard Mr Zabari quoting independent sources saying that chemical weapons and nerve gas have been used against the Kurdish population. What's your reaction to that?

A-M: Well, first of all it is very nice of you to be concerned about the destiny of the Kurds, supposedly the Iraqi Kurds. But I wish that you would have equal concern for the poor Iranian Kurds inside Iranian territory who have been fighting for their right since almost nine years.

SM: I'm sure the world is just as concerned about Iranian Kurds . . .

A-M: No, no, no! You are not concerned because you are bringing a question . . . to me it's not of equal standards . . . to me it's of double standards because if you are concerned about the plight of the Kurds you are not going to bring a member of a tribal mafia, a criminal, who is connected with foreign countries like Iran and Israel, and give him time on your radio to fabricate all of those lies. And then you are using his word of independent sources which are not verified or substantiated by international body.

SM: Well, there's a report in the *Daily Telegraph* this morning which you will have seen . . .

A-M: I am indignant that you are going to bring up that subject and you are not letting me explain to you in the same standard that shows that you are interested humanitarianly [sic]. You should ask this man, or other men, who are traitors to their own people, who are working with foreign governments. How would you feel if on Baghdad Radio I would bring a British citizen who is working with Argentina during the Falkland War?

SM: But, sir, may I ask you on BBC radio about the specific accusation that your country has used chemical weapons against the Kurds?

A-M: Look, it has been stated by the United Nations that chemical weapons were used in the Gulf War but Iran used it first.

SM: Did Iraq use it against the Kurds?

A-M: Listen, listen, we haven't, this is, this is his accusation. It was the Iranian who used it and there is no verification at all what he is saying. This is an extraordinary thing and this to me riff-raff not known, in the word you are bringing him is part of the Kurdish mafia supported by Iran and Israeli governments and outside power and they are working against their own people.

SM: But Dr, Dr Al-Mashad . . .

A-M [*getting louder and louder*]: No listen! No, no!

SM: Are you denying that there is a policy of extermination?

A-M: I am denying, I deny, I deny this categorically and I am indignant even it comes to your attention and mind to raise this question with me.

It was a startlingly undiplomatic performance, but Dr Al-Mashad went on to be Iraq's representative at the United Nations, where he could often be heard defending Saddam during the Gulf War.

The Princess Royal joined us one morning to talk about the Save the Children Fund – prompting the BBC to leap into full Royal Visit Mode once again. The green room might just about have passed muster for politicians but was altogether too unkempt for a royal: the chairs and sofas, where they were not ripped or worn, were covered in late-night food stains and cigarette burns. It was agreed that a brand new suite would be acquired for the princess's visit. On the day, she arrived rather earlier than expected, but remained standing for the entire half-hour before she went on the air, chatting to selected members of the team. The brand new sofa went quite unused until after her departure.

Margaret Thatcher generally avoided personal appearances on the *Today* programme, but she did make one quite unexpected broadcast for us in 1988. Remarkably, she initiated it herself. Her friend Mikhail Gorbachev was in Washington and due in London for a meeting with her on his way home to Moscow. News had just broken of the terrible earthquake in Armenia, and on Radio Four's 6 a.m. *News Briefing* programme a correspondent reported that Mr Gorbachev had decided to fly straight to Armenia without stopping in London. It was not yet known what Mrs Thatcher's reaction to this would be. At about 6.25 the phone rang in the main *Today* office. 'It's Number Ten here,' said an anonymous voice, 'and I have the Prime Minister for you.' The editorial team thought it was a leg-pull, and a rather annoying one, as five minutes from on-air time everyone was frantically busy. But the caller insisted. 'The Prime Minister would like to have a word on your programme about Mr Gorbachev's visit.' It was the genuine thing. Just after 6.30 an astonished John Humphrys was told over his headphones that the Prime Minister was on the line. Seconds later she was part of the programme, expressing sympathy for the Armenians and understanding that Mr Gorbachev could not now come to see her. It emerged that she had managed to circumvent the official Downing Street switchboard, which was under instructions to monitor and occasionally prevent the Prime Minister's spur-of-the-moment calls to the media. On this occasion her flanking action worked triumphantly.

In the days before regular satellite links, arranging live foreign contributions could be a tedious process. Reaching politicians or even correspondents on a decent quality landline involved a laborious series of international connections, as I had discovered on *It's Your World*. When one of our reporters went to Israel in the mid-eighties to present part of the programme from Tel Aviv, the process involved a bewildering network of connecting links in Vienna, Budapest and Brussels. It was nerve-wracking for everybody. As the end of the news bulletin approached, the Tel Aviv connection had still not been achieved. The only voice coming through belonged to an engineer with an Israeli accent saying firmly, 'BBC no here,' and the only item we had to fill the gap between ten past seven and half-past was a short weather forecast, so there was some editorial panic. Through the glass presenters could see their colleagues desperately scrabbling for something – anything – on tape to stall things a little. Then, just as the newsreader drew the bulletin to a close, the right voice came through from Tel Aviv. Sweat was wiped from brows and deep sighs of relief exhaled. To the listeners, the transmission no doubt sounded entirely and seamlessly smooth.

As old-fashioned communications gradually gave way to satellites, and analogue signals to digital, the good connections did not always noticeably improve. Satellite links might be crystal clear, but the annoying half-second 'bounce' effect meant that interviewers' questions were followed by a pause as the signal travelled through space. But much less complicated link-ups could go awry just as easily. At one point the producers of 'Thought for the Day' – the religious affairs department in Manchester – decided that it should spread its wings a little and come from different points around the country, otherwise known as 'holes in the wall'. This often meant some poor cleric having to find his way into an unmanned studio, open it up himself and switch on the power. If this didn't work

– and it often didn't – then he had to find a telephone box and read his 'Thought' into the handset with the traffic roaring past. Nor did temperamental regional studios confine their technical traps to the religious. One man due to give us his views on local government, having negotiated a fiendishly complicated set of instructions about opening a studio at the back of a brand new civic centre, locked himself in and set off the fire alarm. This was clearly heard throughout the live broadcast, accompanied by heavy thumps on the door as the anxious firefighters tried to release the man they were convinced was trapped inside.

I had my own experience of battling to get into a studio for a live broadcast. Phil Harding sent me to Glasgow for a 'copresentation': an edition of *Today* where half the programme comes from some-where well outside London. With a bit of judicious planning and the expert help of our technical staff it usually works well, but on this occasion my producer, whom I shall call A, not usually a nervous type, had been bolstering his confidence with regular nips of whisky. We worked together on the following day's programme until quite late in the evening. At about ten I went back to our hotel, having arranged with A that we would meet again at five o'clock the next morning at the BBC's Glasgow headquarters. Unfortunately, when I arrived the whole building was in darkness and apparently completely deserted. I circled the building several times in mounting panic – it was less than ninety minutes before we were due to go on air, and I had a lot of writing to do. Eventually a rather sleepy commissionaire, rather like the porter in the Scottish play, was roused by my frantic knocking and let me in. We stumbled around the building and found the temporary *Today* studio. Of A there was no sign. A few minutes before transmission he appeared with a cheerful greeting, clutching the morning papers. I could see that this particular ship would have to be steered without a pilot. I tried to sound calm as the programme crossed back and forth between Glasgow and London while A, an extremely amiable fellow when sober, mumbled away in the background. I'm afraid he was soon moved on to something requiring fewer night shifts.

Shortly after my Glasgow experience I had a strange encounter in a studio only yards from our office in Broadcasting House. One morning at about four-thirty I slipped into one of our 'back-up' studios to record a short interview with a correspondent in the United States. As I sat concentrating hard with my headphones on, I heard a strange rustling noise coming from somewhere around my feet. I looked down. There on the floor was a large black plastic bag. It was moving. Out of it gradually emerged a head, and then a pair of shoulders, and two arms. It was an elderly woman: evidently I had disturbed her good night's sleep. As I tried to continue my transatlantic conversation, she picked up the plastic bag, dusted herself down and scuttled out; I think she had been as startled by our encounter as I. My subsequent enquiries elicited her sad story. She was a former employee of the radio newsroom who had found it difficult to cope with compulsory retirement. Sometimes at night she could be found wandering the corridors of Broadcasting House. Occasionally she slept on a studio floor. I never encountered her again, and I've often wondered what became of the ghostly presence on the third floor.

Once – just once – I actually fell asleep in the studio myself, for a split second in the middle of an interview. Working on *Today* is not recommended for anyone who has difficulty in adjusting to different sleep patterns. Even before the programme stretched to three hours my alarm – or rather alarms, for I have always thought it prudent to have two – went off at half-past three in the morning. Occasionally sleep was elusive, and I got up feeling pretty awful and struggled to concentrate on the business of broadcasting. The actor Antony Sher has observed that a perfect performance on stage is a combination of concentration and relaxation. It is much the same for live broadcasters, and finding the right balance can be a problem. On this particular morning I was talking to Lord McGregor of Durris, then head of the Press Complaints Commission, about how he would police its new code of practice. 'Which policies . . . ?' I began to ask him – and then I completely lost the thread of what I was saying. I noticed a rather wild look in Lord McGregor's eyes. He must have thought I was either mad or drunk, and have wondered how quickly he could extricate himself. After about five seconds of burbled nonsense I managed – just – to pull myself together and complete the sentence. I had done what all live early-morning broadcasters dread doing: I had allowed my attention to wander, and had relaxed into the first stages of sleep. No doubt I was thinking longingly of breakfast and black coffee. But it taught me a lesson about concentrating on the immediate task. I later discovered my ramblings in the BBC sound archives, under the heading 'Sue MacGregor stumbles while on air . . .'

By the autumn of 1989 something very exciting indeed was begin-ning to happen in eastern Europe, and particularly within the Ger-man Democratic Republic. This had not been fully foreseen: some of the political experts thought that if the communist edifice were to fracture, the fault line was most likely to lie in Czechoslovakia, where twenty-one years earlier Mr Dubček's liberal regime had been so cruelly smashed by Moscow. Radio, with its relatively simple technology, made it possible to talk each morning live to the people at the centre of it all. The city of Leipzig in East Germany became the hub of opposition to the regime, and an English-speaking pastor called Ulrich Seidel was a regular commentator for us on the extraordinary gatherings in and near his church.

Interview with Pastor Ulrich Seidel, Leipzig, broadcast 10.10.89

US: Such a huge number of people in the streets was really an experience. Two weeks ago we had eight thousand, last week fifteen thousand people, and now I would guess seventy to eighty thousand people in the streets. We expected violence and bloodshed. But when the demonstration went on from the churches in the centre of the city there was a very good mood – people knew they had to renounce violent means. There was a great discipline amongst them, and the police forces were very reluctant to intervene.

SM: Do you think the mood of compromise will extend to the party, the Politburo?

US: Yes, I'm convinced it will happen. Last night for the first time we had a declaration from party members and by Kurt Masur, conductor of the famous Gewandhaus Orchestra, which asked people for calm and non-violence, and they offered dialogue between the population and the party on a local level. Many people [in the orchestra] and in the factories are handing in their party membership. Next week I think there will be more than one hundred thousand people in the streets.

Less than a month later, the Berlin Wall came down. Nothing could match the drama of that night. In the late afternoon of 9 November 1989 the general secretary of the East German Communist party, Günther Schabowski, made an unheralded announcement at a press conference: citizens of the GDR could henceforth leave the country at official crossing points, and visas would be issued for travel to the West. Word spread rapidly among the East Germans, and soon people began to hammer away at the hated wall with pickaxes, shovels and even their bare hands. The story was soon on the international wire services, and through them reached the overnight team in the *Today* office. Everyone blinked. It was hard to take in. Was this really happening? The Berlin Wall was the most potent symbol of the Cold War – it was at the very centre of our understanding of postwar politics. There was a debate for a while within the overnight team about how important the fall of the Wall was, and in what way: whether the event should be treated as a happy occasion or one with frightening implications. Someone argued that it could mean a new threat to Western security. One or two people thought we should do a cautious analysis. But then a reporter talked to East German journalists in Berlin and they were all euphoric about what had just happened. So the doubters were persuaded: it was a moment of stupendous joy, and that was how we should present it.

By the time I came in at around four-thirty we learned that large chunks of the Wall had already been removed. Graham Leach was among the BBC correspondents there to witness the opening of the borders. Thousands of West Berliners gathered at Checkpoint Charlie, and we heard their excited voices as they welcomed the East Berliners across: 'It's what we have waited for for over twenty years!' 'This is history – I cannot believe it – look, she's crying!' 'The day the Wall came down! I mean – this is *it*!' There was an extraordinary moment when we heard a mechanical digger make the first incision in the Wall itself. A man produced a felt-tip pen and drew a square on the Wall where he suggested the breach should be made. A huge cheer went up as the digger, by now on the top of the Wall, in Graham's words 'literally munched off the top of it', and the first row of bricks came away. The crowd below chanted in joy. 'I was born in the year it went up,' one woman told us. 'I've never seen Berlin without this Wall! It's wonderful!' The man controlling the digger then began to distribute bricks as souvenirs. Days later you could buy bits of the Wall packaged neatly into little plastic bags.

The exhilarating times continued, though in some cases horror followed: the break-up of the old Yugoslavia led to the cruel and terrible conflicts in Bosnia between Serbs, Croats and Muslims on which we reported extensively in the nineties. The Soviet Union under Mikhail Gorbachev had also felt the seismic shifts; although he was beginning to be deeply unpopular at home, Gorbachev was regarded by the free world as a significant reformer, and had impressed Margaret Thatcher as a man with whom she could 'do business'. In the summer of 1990 I was sent to Moscow and Kiev, where Mrs Thatcher was due to open the British pavilion at a trade fair, to review *glasnost* and *perestroika* for *Today*. I was to report live into the programme on several consecutive days.

Outside Moscow we stayed in some rather rudimentary hotels: the one in Kiev, I remember, could not provide meals after seven o'clock at night, and the curtains on my bedroom windows were so threadbare that modesty dictated changing in the shower cubicle. Our young interpreter, Irina, shrugged her shoulders and did her best. She was apologetic about some of the public arrangements but – like many Soviet citizens – embarrassingly kind and hospitable at home. We were invited back to lunch in her flat, a three-room apartment in which three generations of her family lived. In the faceless grey block all the lobbies and lifts stank of urine – but inside the flat all was warmth and light. Irina's husband Sacha and her mother had prepared an enormous meal of Ukrainian specialities; after two days of inedible hotel food we fell upon the dishes of meat and pickled vegetables, and on the glasses of vodka and local champagne. All Ukraine was still stunned by the Chernobyl disaster and its aftermath: there had been talk of genetic mutations, deformed babies and a high rise in the cancer rate which might be passed on through the generations. Every mother in Ukraine – and Irina had a young daughter – was fearful.

By now the West knew a great deal more about the circumstances of the explosion in the early hours of 26 April 1986. The engineers on duty that night had switched off the electricity supply as an experiment, to see how long the reactor could work without it. The nuclear explosion which resulted was many times the size of both Hiroshima and Nagasaki. A radioactive cloud drifted across Ukraine and northern Europe, reaching as far as Britain. Welsh sheep were said to be contaminated. The town of Prypyat, built three miles from the Chernobyl reactor to house its workers, was not evacuated until thirty-six hours after the explosion. It was eventually sealed off and became a ghost town. Now, four years later, there was a thirty-kilometre exclusion zone around the damaged reactor, but occasionally foreign journalists were allowed to visit the towns on the perimeter.

I was lucky. I was taken with an interpreter on a car journey, armed with bars of Western chocolate I had brought with me to sustain us. We passed rolling farmlands of green wheat in rich dark soil. There were pretty whitewashed houses with geese in the front yard and a *babushka* sweeping the path. Peasants worked in the fields nearby. The scene could barely have changed in a hundred years, apart from the ill-maintained tarmac road. After two hours we reached a small town which sat starkly in its surroundings: it seemed to consist almost entirely of grey tower blocks. This was Slavutych, to which many of the workers evacuated from Chernobyl had been moved. Chernobyl, despite the explosion, was still providing electricity for Ukraine, and continued to do so until it was finally shut down in the new millennium. The medical staff at the hospital in Slavutych assured us that all the workers were carefully monitored for contamination. 'Look – we are absolutely sure it is now safe here,' said the doctor as she passed a Geiger counter over my clothing. There were no tell-tale rapid clicks, though I could not be at all sure the thing was working. Patient women queued for testing with their babies. I have seldom felt such an overpowering sense of sadness: it seemed a glimpse into a dreary world without hope.

Next day, back in Kiev, we broadcast our report live to London from a well-equipped radio caravan parked in the grounds of the trade fair. The local people crowded round. Many of them were eagerly awaiting the British Prime Minister's visit, and one woman, as I stuck my head out of the door for a breath of air, rushed up to our caravan with a gleam of recognition in her eye. 'Mrs Thatcher?' she enquired eagerly. I had to disappoint her. The Iron Lady had taken a different route, and was half a mile away in a massive pavilion extolling the virtues of British-made goods.

By the time we reached Moscow the Soviet hotels and questionable food had taken their toll: we had all shed weight and I had almost completely lost my voice. Our next broadcast back to London came from what looked like an ancient concert recital hall in the studios of Gostel radio. My despatches were uttered in a barely recognizable croak, and glasses of hot sweet Russian tea did little to improve things. Although our Moscow hotel was much larger than the one in Kiev, I began to despair of ever seeing a square meal again. Waiters claimed that the vast array of empty tables in its dining room were all fully booked. In the end we resorted to subterfuge. Guessing that the head waiter would be ignorant of the British Prime Minister's tour schedule, one of us claimed that I was Margaret Thatcher's private secretary. A table was found for us instantly. As we had guessed, everything on the vast menu was 'off', except blinis and caviare, which we ordered in vast quantities.

In the summer of the following year I went back to Moscow to cover the summit meeting between Mr Gorbachev and President Bush – just weeks too early, as it turned out, to be present at far more dramatic events. This time our budget was a little more generous and we stayed at what seemed like a sybaritically comfortable German-owned hotel: an air-bubble of efficiency and cleanliness and polite staff. It even had room service. I asked one of the girls at the reception desk what the qualifications were to work there, besides good English. 'Not to have worked in Soviet hotel,' she informed me firmly.

That evening a small party of people from the BBC's Moscow office, including Kevin Connolly and Rachel Whewell, whose husband Tim was the World Service correspondent, went for dinner at a restaurant Kevin had recommended in Gorky Street. It served excellent Azerbaijani food and decent wine. Unfortunately, while we dined Kevin's large Volvo, parked outside, lost its radiator grille and two of its hubcaps. He was naturally rather put out, but not for long: he remembered that there was a black market for spare car parts – many of them undoubtedly stolen – on Moscow's outer ring road. It was held only on Saturday nights, so we might be in luck. We set out along increasingly potholed and unlit roads. Just as we reached the outer ring road a policeman stepped into the road and waved us to a stop. He was armed with a machine gun. Where were we going? When we told him we were heading for the black market he said it no longer existed, but that if it did exist it was only on Friday nights. He let us go, and Kevin was relieved, after all the Azerbaijani wine, not to be breathalysed. We turned round and set off back to central Moscow, thinking it advisable this time to avoid the main roads, and with Rachel driving. It was a rather alarming journey along utterly dark and deserted country lanes. Occasionally figures loomed towards us from the side of the road. As we neared the recognizable parts of Moscow another armed policeman stopped us – and this one pointed his machine gun straight at Rachel's head. She kept calm, spoke to him in Russian, and he let us go; we reached our hotel, still minus hubcaps and radiator grille, at about two in the morning.

The following day Rachel and another BBC producer, Lucy Ash, took me to the *banya* – a Turkish bath – just behind the Irish embassy, and I took along my portable tape-recorder. It was an entirely delightful experience. We stripped off and wrapped ourselves in clean white towels, and progressed from the shower room to the huge wood-lined steam room, the heart of the operation. A couple of dozen extremely large naked Russian women showed us what to do. 'Sit here where it's nice and hot. Use your towel to protect your bottom. Why aren't you wearing a woollen hat to cover your hair?' Each one of them had a huge knitted teacosy on her head. The Russian women showed us how to flagellate ourselves with birch twigs: beat gently until the skin turns pink. Finally we were invited to relax in the last room of all, and sip some Finnish beer. It was a reviving end to the day. But I sensed that my *Today* producer, when I handed him the tape-recording of our session in the Turkish bath, was rather appalled by such frivolity. He somewhat reluctantly submitted the tape to London, but it was never broadcast on *Today*. I therefore missed my one chance of appearing on Radio Four completely naked.

A month later I was sitting in the London office at a quarter past four in the morning scrolling through some of the international wire stories on my computer screen, when a story from the Russian news agency Itar-Tass caught my eye. It involved Mikhail Gorbachev. 'Something seems to be happening in Moscow,' I said out loud. The wire story, which was only two lines long, indicated that Mr Gorbachev would not be leaving his holiday home in the Crimea to come to Moscow as expected. He was thought to be unwell. What we were reading was the first indication of the attempted coup against Gorbachev's reforms. By six-thirty the official wires were announcing that he was 'unable to continue in office because of ill health' and that a state of emergency was declared 'for the next six months, in order to avert the country's slide towards a national catastrophe'. We had a dramatic headline at the beginning of the programme: 'Mikhail Gorbachev has been replaced as president of the Soviet Union.'

Our entire programme was recast to concentrate on the events unfolding in Moscow. I asked our correspondent Bridget Kendall, 'Is this a coup?' 'It looks as though it's an attempt at a coup,' she said, 'by hardliners in the Communist party and probably in the military as well, to try and stop what they see as a process of disintegration.' It was the day before the signing of a new treaty which would have changed the relationship between some of the Soviet republics and Moscow. The hardliners were determined to stop it – but some were determined to stop them: 'Mr Yeltsin is clearly going to resist,' said Bridget.

There followed days of tense and sometimes violent confrontation between the forces of reform, led by Boris Yeltsin from the top of his tank outside the Soviet parliament, and those parts of the military loyal to the old ideas. For some time, since the coming of *perestroika*, we had had access to a number of local politicians and academics who spoke excellent English. One of them was Galina Staravoitova, who went on to serve in Yeltsin's government and who was later brutally assassinated in the entrance of a block of flats in St Petersburg. (She had been investigating organized crime. Her killers have still not been found.) Now we found ourselves ringing people we knew in Moscow, telling them what seemed to be happening, and asking them to analyse the situation. 'I knew something unusual had happened,' said one of our contacts, 'for when I turned on the television this morning it was wall-to-wall *Swan Lake*. They always put on *Swan Lake* when there's a political crisis.'

The next day Kevin Connolly described for us how tanks had smashed into the barricades on the city's inner ring road and killed three members of the crowd. The tanks – one of which was driven by a Red Army officer – then surrendered and were driven off in triumph towards the Russian parliament, with dozens of demonstrators clinging on, waving and cheering. In the end the conspirators ran out of steam and the Yeltsinites won; but Mikhail Gorbachev had been fatally wounded politically, and was to resign within a year.

Momentous political events at the beginning of the 1990s were not confined to the old communist bloc. On 2 February 1990 the South African president F. W. de Klerk made a dramatic announcement in the Cape Town parliament. He lifted the ban on the African National Congress, the Pan Africanist Congress and the South African Communist Party. He also paved the way for the release of some of the most famous political prisoners by removing restrictions on those incarcerated for 'non-violent activities'. And he suspended capital punishment. I rang my sister and found my voice shaking as I tried to tell her what had happened. Surely, now, Nelson Mandela's release could only be days away?

BBC news asked me to produce a radio portrait of Mandela, to be broadcast on the day of his freedom. I made appointments to see some old friends and contacts, among them Mary Benson, who had long ago been banned in South Africa and now lived in exile in London, and Adelaide Tambo, the wife of the president of the ANC, Oliver Tambo. Adelaide now worked in an old people's home in Hampstead. Sitting on a bench in the sun, she recalled the old Johannesburg law partnership of Mandela and Tambo, through whom she had first met Winnie Mandela in the 1960s, and spoke of Winnie's role in keeping her husband's name alive during his long years in prison. As she talked, Mrs Tambo gently picked one or two hairs off the collar of my jacket. It was a familiar gesture which touched me deeply; it was also somehow very African. We both laughed when she told me that when she and Oliver had fled South Africa many years before, she had been alarmed to see that the pilot of their Botswana Airways plane was black. The old assumptions of apartheid were surprisingly hard to eradicate.

Nine days later, after an excruciatingly long delay while the world's press and television cameras waited, Nelson and Winnie Mandela emerged hand in hand from the grounds of the Victor Verster prison. The crowd surged forward, and a Xhosa praise-singer danced his welcome. Nelson Mandela raised his right fist in the ANC salute: the crowd was delirious. Six thousand miles away, I jumped up and shouted and wept with them. The impossible had happened at last: after ten thousand days in prison, Mandela was a free man.

That summer my parents came on a visit; it was to be their last together. They were both approaching eighty, and although my father seemed cheerful and in robust good health, my mother looked very frail. She was now badly affected by osteoporosis, and needed a lot of help when walking. But all our old closeness was still there, and we saw a great deal of each other, though she and my father spent most of their time with Kirsty in her home near Camberley. There they had a nice garden to sit in, and they could get to know the twins, who were teenagers now, and their younger sister, who was eleven. The children were enjoyable company for their grandparents over several weeks.

We discussed what looked like the imminent arrival of an entirely new dispensation in South Africa, after the astonishing events of February. Like many liberal whites of their generation, my parents were cautiously pleased at the direction the country was taking.

Full democracy was on the horizon. On the other hand, there was still endemic violence in the black townships, and both white and black leaders would have to convince their people that as communism crumbled elsewhere, South Africa's revolution could be a peaceful one.

It was an enormous wrench saying goodbye: more than ever, we all wondered whether we would see each other again. I was concerned that my mother might soon be an invalid, and about the burden this would put on my father. One day soon it would be sensible, if they were willing, for them to move into one of the many 'retirement villages' which were springing up all over Cape Town; but it would be a big upheaval for them to leave the house in Rondebosch after more than forty years.

As eastern Europe groped for a new order, the middle east was as volatile as ever. In August 1990 Saddam Hussein's forces crossed the border into Kuwait, and Operation Desert Shield cracked into action. Millions of tons of allied hardware was moved to the area. When the air campaign – Operation Desert Storm – began in January 1991, the BBC decided that the progress of what had now become the Gulf War should be covered on radio on a 24-hour basis. The gaps between news programmes on Radio Four's FM wavelength were filled by virtually non-stop commentary on the progress of the allies' campaign. Presenters were invited to take over the long stretches of live ad hoc broadcasting, which in our case meant staying on after the early shift on *Today* until lunchtime. It was a long space to fill, and sometimes the advance notice of topics was minimal. Almost anyone with middle east experience or expertise was drafted in to speculate on the war's progress. On one of my first mornings on duty I was slipped a piece of paper. On it were written the names of two experts and the succinct rubric: 'Discussion on water supplies in the Middle East. Keep going for twenty minutes.' I did my best, but I fear it may not have made entirely compelling listening.

In practice, not a great deal that was not predictable happened in the first few weeks. The long hours of broadcasting soon became known as 'Scud FM', after the endless speculation about the possibility of Scud missiles being used by Saddam and an equally lethal response from the allies. But Birt was impressed by the news service, and after it stopped at the end of the war he asked how it might return in a rather different form. Three years later Radio Five Live, with its successful mixture of news and sport, made its debut.

The allies finally crossed the border into Iraq in the early hours of Sunday 24 February 1991. The Iraqis had ignored President Bush's noon deadline to withdraw unconditionally, and the ground war had begun. My telephone rang at one-thirty in the morning to confirm that a few hours later there would be a special edition of *Today* to reflect the final push of the war; John Humphrys and I were to present it. In the end the allies took only a few weeks to finish the job: by mid-March it was all over. The British troops were congratulated on their successful campaign by a different prime minister from the one who had sent them on their way: for in November 1990, halfway through the Gulf War and rather to the dismay of the Americans, Margaret Thatcher had been replaced by John Major.

By the time the 1992 general election came along Labour began to believe it had a really decent chance of winning. Independent observers thought the result was going to be the most difficult to predict for years. The spin doctors – we had hardly begun to use the term – slipped into high gear. Peter Mandelson, Neil Kinnock's director of communications, did the job with ruthless efficiency. *Today* presenters are not, on the whole, the subject of direct pressure; we are generally only in the office during the early hours of the morning. But colleagues on the long day and night shifts got to know Mr Mandelson quite well. He phoned the programme regularly to try to influence the agenda for the following day and was, according to one of my producer colleagues at the time, 'quite an effective bully'. He used implied connections to the BBC hierarchy to pile on the pressure, making it clear that he knew John Birt extremely well. One form of Mandelsonian attack was the early afternoon call, 'to try to persuade you to do the story he wanted you to do. He nearly always offered you a shadow minister you did not want. Tomorrow, he'd say, it's education and we have decided you should interview the shadow education secretary – that sort of thing. The intention was to try to undermine you – the implication was that if you didn't follow their agenda they would complain to the head of news and current affairs and you would have to spend days writing memos to your bosses justifying your decision not to agree to their demands.' These tactics didn't ever change the programme's original agenda, but they 'did make you wonder if you had the energy to go through the whole thing chapter and verse later'.

The Tories were much less effective at this, and it was therefore easier for a *Today* producer with initiative to circumvent party headquarters and get the interview the programme needed. If *Today* wanted to talk to the health secretary Kenneth Clarke, and Conservative Central Office said he would not be available, it was often possible to telephone him at home in Nottingham and persuade him to talk on whatever the topical health issue was. It was the sort of avoiding action on our part that was anathema to the control freaks at Labour headquarters.

In the event, the issue that dominated media coverage of the 1992 election campaign turned out to be one over which the spin doctors had little control. It was the War of Jennifer's Ear. A Labour party election broadcast had compared the cases of two young girls with a fairly common condition called 'glue ear'. One of them, it was claimed, had a long wait for her operation because of chronic NHS underfunding; the other girl went for private treatment and was operated on straight away. But it turned out not to be as simple as that. The girl with the long wait was named in the press as Jennifer Bennett; it emerged that Neil Kinnock's press secretary had leaked her name to journalists. It was also established that

Jennifer Bennett had a grandfather who was a lifelong Tory. Proper discussion of important health issues became submerged in endless media speculation about whether Labour had played fair in the implications of the broadcast. It was in the end widely perceived that Jennifer's Ear had turned into something of a disaster for them.

It was only the harbinger of greater disaster for the Labour party. By the early morning of 10 April 1992 it was clear, despite what the polls had been suggesting, that John Major had won the general election. The *Today* team had to do some quick rethinking about the running order. Tim Luckhurst, who was on overnight editorial duty, remembers that 'the most appalling moment of the entire night was the realization that we were going to have to change round the two key interviews. We'd put Neil Kinnock down for the all-important eight-ten interview, on the assumption that he was going to be Prime Minister, and John Major for seven-ten, on the assumption that he had lost the election. After the first result from Essex it dawned on us that things weren't going to be quite like that.' At about one o'clock in the morning there was a long battle over who would have to phone Neil Kinnock to tell him he'd been shifted to the earlier slot of ten past seven. Whoever did got a dusty answer from Labour party HQ. In the end the programme replaced a live Neil Kinnock with his impassioned early morning speech to party workers from the front steps of Walworth Road. A delighted John Major, still Prime Minister, happily spoke to us at ten past eight.

In the New Year's Honours List of that year I had been awarded, greatly to my surprise, an OBE for 'services to broadcasting'. I was only too well aware that to many people OBE stands simply for 'Other Buggers' Efforts'; indeed any performer before the microphone is conscious of how much they owe to the support of others. Many journalists also believe that no one in the profession should accept any kind of honour. While I could see that I was only getting a 'gong' for what I was paid to do, I was delighted to accept it, especially as I knew that my mother would be thrilled. She was able to watch the ceremony on the video recording you can buy afterwards, with your own tiny part in the proceedings seamlessly inserted. I was appalled when I looked at it to see that the Queen had to put up with what looked like non-stop chatter from me. I do remember asking her if she ever listened to the *Today* programme, and feeling certain I detected a regal incline of the head.

The following year, as *Today* got a new editor, Roger Mosey, BBC Radio got a new managing director, Liz Forgan. Liz was brought in by John Birt from Channel Four, where she had been commissioning editor in charge of factual programmes; she had not worked in radio before. She was bright, committed and enthusiastic, though she almost fatally blotted her copybook early on when she sent a memo round to everyone expressing her excitement over her new job. She said that after 'listening like crazy for the past few weeks' she was 'simply knocked out by the treasure house of interest, revelation and pleasure you are putting out'. The praise was of course well meant, but producers who had been knocking themselves out working for Radios Three and Four in particular were not pleased to think that she had come so fresh to their work. Liz was eventually to fall on her sword in 1996 over the moving of radio news and current affairs from Broadcasting House to White City.

When Roger Mosey replaced Phil Harding he became the youngest editor the programme had ever had. In his mid-thirties, blond and cherub-faced, he arrived with a strong reputation from his editorship of *The World At One*. He adored the cut and thrust of politics and the minutiae of its daily unfolding. He also struck me as another editor determined to control every aspect of the programme – the most 'hands-on' I had ever come across. Like all his predecessors, he wanted his own team of presenters in place. It was thought that Brian Redhead, already approaching his mid-sixties, might be leaving the programme some time the following year, and a new and substantial figure would have to be found to replace him. Roger knew *The World At One*'s presenter James Naughtie well – well enough to be godfather to one of his daughters – and Jim was a strong candidate to replace Brian. Roger was also an admirer of John Humphrys; when he had applied for the job as *Today* editor he had made it clear he wanted John to be the programme's main voice. He was also, it was thought, quite keen to get rid of me.

As rumours about Brian's departure grew, so did the speculation about the succession. The media press assumed that it would be a straightforward matter. If Jim were signed up to fill the gap when Brian left, he would be Brian's successor. Other names were mentioned, including Jeremy Paxman and Susannah Simons. John Humphrys did not see it quite like that. John was nobody's natural number two, and he knew he was held in high regard. The jockeying for position would be interesting. But where did all this leave me? There had been that reference in the *Independent on Sunday* implying a distinct lack of enthusiasm for me on Roger's part. Now he was in place, he would neither confirm nor conclusively deny it. I could only sit it out.

I was aware that another of my colleagues might have an even shorter shelf-life. Peter Hobday had suspected for some time that his days on the programme might be numbered. I was immensely fond of him and enjoyed working with him, but I knew that neither Jenny Abramsky nor Roger Mosey particularly wished him to stay on. His disappearance for breakfast in the canteen during preparation time had become an irritation, as had his constant references to 'the death of journalism' at the BBC. We assumed he meant to imply by this that *Today* didn't bother with proper investigative work, and to some extent this was true: decent investigative journalism requires a great deal of time and money, and *Today* could only afford this sporadically.

When Roger Mosey finally told Peter that his contract would not be renewed, the news quickly leaked beyond the BBC. There was press speculation that Peter had been dropped because he was 'too middle-class' and 'too old'. It was firmly denied. A great fuss was made, for Peter was popular with listeners. *The Times* launched a Save Hobday campaign, and invited readers, in their own version of the balloon game, to say which of the other presenters they would ditch. When Peter left there was no farewell party, and no hint of a tribute to him from anyone in management; not even, he said later, a telephone call. His last broadcast on *Today* was on a Saturday morning, partnering John Humphrys. About twenty minutes before the programme's end, Peter quietly asked John if he would mind finishing the programme on his own; he had, he said, something urgent to attend to in another part of London. John agreed, and Peter slipped out of the building and drove home. That was it. He had spared himself, and the rest of the team, the embarrassment of his finishing without any kind of final flourish. No vote of thanks had been arranged, and there was no telephone call from his editor. Peter had been on *Today* for fourteen years, and with BBC news and current affairs for twenty-five. He was now able to spend more time in his restored farmhouse among the olive groves of Umbria, and he resumed some of his lucrative media training jobs for big corporations. He has never spoken publicly about the bitterness he must undoubtedly have felt.

Roger Mosey, in his search for fresh voices, made arrangements to hire Anna Ford. Anna, one of television's best-known and most attractive faces, was a veteran of both ITN and BBC television news. She had been one of the 'Famous Five' on TV-AM's first breakfast team, and when things began to go wrong she had shown her contempt for the board by throwing a glass of red wine over Jonathan Aitken. Anna was thought to be unhappy paired with Martyn Lewis on BBC television's *Six O'Clock News*: the *Today* programme looked like a useful alternative. No one could doubt her feistiness or her long experience of live broadcasting, but she was the first to admit that she was not someone who easily took to very early rising – and getting up well before dawn is even more demanding if you are, as Anna was, the mother of young daughters. Still, she took on the challenge.

And challenge it certainly was. She would, she said later, have welcomed a great deal more help when she first joined the *Today* team; but, like many a brand new presenter, she felt she had to find out for herself how best to adapt to a fast-moving news programme. What experienced presenters take for granted, like telling the correct time at the right time, can be a nightmare for the uninitiated. Radio skills are quite different from television skills, and not everyone makes the transition successfully: Anna herself likened her first performances on *Today* to 'learning to ride a bike'. But after she joined the team *Today* enjoyed an even higher profile in the press.

She had one or two memorable tussles with the politicians, particularly when she tackled Ken Clarke as Chancellor of the Exchequer on the number of times the Conservatives had or had not put up VAT. The rather fractious interview ended with Mr Clarke apparently refusing to answer Anna's last question, which was about 'elevating the argument', a point Roger Mosey himself had suggested. There was an abrupt silence. It sounded as if Ken Clarke had walked out; what had actually happened was that the radio car in which he was sitting had been accidentally cut off. The press picked up the exchange and had a bit of fun with it; the Conservative party chairman, Brian Mawhinney, accused Anna of being 'extremely rude'. Ken Clarke himself, ever the good sport, made no complaint at all.

And then, only months before his intended retirement date, Brian Redhead became gravely ill. He had not long before been diagnosed as a diabetic, and needed to take regular doses of insulin. He had given his producer – and everyone else – a desperate fright during the 1992 Earth Summit in Rio de Janeiro, when he was found in what appeared to be a coma in his hotel room. He had forgotten to take one of his insulin doses, probably as a result of the time change and jet-lag. He recovered quickly enough, but it was an indication to everyone that he was less robust than he made out. Over the next year or so it became obvious that he was also in pain from one of his hip joints, though he was determined to wait as long as he could before submitting to an operation.

Brian's interviewing style changed: he was perceptibly gentler. It was as if it all didn't matter quite as much any more. We assumed he was anticipating his retirement. Then, in mid-December 1993, Brian went into hospital. It turned out that a perforated appendix had been leaking poison into his system for months, and his diabetes had helped to lower his resistance. It was too late to treat him effectively, and on 23 January 1994 he died.

Thousands of messages came in from listeners, and from the politicians and other national figures whom Brian had interviewed over the years. *The Times*, in its obituary notice, said that 'Redhead made *Today* a programme that no member of the political class could miss. The beneficiary . . . was the very medium of radio.' This was quite true; he was a uniquely talented journalist, and more at home in the radio studio than anyone else I have come across. He knew that one of the secrets of sounding good was being able to put on a bit of a performance, and his enjoyment of that theatricality was infectious. We all learned a great deal from him.

Brian's funeral was largely for his family and closest local friends, and was held in Macclesfield. His memorial service was held at St Paul's Cathedral, and beautifully organized by the BBC. David Hatch and I were asked to read some of Brian's own words, and I remember not just the high emotion and affection for Brian permeating the whole service, but also the challenge of that St Paul's acoustic. It was particularly trying, I remember, for John Cole, who paid public tribute to his old friend. During the rehearsal I turned to the woman next to me and made some comment about John's strong and unmistakable Ulster accent fighting with the echoing spaces of the cathedral's high dome – and then realized to whom I was speaking: John's wife. She was kind enough to ignore my gaffe.

Brian's death precipitated the arrival of James Naughtie on *Today*. Despite all the official denials about who was first in the pecking order, or even that there was a pecking order, I anticipated an interesting relationship between Jim and John when they were paired together. Jim was an accomplished broadcaster: a first-class political interviewer on *The World At One*, and he was also impressively knowledgeable about sport and opera. He had made news himself in 1989 when he had pressed the opposition leader Neil Kinnock on *WATO* for details of Labour's alternative economic policies. Kinnock had lost his temper and refused 'to be bloody kebabbed' by him, though the full fury of his answer was cut from the tape when it was transmitted. Later, to his credit, Kinnock allowed the whole thing to be broadcast.

I barely knew Jim before he joined *Today*, although we had shared a train journey to the Lib Dems' autumn conference the year before. 'What's your best advice about dealing with the early morning regime?' Jim had asked me. 'Well,' I said, 'I think it's important to be physically fit. I actually go to the gym two or three times a week.' It sounded, I realized, horribly smug, and Jim looked appalled. But once he started with us he settled in quickly and managed from the moment he came into the office to sound almost as cheerful as Brian – in sharp contrast, I fear, to both John and me.

As the momentous South African elections of 1994 approached, Roger Mosey sent me back to record some personal impressions of a changing country. It was a thrilling assignment, and I had every hope that I would return the following April to watch the actual voting. My producer and I visited my old school, Herschel. The blue uniforms of almost forty years ago were still there, as were the battered panama hats. Otherwise Herschel was transformed, with a lecture theatre where once a tennis court had been, and a smart science department a long way from our battered old lab smelling of formaldehyde and Bunsen burners. And the school had gone multiracial. If they could afford the fees or win a scholarship, black girls were welcome, and the Xhosa language was on the senior school curriculum. When I visited, the school choir, still under the baton of Miss Sweet, and now a multiracial choir, was rehearsing the Xhosa anthem 'Nkosi Sikelele iAfrika' – God Bless Africa. Hearing it brought a very large lump to my throat, as it does to this day.

I recorded my impressions, and my conversations with members of staff and pupils – black and white.

Interviews with staff and pupils at Herschel School, Cape Town, broadcast December 1993

SM: Herschel is an Anglican school. In my day it was for white girls only. Now black girls are welcome. And the lessons? They've changed as well. Miss Wilkinson's history class is quite unrecognizable from the ones I used to sit in. For a start, South African history no longer begins with the arrival of the white man.

Miss Wilkinson: We're now doing a lot more on early African history – the original inhabitants, particularly of our country – the San, the Koi Koi, the Bantu settlers that came down. And then, and only then, do we come to the Europeans' arrival.

SM: And what's more the white girls are now learning to speak Xhosa – the language of Nelson Mandela and most of the black people of the Cape.

What are the Herschel girls themselves making of their new multiethnic school? I asked a group of sixteen-year-olds, beginning with Marcy Shimange who came to the school last year.

Pupil: I was so scared when I came here. I wasn't sure how people would react to me. When I speak to my black friends I hear what they say about white people and all that, well now most of my friends are going to white multiracial schools since the schools are open and I find it's so much easier for us to relate to white people.

Another pupil: When I came here I was at the age of ten and that's when you suddenly realize how separate the black people were at that age and only about three years ago did we become . . . we were allowed to mix together.

SM: But the adjusting and adapting hasn't just been between black girls and white. Karina and Christine came to the school from Afrikaans-speaking backgrounds, from the culture of the oppressor.

Pupil: Since I came to Herschel I've actually realized I've often felt embarrassed to be an Afrikaner. I just wanted to hide it I was so embarrassed, I was scared that my friends would look at me and go, 'All of you, it's all your fault'.

Another pupil: It was so interesting to hear their point of view because they've been suffering through the years and I felt so bad as a white Afrikaner.

SM: Sixteen-year-old Thandi has written the new song for the school, and the words 'we are assembled here in love, we are united, we live for one another' speak to her generation of a future where the old barriers won't matter any more.

Thandi: It begins by saying 'we are assembled here in love' and I think that that definitely hits it with a bang. Definitely, because I know in the community of the school we all want to work together and I think as a school when we sing that song we almost sing it for the country as well.

Another pupil: If you really believe in your country you will want to stay here and want to work with everyone. Our roots are too much in South Africa and we want it to work so much that we want to see it work and we want to be part of the change and we want to be part of the working together.

The University of Cape Town now had a black deputy vice-chancellor, Dr Mamphela Ramphele, once the partner of the black activist Steve Biko, who had been fatally beaten up by the police after his arrest. She told me ruefully that apartheid had been 'a remarkable success. Believe you me, the divide and rule policy works. It has given objective evidence for the myth of racial superiority. You only have to look around you. Who are the people in power? Who are the people with the skills?' Apartheid, she implied, may be officially over, but it would take a long time to make South Africa a fair and just society.

I also visited the massive black shanty township of Khayalitsha, close to Cape Town's airport and fast encroaching on the road. Perhaps a million people lived in Khayalitsha ('my new home') and its neighbouring areas, in brick houses, tin shacks and cardboard shelters, all pressed together in a bizarre jigsaw. It was to be another five years before even a proportion of them had decent running water and electricity. Anger and violence simmered in these townships; it was not unknown for white people to be attacked if they visited unannounced. A young American girl, a social worker, had been murdered not long before. But we were welcomed into a crèche and feeding scheme with the help of my old school friend Anne Templeton; the children ran up to us shouting and laughing and eager to be photographed.

Only five miles away, the neat white suburbs of Cape Town could have been another country. Here the new South Africa meant high walls and sophisticated burglar alarms everywhere, though Cape Town was said to be considerably safer than Johannesburg, where almost every well-to-do white home had its own electronically operated security gate. Black people suffered far more than whites: the crime statistics in the townships were deeply disturbing. I spent as much time as I could with my parents in their new home, a pretty cottage in a retirement village behind a security gate, manned twenty-four hours a day. The move to the little village near Constantia had been much smoother than I had thought possible.

Two years earlier, on a brief visit to Cape Town, I had heard of what sounded like somewhere more suitable for my parents to live: my mother's health was now poor and the garden seemed too big a responsibility, even with help, for my father. I broached the subject of a move; to my astonishment they both agreed in principle, providing we could sell Farthings for a decent price. As it turned out we could; a few months later Kirsty went out and managed, astonishingly, to clear out the old home and help them move into the new one in a fortnight. ('You are the one who can *arrange* things,' said my mother, 'but Kirsty is the practical one.' She was right.) Here in the village called Cle du Cap ('Key of the Cape' – it referred to an eighteenth-century local battle between the Dutch and the British) they lived in a two-bedroomed whitewashed cottage of some charm, with someone else to tend to the communal garden and a well-equipped nursing home as part of the complex; the surplus money from the sale of the old house could keep them there comfortably.

My father, now in his eighties, still drove into town twice a week to help supervise the clinic at Groote Schuur hospital specializing in Huntington's Chorea, a degenerative disease of the nervous system that is genetically transmitted and is not uncommon among the Cape Coloured population. My mother, from her bed, could gaze proudly at framed pictures of the grandchildren; next to her was the corner cupboard filled with the beloved Crown Derby. Eventually both the cupboard and china came to me, and they have a new home in the corner of my dining room. I sat with her and chatted as cheerfully as I could, but I felt desperately sad: there was so little time. We held each other tight before I left, and I promised to ring as often as I could from Johannesburg before I returned to London. I think we both knew that this really was our last meeting.

*   *   *

My position on the *Today* programme now seemed much more secure: I could only assume that Roger Mosey had changed his mind about me. But four months later I suffered a terrible disappointment: it was John Humphrys, not me, who was sent to cover the South African elections of April 1994. John had been a correspondent in Johannesburg and had some knowledge of the local political scene, but I had longed to be there to witness for myself the transition to democracy. Instead, I had to watch the drama unfold on television from six thousand miles away. The pictures were dramatic and tremendously exciting: long lines of blacks and whites together snaked up to the polling booths; madams and their maids stood together, and white farmers with their black workers. Every single black person was voting for the first time. The queues were long and slow – but, as one woman in Soweto told a reporter, she had waited all her life for this moment, and a couple more hours standing in a line were not going to hurt her. In Cape Town my mother was wheeled out into the sunshine to mark her own first ballot paper in over forty years: a vote, she told me, for Helen Suzman's Progressive Reform party. There was little doubt about the outcome. Nelson Mandela's African National Congress won by a huge majority, and the former prisoner on Robben Island was the new president.

One Sunday morning three months later I returned to my north London flat at half-past eight after a thirty-minute jog around the neighbourhood pavements. The red light on my telephone answering machine was flashing, and at that hour I knew it was bad news. My sister was in South Africa with one of the twins; the rest of her family was due to join her for a holiday with the grandparents the following day. Kirsty's recorded message was stark: our mother had died in the early hours of the morning. By that evening I was on a flight to Cape Town with my brother-in-law and my other two nieces. It was a journey clouded by grief and guilt: guilt that I had not gone earlier and stayed longer when it was first apparent that my mother's health was deteriorating. 'You can never time these things perfectly,' people said kindly, but I knew that I had timed it badly. 'Your mother was asking after you,' said a nurse when I got there. It struck sharply home, and added to my misery: not having been there at the right time is an enduring and painful memory.

In many ways, I suppose, I had really lost my mother a year or two earlier. A gradual deterioration of her faculties had made life increasingly difficult for her. Letter-writing became awkward and then impossible; the old intimacy of our twice-weekly telephone calls had gradually tailed off. All this had put a great burden on my father, who, with the help of day nurses, had looked after her with enormous patience and good humour.

My mother wanted no funeral service, so instead we invited round all her closest friends, passed round glasses of wine and told affectionate stories about her. I took her ashes back to Britain and Kirsty and I scattered them, as she had wished, in a small wood near Wheatley. She had particularly chosen those woods, for in the spring the bluebell display was spectacular, and in the village of Wheatley she had been, she said, happier than anywhere else.

In 1995 the Queen paid a state visit to South Africa, and this time *Today* did send me to cover her tour. South Africa had been re-admitted to the Commonwealth the year before, and the Queen, it was said, was rather a fan of Nelson Mandela. Forty-eight years before, on her first visit with her parents, the young Princess Elizabeth was part of a royal progress which took a leisurely two months, and included her twenty-first-birthday broadcast to the Commonwealth. This time she was whisked round the country in six days, but she seemed to enjoy every minute of it, beaming whenever she was in the company of Mr Mandela.

We had a makeshift studio in a lifeboat station down in the newly developed Cape Town waterfront. As the royal yacht *Britannia* steamed round the corner into Table Bay, my opening remarks on *Today* were almost drowned by a perfectly timed flypast by the South African Defence Force. Table Mountain provided its reliably spectacular backdrop. This time the 'tablecloth' – massive white clouds tumbling down from the summit like luxuriant folds of linen – was lit by the morning sun. My old city looked fabulously beautiful.

President Mandela had agreed to talk to us just before the Queen's arrival. We met in the grand eighteenth-century Cape Dutch house which had once been the home of the governor-general. 'Don't, whatever you do,' said one of his minders as we waited for the President, 'mention Winnie.' The former Mrs Mandela, from whom the President was separated, now preferred to be known as Mrs Madikizela-Mandela. She had been mired in scandal for months, accused, with her former 'football team' in Soweto, of kidnapping and complicity in the murder of a black teenager. An assault conviction was later set aside on appeal. At the Truth and Reconciliation hearings under Archbishop Tutu Mrs Madikizela-Mandela was directly accused of murder. She denied all these allegations.

Mr Mandela duly appeared, all charm and modesty, wearing one of his trademark informal shirts, and greeted us warmly. I was in the presence of one of the world's most iconic figures.

Interview with President Nelson Mandela, broadcast 20.3.95

SM: The Queen will see a very different South Africa, of course, from the one she saw in 1947. And she'll be aware, as you are more than anyone, of the immensity of the task ahead. There are still great inequalities in housing and in education. This is something you must feel is a burden on your shoulders?

NM: We do. And we are aware that Britain has been assisting in order to raise the living standards of our people, especially in the field of education, which is of critical importance. Now having opened the doors of education to all national groups of this country, we are having serious problems which may explode in our faces. Because in some areas in the countryside there are no facilities, there is no infrastructure at all. No schools. Some children have to be accommodated in tents. What is more, there are no teachers, and they sit the whole day without instruction, and go back home depressed. One is going to raise these issues with Her Majesty.

SM: The government has had its critics from within the African National Congress for the slowness of reform, including indeed Mrs Mandela herself. Is it a matter of personal sorrow to you that she can't be for various reasons at your side when you welcome the Queen?

NM: No, I mean one has to be realistic. It is not possible for her to be with me. And I have accepted that. It means very little to me. I hardly think of it. I have got my children, and I have got my granddaughters, and I will be with them when I meet the Queen. On previous occasions, when I received heads of state, or when I'm abroad, my daughters have been at my side. I'm very proud of my children and my grandchildren.

I had got away with it. And he didn't seem to mind: he was all smiles as we parted. I handed my producer John Cary my camera, and he took a photograph of us together. I have it in a frame in the corner of my living room, and it is one of my most important possessions.

Four years later, trying to interview Mandela's successor Thabo Mbeki in Cape Town just before the 1999 South African general election was a very different experience. Mbeki is notoriously wary of the press, and pinning him down for *Today* was a frustrating business. Just as I had given up all hope, I received a telephone tip-off in my hotel room: Thabo Mbeki would be in Irvine and

Johnston's fish factory in Salt River in twenty minutes' time. I had been to school with the daughter of an Irvine and Johnston manager and I knew exactly where the factory was. We sped towards it in our hired car and arrived seconds before the new president-to-be. As I approached him with my microphone he waved me away, telling me I had 'come to the wrong place', but having got this far I was determined to snatch at least a few words with him. We followed the Mbeki entourage into the factory with my producer, David Gibson, a burly Ulsterman, doing his best to protect the rest of the recording gear from the seething crush of people. As Mr Mbeki started up the stairs to the office area I managed to snake my way past his bodyguards and thrust the microphone at my quarry. This time he couldn't brush me aside: there was no room. I managed to get about one and a half minutes of reasonably lucid conversation before two security men bodily lifted David and his equipment – no mean feat – high into the air. The connection between my microphone and the rest of the apparatus instantly snapped apart. But we had an interview, of sorts, which no one else had got, and the result was broadcast triumphantly on *Today* the following morning.

Following the Queen in 1995 was a less hazardous business – though once the royal tour left Cape Town, much of the rest of it was washed by torrential rain as she was rushed from school to farm to hospital. In Durban the local racing fraternity had arranged a special afternoon for Her Majesty to enjoy her favourite sport at the Greyville track, but the sodden ground meant that no horses could run. The Queen nevertheless made her royal progress before the grandstands in a special carriage, Ascot-style, while the racegoers heard a commentary specially relayed from the track at Milnerton hundreds of miles to the south. Of Winnie Mandela there was no sign during the entire trip. She's merely biding her time, muttered the political commentators. One day she'll stand for president herself.

CHAPTER TEN

Tomorrow?

Eddie: We're better news than the other lot, Liz.
Liz: Better news managers, too, of course.
Feelgood by Alistair Beaton, 2001

The art of news management and attempts to dictate the agenda were not born in the 1990s: a decade earlier Bernard Ingham, as Margaret Thatcher's press secretary, had his own views on how current affairs programmes should treat his political masters. Few Tory ministers appeared on any current affairs programme unless Bernard thought it a good idea, and the Prime Minister's appearances were especially carefully rationed. The *Today* programme, with its large and significant morning audience, was an important platform for them.

Virginia Bottomley, as Conservative health secretary, rang in regularly to try to book a place on the running order – she once told *Desert Island Discs* that her one luxury would be a constant supply of the *Today* programme. Paddy Ashdown for the Liberal Democrats and Robin Cook for Labour were also persistent callers-in, but normally it was the press and policy advisers who telephoned. By the mid-nineties the spin doctors in all the parties were both numerous and persistent. Shaun Woodward, who went on to become a Conservative MP before he crossed the floor to Labour, was one of the Tories' most assiduous spinmeisters, keeping up a constant barrage of suggestions and complaints from the party's Smith Square headquarters.

A year before the 1997 general election the Conservatives were in an edgy mood, dubious about their ability to claw themselves back to a winning position in the polls. Five years earlier John Major had scored a surprise election victory despite the confident predictions against him: this time triumph against the odds looked unlikely. As the tension mounted, some of their chief spokesmen developed noticeably short fuses – among them the abrasive Ulsterman Brian Mawhinney, chairman of the party. He did a telephone interview with me after a bad by-election result, just a fortnight before the May local elections.

Interview with Dr Brian Mawhinney MP, broadcast 17.4.96

SM: In 1990 you did something dramatic – you got rid of the poll tax, you also got rid of Mrs Thatcher. Aren't you going to have to do something as dramatic as that not to lose a lot more seats?

BM: Oh, come on, Sue, let's stay in the real world, can we?

SM: Well, I hope I'm talking about the real world!

BM: What you have just suggested to me in front of the nation is that we should dump the Prime Minister. Don't be ridiculous, Sue! That isn't even worthy of an answer.

SM: I wasn't suggesting you should dump the Prime Minister.

BM: Of course you were. That was exactly the parallel you drew with Mrs Thatcher.

SM: I was saying dramatic gestures sometimes work.

BM: On the contrary, you drew the parallel with Mrs Thatcher and that is a ludicrous and indefensible question. And if you think I'm annoyed with you it is because it is that kind of smeary question by *Today* programme presenters which so annoys people who listen to this programme up and down the country.

SM: Dr Mawhinney, thank you.

BM: Thank you.

Brian Mawhinney renewed his attack later that morning at a news conference, saying that there were times 'when politicians ought to make it clear to the British public that they consider some questions, even by professional journalists, to be illegitimate and to say so'. Next day the incident produced some amusing cartoons in the national press, including one of John, Jim and me as the victims of a vengeful bucket of paint from Dr Mawhinney. But his angry ripostes were considered politically inept, for it is generally not thought wise to lose your temper with an interviewer, however daft or annoying you may perceive the question to be. If the Tories were in a trough in the polls it might have been better to remember, as the columnist Peter Riddell put it in *The Times* next day, that 'sounding reasonable rather than aggressive is the way to win back former supporters'. As the interviewer, I knew that all I had to do was keep calm and sound persistent. A flurry of emails from listeners confirmed by a proportion of three to one that Dr Mawhinney might have won more friends by doing the same.

A suspicion of bias on my part was not confined to the Tories. Some time before this I had spoken to John Smith as shadow Chancellor about the practicality of Labour's latest tax proposals.

Chapter and verse, I put to him some well-researched points which seemed to indicate their ineffectiveness. He did not show his annoyance at the time, but later that morning there was a furious phone call from Labour's headquarters at Walworth Road. Mr Smith would no longer be available for interview with me, nor would any other members of the shadow cabinet. I was clearly, they said, following a *Daily Mail* agenda in my questioning, and this was absolutely unacceptable. It was an absurd spin doctor's tantrum which the editor and his team naturally ignored. But I did have to wonder once again whether some politicians, or perhaps more likely their minders, were more sensitive to pointed questioning from a woman.

When John Major announced in March 1997 that the general election would be held at the beginning of May it meant a long campaign: over six weeks of electioneering. There were a few groans, even from those who adored the detailed ins and outs of politics; the daily party press conferences and the ever more assiduous attempts at news manipulation would be wearying for everyone. But for us on *Today* there would be a richer than usual political diet, with so much evidence of deep divisions within the Conservative party. Jim Naughtie could also look forward to being the main anchor for BBC radio when the results came through on election night.

By the time the election was called *Today*, slightly to our surprise, had a new editor. Jon Barton, who came to us from television when Roger Mosey was promoted to run Radio Five Live, was unlike his predecessor in almost every way. A former teacher, he was rather earnest, and impressively fit: he arrived in the office each day after a long journey from Oxfordshire by coach and a fold-up bicycle, which he stowed carefully in his den before getting down to work at a computer terminal. Jon was less interested in the political minutiae of issues for the programme than in the broad strategies, and left many of the last-minute editorial decisions to his team. He was keen to make politics and some of the issues we covered feel less remote to some of our listeners, and thought it important for presenters to get out on to the road and test the political temperature with 'real people'. Thus the *Today* battle bus was born – a large white 'people carrier' with a minimal crew on board. In my case this consisted of one producer, Tom Heap, and me. Tom drove the van and was also in charge of the technical link-up back to the studio, which meant manhandling a heavy metal case from which emerged a large satellite dish. This had to be pointed skywards in exactly the right direction, a fiddly process which I was happy to admire from the sidelines. But it usually worked, and meant we could broadcast back to London from just about anywhere. We criss-crossed the United Kingdom, visiting Chichester, Glasgow, Blackpool and Belfast, with a quick stopover in Londonderry. This gave me a chance to come face to face for the first time with Martin McGuinness, the man at the centre of the *Real Lives* controversy some years before, who was now standing for election as the Sinn Fein candidate for Mid Ulster.

McGuinness' own voice had been heard on the BBC only since 1994, when the six-year ban on using the voices of terrorists or their sympathizers was lifted. Most of us thought the 'voice rule' absurd, particularly as there was no ban on reporting what Sinn Fein actually said; but Margaret Thatcher had been determined to deny them what she called 'the oxygen of publicity' – and her views on the matter weighed heavily with the BBC. The ban meant that one or two actors with Northern Irish accents made a decent living 'voicing over' each interview.

This time it was possible to talk to McGuinness live and in person. The slot was agreed: just after the seven o'clock news bulletin. Although we were well into spring it was a dark, wet morning as we set up the equipment. The meeting point, a semi-deserted car park, was overlooked from the old Derry city walls by a British army post. I could well imagine their night-vision binoculars staring down at us. I should have felt safe, but I did not. This was a strong republican area and there were anti-British murals everywhere; we were close to the part of the march route where so many had died on Bloody Sunday, and the damp and the black shadows made it seem as if we were part of a scene in *The Third Man*. At five past seven dawn began to filter through, but there was still no sign of McGuinness. 'Don't worry,' said Tom, 'these guys like to play it cool. They're usually on time in the end.' Then, quietly, out of the gloom fifty yards away, a figure in a raincoat walked towards us across the car park. I had a sudden doubt about whether I should shake his hand – do you shake hands with someone who was once in the top ranks of the local IRA? – but as he came up to me *politesse* took over. I held out a hand and he took it. We had a brief interview about employment opportunities in the province, and then he was off. Three weeks later he was returned by the voters of Mid Ulster with a majority of almost 1,900.

Back in London the slick and sophisticated Labour election machine was in high gear, brilliantly coordinated by Peter Mandelson, Alastair Campbell and David Hill. Their jobs were made somewhat easier by the less proficient team at Conservative Central Office – 'nice Sloanes, helpful, but definitely amateurs', said one of my colleagues, an editor who had to deal on a daily basis with some of the young women there. The Liberal Democrats made up for their smaller resources with tireless badgering: Paddy Ashdown would ring up at any time up to midnight, trying to negotiate a good slot on the programme. The Lib Dems kept up a constant complaint of under-representation on *Today*, but all three main parties tried to steer the programme's agenda. One day it was Labour objecting to the Essex firemen's strike leading the news bulletin; on another, the Conservatives' Michael Howard insisting on talking about illegal immigrants close to his Folkestone constituency.

It was a campaign dominated by sleaze, BSE and Tory splits over Europe. Our foreign correspondent colleague Martin Bell came forward as the anti-sleaze candidate for Tatton in Cheshire, putting himself up against the Tories' Neil Hamilton, who had become the centre of the 'cash for questions' allegations involving Mohammed Al Fayed. The confrontation before the cameras on a Tatton walkabout between Hamilton, his wife Christine and the white-suited Bell was one of the most entertaining moments of the campaign. Labour began to sniff not just a win but a big majority. The Wirral by-election result in February, which had seen Labour convert a Tory majority of just over 8,000 to a win for them of over 22,000, turned out to be an accurate indicator of what was to come.

On the morning of 2 May, with most of the results counted, I shared the *Today* presentation with John Humphrys. The extent of the Tory rout was extraordinary. No fewer than six Conservative cabinet ministers had lost their seats overnight, including Michael Portillo and David Mellor. Labour had won with the biggest landslide in history. The morning programme overflowed with the voices of the overnight cast of characters: jubilant in triumph or reeling in defeat, they all sounded exhausted. Tony Blair's voice was hoarse and cracking with emotion as he referred to a new dawn and the new millennium. Brian Mawhinney, clearly devastated, refused to be drawn on the possibility of a fresh leadership struggle in the Conservative party. One of the massive new intake of Labour women MPs, Angela Smith, speculated on the difference more women would make to the workings of the House. Two sour Essex market stallholders were not at all surprised by the result. The Conservatives under Major were all over the place, they said; at least you knew where you were with Margaret Thatcher.

Four months after New Labour came to power, the woman Tony Blair called 'the People's Princess' died in a bizarre car crash in Paris. For a few days the world seemed utterly consumed by the event. It is a little easier now to put the death of Diana into some sort of perspective: a young and attractive woman, with perhaps the most recognized face in the world, died tragically. But as with her engagement, her marriage, her unhappiness and her subsequent

divorce, so with her death – Diana was an Event, and the abrupt
ending of her life seemed at the time almost cataclysmic. It was
as if Britain had gone into collective mourning. The gardens of
Kensington Palace were strewn knee-deep with floral tributes and
mawkish messages; the pile stretched and spread for hundreds of
yards. People came to leave more flowers, and to gaze. It was
extraordinary. I have no doubt that the grief was genuine, and it
was remarkably international. Friends on holiday in Tanzania told
me that only a few hours after the fatal accident in Paris, when
they still knew nothing of it, an African gardener approached them
with a touching message of sympathy. He had heard the news on
the BBC's Africa Service. Another friend, driving in a remote part
of Namibia, found a simple roadside shrine of flowers set around a
crumpled photograph of the princess only twenty-four hours after
Diana's death.

BBC radio devoted much of the day the news broke to tribute
programmes. As soon as the facts of the story were confirmed, it was
decided that Radio Four would put on a special news programme
beginning at 5 a.m. Frantic phone calls went out to presenters,
but not all of us were reachable. The thirtieth of August is my
birthday; I had been out enjoying a dinner with my old friend
Nonie, on a visit to London from her home in Portugal, and
her two daughters, and on my return home before midnight I
had unplugged the phone next to my bed. I had felt professionally
quite safe in doing so as there is normally no *Today* programme on
a Sunday morning; but when I got up just before seven I noticed
the light on my telephone answering machine blinking furiously
in the study near my bedroom. There were several messages from
the office; they had been trying to reach me since 2 a.m. They
had managed to get hold of Jim Naughtie, who was already on
the air. I pulled on my clothes and drove as fast as I could to
Broadcasting House, where producers and reporters dragged from
their beds were arriving every minute. I began to prepare and script
a special obituary programme; our hour-long tribute to Diana was

broadcast live at three o'clock. London, I noticed as I drove home afterwards, was strangely silent, the streets almost deserted.

Diana's funeral at Westminster Abbey the following Saturday was an international broadcasting event, and primarily one for television, though radio would have its role – especially for millions of people listening around the world with no access to TV. The centre of London was closed to traffic. The radio commentary team was asked to stay in a hotel close to Broadcasting House, and as it was a warm summer night I walked at four in the morning to our position outside the Abbey through the London parks. Each spare patch of grass was taken up with little huddled groups; the glow of candles was everywhere. Close to the Abbey the pavements were already thick with mourners. There was a real sense of communal grief, and the eerie silence continued throughout the long, slow rituals of the morning.

The princess's coffin arrived at the Abbey's main doors precisely as Big Ben struck eleven. The funeral ceremony was relayed to the crowds outside, and many joined in the hymns and prayers from orders of service torn from the morning papers. There was a ripple of applause when Earl Spencer in his oration made veiled criticisms of the royal family and the press. When the ceremony was almost over I was despatched into the crowd to ask people for their reactions. Almost no one would talk to me; I felt – as I never had before – a widespread hostility to anyone from the media, but whether it was an objection to intrusion at an inappropriate time, or because of a widespread perception that press hounding had caused Diana's death, I could not tell. It was months before the high emotion of that week began to fade.

Diana's sister-in-law and close friend Sarah Ferguson, the Duchess of York, had a less complicated relationship with the press. Her more public indiscretions had turned the tabloids against her to what I thought was an unnecessarily cruel extent. I talked to Fergie at some length for *Today* when her autobiographical book was published in 1996. We recorded the interview on what her publishers chose as neutral ground: a suite in the Berkeley Hotel in Knightsbridge. She was friendly and eager to give a good account of herself, and there were no preconditions to the interview. But at one point, when I asked her if she thought she had been a good mother to her daughters, she came close to tears, and we had to stop the recording while she recovered herself. Evidently I had hit a tender spot. I felt sorry for her; I don't usually reduce interviewees to tears. The result was run at some length and at peak time on *Today*, just after the eight o'clock news.

Interview with the Duchess of York, broadcast 14.11.96

SM: Prince Andrew was away a lot, wasn't he, on naval duty?

DY: I saw him forty-two days a year for the first five years of our marriage.

SM: Was it lonely?

DY: I think it added a great weight to my already lonely and rather isolated lifestyle on the second floor of Buckingham Palace. I don't use that as an excuse; however, I think it was very difficult for me because I married my man and I got the 'firm' [the Royal Family] and an apartment on the second floor of Buckingham Palace, which most people would say would be absolute heaven, but it was quite difficult because it was a Department of Environment building and it closes at six.

SM: And after that you're on your own?

DY: It's black and the light bulbs are rather . . . they need to pep up the light bulbs, I feel. You're on your own and it's very different from Clapham with a different life to suddenly be going into without the man that you married.

SM: But being without your husband doesn't inevitably, in marriage, lead to unfaithfulness and you've admitted that you were unfaithful to Andrew.

DY: Mmmm . . . I think that . . . have I admitted that? Where have I admitted that?

SM: I think in the book it's clear. You haven't denied it.

DY: Mmmm . . . I haven't admitted it and I think the most important thing is that . . . I agree with you that being lonely and isolated . . . but there are very firmly two sides to every story. I think that you can be very lonely and isolated and incredibly vulnerable and therefore very open to a small amount of kindness shown.

SM: Were you unfaithful to him?

DY: I don't think that's relevant to this interview. It's certainly not mentioned in the book and my book, I think, explains it all.

SM: You refer to yourself very honestly in the book as 'a grand master of self-destruction'. I don't know whether you still feel you are in this position? Do you still describe yourself that way? That's the way you described yourself about five years ago.

DY: I was the most classic example of self-hatred and that is exactly why I say about the 'Hob Goblin' that I've had since puberty is weight and then they write 'The Duchess of Pork' and all those things are exactly playing to the self-hatred within me. And I think that I had to get to a stage of such learning and such humiliation to learn really what life is about, and what is the self about . . . the book was like a therapy session for me.

SM: What was your lowest point when you felt that way about yourself?

DY: After the photographs.

SM: With John Bryan?

DY: The South of France photographs with John Bryan, yes. That was purely faith that got me through that.

SM: Faith?

DY: Yes, asking for forgiveness. Realizing that you've made a mistake, how selfish and very unfair you've been. And asking for help and guidance and going forward and saying OK, I'm sorry, show me the way?

SM: Did you ever consider . . . it's been reported that you considered doing away with yourself around that time. Has that ever been in your mind?

DY: No. It's never . . . I don't know how to spell the word really . . . I mean I do! But I'm not like that. I don't have red hair for nothing. At the end of the day I will fight on. And the way I fight on is through acceptance . . . you know we all . . . 'be anyone the first person to cast the stone if they are without sin' or whatever. I sit here, not asking anyone to believe in me, not to believe in me, I'm simply saying, I'm admitting, and I'm saying I'm here and I'm sorry and I want to go forward. And that's just the way it is.

SM: You must, as a mother who loves her daughters very much, have been very conscious of the effect that all the publicity might have. Perhaps not then, because they were too little, but later. That must still be at the forefront of your mind.

DY: Very much so. Very, very much so and that's why I always try and explain to them what's going on. I always try and say, look, this is John Bryan and this is the situation. Andrew and I both are very, very honest with them about what's going on so that no one can come up to them at school and tittle tattle. They turn around and say, 'Well, we know that Mummy said this or Mummy has done this.' I've explained the situation and I have said exactly the way it is so that they can see that we all make mistakes. And if they make mistakes, Mummy makes mistakes too.

SM: Do you think you've been a good mother to them so far?
[It was at this point that she came close to tears; briefly we stopped the tape]

DY: I think, Sue, the only thing I can probably say I'm good at is being a mother. And I think I probably somewhere deep inside me said, when I have my own children, I will always give them what I didn't get then [as a child]. I think that my children are great testimonies to the fact that the one thing I can safely say I have done right is be a good mother.

I'm not sure what John Birt made of our giving Fergie peak time on a serious news programme, but his determination to reorganize the BBC's current affairs department continued. The idea of moving us from Broadcasting House to White City had become reality: the upheaval was only months away. There was, though, one Birtian scheme which came up against such fierce opposition that within thirty-six hours of floating it he had to ditch it. As the *Observer* put it in the autumn of 1997, 'After years of arbitrary job-cutting and cost-cutting . . . the Corporation's own producers and journalists, household names and anonymous alike, finally called a halt.' The plan was to remove the power of each programme's individual editor and replace him or her with a new tier of so-called 'executive editors'. In other words, five people would decide daily on the agenda for news and current affairs programmes, and obedient functionaries would see that it was put in place. The idea of removing individual editors seemed to most of us absurd. Current affairs programmes thrive on a friendly but intense rivalry with other current affairs programmes. An imaginative and competitive editor for each programme is a crucial element to its success.

The new plan had been conceived in characteristic Birtian secrecy, and the head of BBC news programmes, Richard Clemmow, and his deputy, Steve Mitchell, were asked to address the troops and explain the scheme to them at ten o'clock one morning. The thrust of their message had already leaked out, and the meeting was packed. There was an air of suppressed fury. Once the explanation was over John Humphrys, Jim Naughtie, Anna Ford and I stood up and attacked the idea at once; I can remember, rather to my surprise, hearing my own voice tighten with emotion. I had not, I concluded, come across anything as idiotic in more than twenty-five years of working for the BBC. I got a round of applause; I think people listening were as surprised as I was by my genuine fury. Clemmow and Mitchell went off looking rather shaken to try to sell the plan to another roomful of people.

To reinforce our opposition a raft of presenters from radio and television, including Jeremy Paxman and Kirsty Wark, organized a letter listing specific objections to the idea, which was sent directly to John Birt . 'News', said Paxman, 'is not a sausage machine.' It was leaked to the press. Soon politicians from all parties came out in support of the staff revolt. The BBC's chairman Christopher Bland, an old friend of John Birt, wisely announced a 'cooling-off' period. By the weekend the idea was dead. But the intended move to White City was not, as we were to discover.

I had now worked for *Today* full-time for over a decade. Despite the awful hours it was a highly enjoyable job, both demanding and fulfilling. But it had also been from time to time a bumpy ride for me as the one full-time woman presenter. With two assertive, highly talented and territorial males as my on-air companions, I thought my role as their supposed equal was worth re-examining. Interviews about politics are undoubtedly the backbone of *Today*, and both John Humphrys and Jim Naughtie expected that they would do most of them. Roger Mosey, as the programme's editor, had told me that he thought it was generally 'better theatre' to have John Humphrys interviewing Michael Heseltine, for instance, 'especially if there was no particular political point to tease out'. It was an indication of a wider trend: news and current affairs programmes should be entertaining as well as informative. As the number of outlets for both radio and television multiplied, it became increasingly important to establish strong interviewing 'personalities' who could tussle with politicians as their equals. It was a thesis with which I could not strongly disagree. But it left less room for alternative approaches.

Tony Hall, when he was chief executive of BBC News, was asked in the mid-1990s by Paul Donovan of the *Sunday Times* about a 'pecking order' of *Today* presenters. Hall claimed, somewhat against the evidence, that it was 'basic policy . . . that there is an equivalence between them all'. Donovan, in his book celebrating forty years of *Today*, looked at the running orders for all the *Today* programmes broadcast during 1996, focusing on the 8.10 a.m. interview, which is generally considered to be the most important of the morning. It was done by John Humphrys on 67 per cent of the days he was on duty, by Jim Naughtie on almost 48 per cent, and by me on just under 30 per cent. Five years on, the statistics for the first six months of 2001 were not dissimilar, though John's proportion of 8.10 interviews had risen: the 'big' interview was now his on 77 per cent of the days he was on duty, Jim's on 56 per cent and mine on 38 per cent. Interestingly, Edward Stourton, a newer member of the *Today* team, had a figure of 61 per cent. Equivalence depends, I suppose, on how you define it; in any event, Tony Hall is no longer there to define it his way, having left to run the Royal Opera House.

The press seized on another bit of evidence of discrimination unearthed by Paul Donovan: the question of pay. John Humphrys and James Naughtie, he said, get around £20,000 a year more than Sue MacGregor. I was astonished by this claim, having naïvely supposed that we all earned much the same. I was also embarrassed to see my alleged worth splashed in the papers, for I had never discussed my earnings with anyone other than my accountant and the contracts people at the BBC. Donovan's estimate in my case was somewhat wide of the mark, but the message was clear: women are still valued less than men.

Tony Hall had explained the discrepancy to Donovan with an uneasy comment about anomalies arising over a period of years. It was a sensitive subject for him. He had recently sanctioned a very large pay rise for John Humphrys after the newly established commercial station Talk Radio had apparently offered him £300,000 a year – an enormous sum for a radio presenter. Humphrys, an astute and determined negotiator, had managed to get the BBC to persuade him to stay with a tempting pay hike. Jim Naughtie, on learning of this, would certainly have wanted a matching offer; he was given what I was told later was a 'significant increase'. But there was another factor operating in favour of my male colleagues. Jim had joined the BBC from the world of newspapers, and had doubtless been decently rewarded as the *Guardian*'s chief political correspondent. John had come to radio from television, where front-line people were more generously paid than their radio colleagues. Indeed, one member of BBC management with access to the details of presenters' fees told me that television personalities were paid 'phenomenal' salaries in comparison with their radio equivalents. So perhaps, I admitted to myself, sticking with radio had not always been entirely to my advantage.

I wrote to Tony Hall and asked if we might discuss the matter of pay; I received a polite and non-committal answer. When I wrote again I received no answer at all. Evidently it was something in which he did not wish to become embroiled. But I did eventually successfully negotiate a deal which, I was assured, meant that the three main *Today* presenters were within 'a tiny percentage' of each other. Whether or not this was true, the well-publicized pay differential dogged me for a long time, and print journalists never tired of asking me about it.

By the beginning of 1998 my father, approaching his eighty-seventh birthday, began to hint that he was troubled by back pain. But his cheerful letters – closely typed and carbon-copied to Kirsty and me – still arrived weekly. He seemed as alert and interested in life as ever, ordering up the expensive books that had so exasperated our mother. His work, too, was still important to him, and he continued to run the twice-weekly Huntington's Chorea clinic at Groote Schuur hospital. The long walks with the dog were no longer possible, but since our mother's death he had found new friendships in the retirement village, and was particularly fond of an attractive woman some years his junior. I was aware that his letters had begun to suggest an impatience with getting old; but he had lost none of his enthusiasm for his family, or for the things that mattered most to him.

All three of Kirsty's children had delighted their grandfather by taking up medical careers. The twins Emily and Susanna trained to be doctors at Cambridge and Oxford respectively, and their younger sister Isabel graduated from Southampton University with a degree in physiotherapy. Just six weeks before he died my father wrote long letters of advice to the twins, then still undergraduate students. He had been immensely loved by his own patients, and they read the letters carefully. 'What are the most important factors for a young doctor, any doctor, to bear in mind when approaching a patient?' he wrote to Susanna. 'I would start with Observation. Watch your patient from the moment he or she steps into your room. Second, take a good history. But most important of all is taking trouble to develop some kind of rapport with your patients. Ask about their interests, and show you regard him or her as a living normal person and not a bundle of aches and pains and fears. It opens a door between you and them which might never be opened again.'

In February, during one of our regular phone calls, he admitted that his back pain was making driving his car more difficult, and that he was going briefly into hospital for tests. There was no need to worry, he said. A week or two later Joy Hatwood, a BBC colleague, rang me from Cape Town, where she was on holiday; she had discovered that my father had been detained in hospital. He had confessed to her, when she visited him, that he was gravely ill, and she thought I should know this. It had been discovered that a sarcoma, a large cancerous growth, was pressing on his spine. It was thought not to be operable. She thought it best if my sister and I came out to see him as soon as possible.

Kirsty and I were in Cape Town within thirty-six hours; we went straight to Groote Schuur hospital from the airport. Dad had been given a small room within his old neurological department. He was attached to various drips and catheters and obviously in some pain; his legs were badly swollen. It was heartbreaking to see him like this. He struggled to greet us as cheerfully as he could. We held his hands and gave him a bundle of letters from the grandchildren; we assured him that we could stay as long as he liked. 'This is all rather overwhelming,' he said quietly. It was the only reference he ever made to dying. As tactfully as we could, we made arrangements for him to be taken back to the small nursing home in the retirement village. There, slowly, over several days, he drifted in and out of sleep and towards death. We placed his bed near the window so that he could see the distant mountain; with the increasing doses of morphine he hallucinated and told us he could also see wild horses galloping by. I felt an extraordinary new tenderness towards him, a sort of relaxed closeness that I had not experienced before. Now, suddenly, he was helpless, and I was terribly aware that I was losing him. At least now, Kirsty and I told each other, he was out of pain. On the morning of 5 March, as I stroked his hand and Kirsty talked gently, he died.

Like my mother, he had wanted no religious ceremony. His friends and colleagues joined us for a memorial meeting in a place he knew intimately: the magnificent Botanical Gardens at Kirstenbosch. I suppose if he had had any religious feeling at all he would have been a Quaker, and this was rather like a Quaker gathering. Some months later I returned to Cape Town and with a group of close friends took his ashes to a spot on the contour path high above Kirstenbosch. It was a sparkling day, and the wind flung the ashes wide over the silver trees. Well, I thought, he's here, and my mother's there, and that in the end is what they wanted.

Back in London the big move from Broadcasting House was imminent. The rationale behind it lay in John Birt's conviction that in news and current affairs radio and television should embrace each other. It was all about going 'bimedial'. Duplicated radio and television news directorates were wasteful. Wherever possible, reporters and correspondents should be encouraged to work with the most sophisticated technology available. Convinced that the Far East, and in particular Japan, would provide a plethora of news stories in the next decade, Birt decreed that millions be spent on refurbishing the BBC's Tokyo bureau. This was to become one of the BBC's biggest white elephants, a monument to the folly of second-guessing world events.

The new hi-tech home for journalists in London was to be called Stage Six, which had a ring of a ten-year plan to it. Were some grandiose Stages Seven and Eight just over the horizon? The greatest fear of most of us who thought the move a mad and bad idea was that current affairs radio would simply be swallowed up by televison. The *Today* programme might well lose its unique identity: it could become a mere copy of Breakfast Television in sound.

Senior management at the BBC went through the motions of 'consultation'. Presenters were taken out to lunch in the attempt to persuade us over a plate of seared tuna that the upheaval would be good for us. John Humphrys and I were lunched by Peter Bell, then deputy to Tony Hall, who dutifully listened to our complaints. People, I told him, would be poached by the more glamorous medium: we would inevitably lose talent. Fewer of our programme guests would be there in person. Politicians had always enjoyed coming to Broadcasting House; it was conveniently placed in central London, and the *Today* green room between seven and nine in the mornings could be a productive meeting place. Here you could rub shoulders with a great gallimaufry of people, and not just your fellow politicians – top businesspeople, influential journalists, religious leaders, writers and sports stars could all be spotted there. It was a good place to pick up the fresh political gossip. White City was inconveniently far from Westminster; few cabinet ministers would wish to come in to our studio and then be turfed out on to the A40 in the middle of the rush hour. Too many of them would in future have to be interviewed 'down the line': in a remote studio, over the telephone, or from the radio car. All of these options carried with them a greater risk of technical breakdown; it was also, frankly, much more fruitful to talk to people face to face. Body language – facial expressions, hand movements

– can make a surprising difference to an interview. It was easier to ask an impertinent question, I always claimed, with a smile on your face.

And besides, White City was a bleak and unlovely place. Staff do not live by work alone; they like to pop out to shop, have a meal or just get some air. There were few opportunities for any of that along the depressing grey pavements of Wood Lane, W12. And if the idea was to save money – Tony Hall had told the governors the savings would be somewhere around £10 million a year – we were highly dubious. The initial costs of a brand new home were bound to be high. No one beyond John Birt himself and one or two carefully chosen members of management, including the director of finance, was allowed to see the real figures. The governors were told to expect around £41 million. It would be many years before even that sum was recouped – if it ever was.

Peter Bell went through the motions of listening, but we knew the move was unstoppable. When we saw the designers' plans for our new home, my heart sank still further. We would be sharing an enormous floor space with several other programmes: not only *The World At One*, but Breakfast Television, *Breakfast With Frost* and endless 'planning' departments. There would be no privacy; everything we did would be observed and probably overheard by rival programmes. That, of course, was the idea: in this Brave New Bimedial World, everyone would cooperate. Televison's *Breakfast News* and radio's *Today* would share editorial desks. And if a top politician came in early to give just one interview, it would almost inevitably be for Breakfast Television, and *Today* would simply run the sound version. It was not an idea likely to appeal to *Today* presenters, nor a way of working that any of us recognized.

Liz Forgan, as managing director of network radio, had been so disturbed by the implications of the move that in 1996 she had asked John Birt to convene a special meeting of the BBC's board of governors. She was determined that the arguments against the move should be properly laid before them, and she was sure of her ground. As she told the *Guardian* four years later, 'Stage Six – as the new journalism factory was called – was more than a new office. It was a physical symbol of corporate purpose. Practical arguments about the needs of programmes and programme-makers were secondary.' She believed that the move would be bad for Radio Four as a network. White City, she said, 'was a mad place to site the *Today* programme'. 'Who would be willing to toil down to Shepherd's Bush at 7 a.m. to face Jim Naughtie?' She lost the argument, though she was eventually to be proved right. She was appalled, she told me later, by the 'bogus economics' which were produced to justify the move. 'As members of BBC management,' she said, 'we were presented with a stream of financial fictions.'

John Birt's driving ambition to establish news and current affairs as one of the core functions of the BBC was a perfectly understandable one, but all other considerations, like real costs and programme-making conditions, were ignored. Sadly, it seemed that too few members of the BBC's senior management team understood the subtleties and skills required for good radio, and they went along with his idea. Four years later the magnitude of the mistake was acknowledged. It was announced that in the year 2008 radio news and current affairs would return to Broadcasting House. Radio's special status seemed safer.

Change was not confined to our new premises. It was also decided that *Today* should be lengthened from two and a half hours to three. *Today* 'delivered' the best audiences of the day to Radio Four; the numbers of people listening showed a marked dropping-off once *Today* came off the air. Making *Today* longer by bringing it right up to the nine o'clock news, and moving *Yesterday in Parliament* to longwave, would persuade the audience to stay on past nine o'clock. And why not make *Today* longer at the other end too – start the programme at six instead of six-thirty? The nation was getting up earlier; there would be a good audience at dawn. It would mean moving *Farming Today* back to an earlier hour, and losing the popular six o'clock *News Briefing*, but the audience would adapt to that.

It was an idea flattering to *Today* and its staff, and there was little objection to it from the team. But Tony Hall made it clear that there was no question of extra staff for the longer programme, for savings had to be made at the same time. John Birt's vision for the future of the BBC was a digital one, and digital broadcasting is expensive. Cutbacks would start immediately.

I was not as convinced as some of my colleagues that lengthening *Today* was a good idea – and not just because an earlier start would mean losing even more sleep. I could also see that a longer programme without extra resources could stretch the production team pretty thinly, and some of the material too. Nor was the idea of a longer *Today* greeted with universal delight outside the BBC. There were objections to the disappearance of the full version of *Yesterday in Parliament* on to longwave. But within weeks of the relaunch of *Today* the Radio Four audience figures before the nine o'clock bulletin began to go up, and the bosses were pleased.

We finally moved from Broadcasting House in July 1998. The detritus of over forty years in the famous old BBC building near Oxford Circus was packed into boxes and taken to Shepherd's Bush. The brand new glass-fronted Stage Six was umbilically attached to Television Centre by a long corridor flanked with flickering television screens. The *Today* office was now a series of islands in the middle of a vast sea dominated by computer consoles. Breakfast Television was to one side; to the other, *The World At One*. Clusters of researchers and planners filled the spare spaces. Two of our *Today* studio walls were made entirely of glass, so that our studio guests looked beyond their interviewers to a distracting vista of other people's comings and goings.

Writing the studio links for *Today* was always done under time pressure: now there were distracting noises off as well. Someone had built a small television editing suite just behind my desk, so that

I was frequently doing my writing while video clips, with sound, were played again and again just over my shoulder. The rather shabby charms of Broadcasting House took on an even rosier glow, even though colleagues who had stayed there announced gloomily that the poor place was utterly changed: all that remained of our presence were acres of dusty and abandoned offices and miles of trailing wires. It was, someone said, as if the heart had been torn out of the building.

Before the move we changed editor again as Jon Barton was replaced by Rod Liddle – shaggy-haired, long-limbed and generally dressed in black, he was at first sight a rather unlikely figure to be in charge. His previous experience included speechwriting for Labour and being a member of a rock band. He had joined the BBC in his late twenties and worked his way up to being deputy editor under both Mosey and Barton. A chain-smoker, who in a crisis had a habit of sneaking out of the smoke-free office for a lengthy puff, he was uninterested in the minutiae of day-to-day management; so that the office, or what passed for our office in the vast spaces of Stage Six, was at first run somewhat shambolically. But he was a keen courter of press publicity, and under his editorship *Today*'s public profile grew.

The first weeks after the move to Stage Six were – in Rod Liddle's own words – 'the most demoralizing time' the programme had ever had. The longer programme, with a 'softer' last half-hour requested by the then controller of Radio Four James Boyle, was not considered an editorial success: the programme often ended on a limp note, with meandering debates on abstruse matters which seemed to have little to do with hard news. The number of politicians willing to trek out to Shepherd's Bush did indeed dwindle. Jack Straw as Home Secretary initially made valiant early morning efforts to join us, though he spoke wryly about the 'sense of occasion' that visiting Broadcasting House had once brought. After about a year he gave up and, like most of his fellow politicians, resorted to the radio car or our studios at

Millbank, conveniently close to Westminster. William Hague did his best to be with us in person, accompanied either by Sebastian Coe or his personal press adviser Amanda Platell, but in the end he too preferred a less unpredictable journey to a studio closer to home. The programme's taxi bills mounted steadily as people came in from distant places, and our transport budget was soon heavily in the red. From time to time contributors got stuck in the tube and missed their slot entirely; others, on poor mobile phone links or in a radio car with a weak signal, found themselves cut off in mid-sentence as connections crashed.

There were other risks to all this semi-detached broadcasting. Rather more has to be taken on trust when you cannot see a speaker, including even their identity. One morning I embarked on what I thought would be a fairly run-of-the-mill discussion about wisdom teeth. The cast list on the piece of paper in front of me consisted of the president of the British Dental Association and a man from NICE, the National Institute for Clinical Excellence, which monitors clinical standards in medicine. A new report had suggested that too many wisdom teeth extractions were unnecessary. The man from NICE was, I was led to believe, sitting opposite me, the BDA man in a remote studio. In fact, it was the other way round – but not quite. I asked a question of the man in the remote studio, the supposed representative of British dentistry. Rather puzzled, as he was the man from NICE, he answered my question but from his own point of view. Ah! I thought, I've got these speakers the wrong way round. I looked to the man opposite me and assumed *he* must be the man from the British Dental Association. Changing tack slightly, I asked him why there were so many unnecessary wisdom tooth extractions. He looked utterly nonplussed. He shrugged his shoulders, spreading his hands dramatically to indicate that he had no answer to my query. Wherever the top dentist was, he was not opposite me. I struggled on for the rest of the allotted four minutes, concentrating on the expert down the line, and rather sheepishly confessed to the listeners at the end that I was quite as confused as they must be. It turned out that the mix-up was not entirely of my own making. The man opposite me was a Russian who spoke no English. He had been waiting in the downstairs foyer for someone else. A girl from *Today* had rushed down to the reception area to collect the next interviewee. Seeing a likely-looking candidate, she asked him if he was there to talk about wisdom teeth. He gave her an encouraging nod, so she hurried him upstairs and straight into our studio. Suddenly a poor non-English-speaking Russian was on *Today* facing detailed questions about British dentistry. He was eventually put in a taxi and steered towards Bush House, where an impatient member of the BBC's Russian-language service awaited his arrival.

The move to White City also took me a little further away from my post-programme keep-fit routine. I enjoyed unwinding sessions in the health club under the Grosvenor House Hotel in Park Lane. There is a decent gym and an unusually large pool, and the regulars are occasionally joined by top sporting stars and even politicians – I have found myself stretching on a mat in the unlikely company of Chris Eubank, Boris Becker or even Gordon Brown. The regulars include an engaging crowd of Iranian expatriates. One of them, Bijan Golshaian, invited me one evening to join him for a drink to celebrate the acquisition of his British citizenship. In return he accompanied me to Nottingham University when it awarded me an honorary degree, and we have become good friends. He met my father on one of his last visits to London, and I was touched when a few years later, en route to Australia, Bijan made a special point of visiting the small library named after my father in the neurology department at Groote Schuur hospital in Cape Town. Kirsty and I have now arranged that the department awards an annual prize in his name for the best undergraduate student of neurology.

As the 2001 election campaign approached it was clear that at least two of the dominant themes – sleaze and agricultural problems –

would mirror those of four years earlier, though in different forms. Sleaze was now an issue for Labour. The Europe minister Keith Vaz was in trouble over alleged links with the wealthy Hinduja brothers. For most of the campaign he went to ground, complaining of harassment by BBC journalists. The Downing Street spokesman Alastair Campbell accused the *Today* programme of being obsessed with matters in which the public had little interest. The old master spinner himself, Peter Mandelson, was less in evidence. He had twice been sacked as a cabinet minister over indiscretions: one involving a substantial house-buying loan and one involving alleged preferential treatment for the Hindujas. He was now confined to campaigning in his Hartlepool constituency. Foot and mouth disease delayed the expected May poll to June. This meant that our careful plans had to be hurriedly redrawn, though eventually the *Today* cast list was unchanged. A press release went out: *Today* would be 'anchored' by John Humphrys, with James Naughtie and Sue MacGregor reporting from around the country in the battle bus.

The *Today* battle bus was now a stubby saloon car with room in the boot for equipment. The satellite dish and its entrails had shrunk to a couple of small suitcases and what looked like an electronic notebook. It was much easier to handle. When the notebook was opened out and, with the help of a compass, pointed in exactly the right southerly direction, it came up with a good clear satellite link to the studio in London. My producer this time was a young woman, Emily Wilson, who did all the driving and dealt with the satellite equipment while I kept in touch with base on the mobile phone. Each assignment was confirmed only the previous day. Our first was in Oldham in Greater Manchester, where *Today* over several months had been following a series of tense stand-offs between Asian and white youths. There had been accusations that some young Asians had turned parts of the deprived and rundown Glodwick district into a 'no go' area for whites. There was some evidence of aggression in both communities. It was ripe territory for the British National Party. We arrived in Oldham halfway through a long bank holiday weekend of rioting: over three days corner shops were trashed, firebombs hurled and cars set alight. The police had come well equipped and stood in groups at intersections, hard helmets and shields stacked ready on the pavement. For our first battle-bus broadcast of the week, as the police pulled off their rain-soaked overalls fifty yards away, I talked to Nick Griffin, chairman of the British National Party and one of their local candidates. Griffin is a Cambridge law graduate, more articulate than some of his followers, and keen to present the acceptable face of the far right, claiming the BNP has nothing to do with the National Front.

Interview with Nick Griffin, broadcast 28.5.01

SM: There were a lot of white youths leaving pubs last night, and a lot of racist chanting coming from them about Pakis and Bangladeshis and that sort of thing. Would you condone that?

NG: I wouldn't condone it, but what's been going on in Oldham and has been going on for months has been tit-for-tat racist violence in which sixty per cent of the attacks have been by the Asians, and yet the Asians are only twenty per cent of the population. That means if you're looking at a racist thug in Oldham, it's six times more likely that he's an Asian racist thug than a white racist thug. There's blame on both sides.

SM: The truth is, though, that you are standing on a platform which says 'I'm in defence of ordinary white people.' You'd prefer the people of Asian origin here in Oldham to go back home, as you see it, wouldn't you?

NG: It would have been far better if the multiracial experiment hadn't been forced on Oldham in the first place. When it was a white community this kind of problem naturally didn't arise. It was forced on Oldham by the owners of the mills who brought people here as cheap labour. And by the media and the politicians who said, 'Let's have a multiracial experiment – it will all work.' Plenty of people like me said, 'It won't work. It will all blow up in your face.' This is now what is happening. Don't blame us for it. It's the fault of the politicians and the liberal elite who've done this to places like Oldham.

It was only too reminiscent of the sort of Powellite argument I had heard so many times in Cape Town a quarter of a century before. But the BNP could be well pleased with its electoral success. On polling day in Oldham West it achieved a record-breaking 16 per cent of the vote.

The next day we were in Belfast, where tribal confrontation has a longer and more complicated pedigree. The bright patchwork of green fields outside the main towns of Northern Ireland was a dazzling contrast to the bleakness and gloom of much of the industrial north-west on the mainland. But here it was a different election altogether. It was an election about the intensely felt local issues of power-sharing and arms decommissioning, and even about the future of David Trimble's Ulster Unionist party. I had appointments with Trimble, Ian Paisley and – once again – Martin McGuinness, who had recently admitted to being the IRA's second-in-command in Londonderry at the time of the Bloody Sunday shootings in 1972. Was he still, I asked him, a member of the IRA? His response did not miss a beat. 'No, I am not still a member of the IRA and I have to say that I am very pleased by the reaction here in Ireland and indeed from many people from within the Unionist community who have seen my statement.' But – I said – people never resign from the IRA, do they? This time there was a slight pause from McGuinness. 'Well, I'm telling you that I'm not a member of the IRA. How I left the IRA I think is a matter for me. The important thing is where we're going in the future, not where we've been in the past. I'm playing a very positive, very constructive role to ensure the success of the peace process.'

The Northern Ireland first minister, David Trimble, talking to us in Portadown, spoke of disarmament and deadlines and confirmed his threat to resign if there were no sign of weapons being handed in by 1 July. He seemed remarkably relaxed, but he confessed to us away from the microphone that it looked highly likely his Ulster Unionists would lose seats to Ian Paisley's hardline Democratic Unionists. It proved to be an accurate forecast. Dr Paisley himself, looking far frailer than I remembered him, met us in his leafy garden wearing a raincoat and a flat cap against the early morning drizzle. In his lapel a small gold badge proclaimed 'Jesus is Lord'; behind him fluttered a large Ulster flag. He predicted a 'meltdown of official Unionism' – David Trimble's Unionism – because they were willing to compromise with Sinn Fein.

Interview with Dr Ian Paisley, broadcast 29.5.01

SM: But you're always, Dr Paisley, the man who says no, no, no, to everything . . .

IP: No, no, no . . .

SM: . . . you must feel after thirty years in this business that you haven't really achieved a huge amount. You haven't smashed the IRA for a start – the Real IRA are still out there.

IP: Well, the Real IRA has to be smashed by the government. What I'm saying is you need trust. We have to go back to the drawing board. You can't trust Mr Trimble. He has betrayed us.

As we were leaving Belfast we realized we had left the *Today* compass on the wet grass in the Paisley back garden. He probably had little need of it. Ten days later his confidence was fully vindicated by the poll results: the DUP, and Sinn Fein too, had made some spectacular gains.

With the battle bus back on the mainland, I had consecutive encounters with two of the grandest *grandes dames* of British politics. Margaret Thatcher had just stormed through marginal Tory territory off the M1: in Northamptonshire there was a near riot as the press, local residents, small girls bearing flowers and a man convinced she was in the secret pay of General Pinochet mobbed her in the marketplace. By the time she got to Bletchley and a teatime appointment at the local Conservative association things had calmed down. Still, I was the lone journalist allowed inside as the baroness cut a cake on the first floor. I was not at all sure if she would remember me; I had last snatched a few words with her at the Conservative party conference the previous autumn. As she descended the stairs, someone stage-whispered, 'Sue MacGregor is the one on the left.' She beelined towards me. I noticed that her makeup was now a virtual mask of white, a startling contrast to the bright red slash of her lipstick. Was this the toughest campaign in which she'd ever taken part? Good heavens, no – others were much harder. She'd fought her first campaign – not as a candidate but as a helper – in 1945. Every election's hard, she said, and every count is nerve-wracking. But this time she and William Hague, I reminded her, had different approaches to the European single currency: he wanted to rule it out for one parliament, she for ever. Could she explain why? 'The idea that we should give up our own currency – sterling – is utterly repugnant. And I don't think many people would want to give it up. The euro – it's a spineless thing, isn't it?'

So would she keep stirring it up? 'If they think they're going to go to the euro, I shall keep stirring up sterling. And I shall win. You don't just change your currency. Is that clear?' And off she darted to work the room next door. She departed to enthusiastic cheers.

Barbara Castle, now nearly ninety-one, met us in her enchanting old house on a hill overlooking unspoiled Buckinghamshire fields. Its name, Hell Corner Farm, somehow seemed appropriate. Her fury over what she saw as the Labour government's tightfistedness over pensions had not abated. Her study was packed with folders and leaflets and reminder notes to herself about tasks ahead, written in a large hand – her eyesight was not as good as it used to be. I asked her about the low profile of women ministers at Labour's daily election press conferences: Gordon Brown had provoked laughter a few days earlier when he firmly interrupted Estelle Morris after a question on the scarcity of women speakers was put specifically to her. But Barbara Castle refused to play the feminist card. 'Once women are in parliament, it's their job to assert themselves,' she declared, clutching my hand so that I could steer her back to her study to find a pensioner's letter. Afterwards we sat outside in the evening sun posing for a battle-bus picture, and she smiled her old bright smile at the camera.

In the end it was the incidents off the parties' main agendas which dominated the campaign: John Prescott's punch after a man threw an egg at him; Margaret Thatcher in the middle of a seething media mass. For *Today*, the long hours of work behind the scenes were made rather merrier by the unscheduled appearance of one of our reporters on a late-night phone-in programme. Michael Buchanan was trying to send a story back to London from the studios of BBC Radio Leeds, but without anyone to help him became increasingly baffled by the technology. He accidentally hit an over-ride button and went out on the network, treating listeners to the late-night Andy Peebles show to twenty minutes of heavy breathing and furious four-letter words, until someone cut him off.

The campaign was received largely with indifference by the voters. The turnout was low, and so were the audiences for programmes dominated by politics. Even our own website showed a drop in the number of visitors around the election period, though at other times it was astonishingly popular. Two months earlier, when we offered a new kind of sociological quiz called 'What Kind of Class Do You Really Belong To?' there were over 830,000 visits to *Today*'s website during a single week. Normally the weekly average was over 200,000; during the campaign it plummeted to something like 80,000.

As I tuned in to the BBC's election night broadcasts, I thought again about Barbara Castle's views on women asserting themselves. In the early spring there had been much trumpeting about the number of women who would for the first time fill prominent roles in the election coverage. David Dimbleby's all-night marathon on television would be shared with Fiona Bruce and a psephologist called Alison Park. But on the night Fiona was given the roving microphone and ended up talking largely to celebrities, and Alison Park found herself playing a bit-part. Kirsty Wark of *Newsnight* was on a separate programme in Scotland concentrating on the results north of the border. For Radios Four and Five, joined together for the evening, there had been indications that the results would be presented by Jim Naughtie and Jane Garvey. In the end, Jane was given the secondary role of results summarizer. Despite the advance publicity, the only perceptible difference from the results programmes of four years before was that there were more women political correspondents doing analysis on radio. Otherwise it was business as usual.

The role of women as front-line presenters had been challenged many years earlier by the pressure group Women in Media. In 1971, when I was still a reporter with *The World At One*, they began a campaign for the selection of a 'perfectly ordinary, intelligent' woman as a TV newscaster. Lord Hill, the BBC's chairman, suggested that no such woman existed, so a long list of suitable candidates was produced. None was auditioned. Lord Hill wrote to one of the group, the journalist Anne Sharpley, the following year, asking: 'What do you want me to do? Sack a man or ruin the thing economically and introduce a woman?' But the issue had been raised. A paper was written for the board of management in January 1973, entitled 'Limitations to the Recruitment and Advancement of Women in the BBC'. It pointed out that in 1971, out of a total of 140 men and 22 women who applied for the job of sub-editor in the radio newsroom, 21 people were selected, not one of them a woman though the editor of radio news, Peter Woon, was quoted as saying that he 'would like to have more women'. The paper went on: 'A huge percentage of the audience is female and journalists of their sex are qualified to identify interesting stories on their behalf. *When a woman is married* [my italics] her knowledge of the subjects that interest women is thereby increased, but of course marriage makes it more difficult for women to work on shift.'

Woon had also warned against opening the floodgates. 'He would have to limit the proportion of women. Those who are dedicated, he believes, are not really women with valuable instincts, but become like men.' He would accept women as newsreaders, but believed 'most female broadcasters tend to sound as though they came from Cheltenham Ladies' College. What is needed is a classless voice.' In his reservations he no doubt had the support of the presentation editor of Radio Four at the time, Jim Black, who believed that women would not be much good at the job. 'If a woman could read the news as well as a man,' he declared, 'there would be nothing to stop her doing it. But I have never found one who could. A news announcer needs to have authority, consistency and reliability. Women may have one or two of these qualities, but not all three.' The following year, despite Lord Hill's curious fears about economic ruin for the BBC, doubts about female staying power, and an antipathy to posh voices, women as newsreaders had arrived.

Eighteen years and four general elections on from the time I first joined *Today*, there are still remarkably few women fronting current affairs programmes. As programme producers and editors women are now universally accepted: in 2001 there were women editing *Newsnight*, the *One O'Clock News* and the *Six O'Clock News* on television, as well as the rolling news service BBC News 24, and there have been women newsreaders for years. Sometimes when I look through the studio's dividing glass as *Today* takes to the air I see an editorial team – and technical staff – that is almost entirely female. After the terrible events of 11 September in the United States, and the subsequent campaign against the Taliban and Bin Laden in Afghanistan, there emerged a new generation of front-line women war reporters. Kate Clark, Jacky Rowland, Susannah Price and Catherine Davis from the BBC World Service all distinguished themselves with daily accounts of the battle, and their names became almost as familiar as John Simpson's. But the number of women as front-line political interviewers is still lamentably low.

Perhaps it is partly a matter of style: interviews are expected to be more confrontational these days, and confrontation is an approach with which men are generally more comfortable. If a woman interviewer presses hard and loudly, she is liable to be labelled shrill, or a harpie, or worse; even Ken Clarke, that most reasonable-sounding of politicians, confessed when he was regularly on *Today* as a cabinet minister in the nineties that he sometimes found me 'waspish' and 'testy'. I doubt that he would have applied the same adjectives to a man.

Robust political interviews are not new: in the seventies and eighties both Robin Day on television and Brian Redhead on radio sliced through a politician's defences with ease. The result was both illuminating and entertaining. None of us who saw it could forget John Nott's huffy departure from an encounter with Robin Day after he had been characterized as a 'here today, gone tomorrow' politician. Since then the politicians have become much more accomplished at counterattack. Many of them go on media training courses, where they are guided through all the most difficult areas of interrogation their instructors can think up. They can be irritatingly adept at refusing to answer an awkward question or – as the international development secretary Clare Short did during an interview with me about AIDS in Africa shortly after the 2001 election – imply personal malice: I was accused of 'entrapment'. So the political interviewer has to change tack. He – or she – must try other ways to get an answer. A sort of relentless ferocity sometimes works: being prepared to interrupt and push for an answer at a furious pace. It helps if the interviewer gives an impression not only of great confidence in his own rightness but also of a certain disdain for the victim. As a result, many set-piece political interviews are more reminiscent of the gladiatorial arena than the debating chamber. John Humphrys is a master of the genre, taking on politicians with what one fellow journalist recently called an air of 'magisterial distrust'. It is immensely effective; but it is not an approach with which many women interviewers feel comfortable. The interviewing style with which I feel happiest is a great deal less aggressive. The results are predictably different, but within a long programme like *Today* there is room for contrasting styles. An unbroken diet of any one method would be both tedious and unrevealing. Perhaps if a reincarnated Adolf Hitler found himself opposite us in the *Today* studio, John would wrestle him to the floor, Jim might remind him of what he had said at the Nuremburg rallies, and I would try to find out why he'd turned into a monster. All in the space of five minutes, of course.

When Jim Naughtie first joined us I had anticipated a certain prickly suspicion between him and John, and I was not wrong. Their professional rivalry is intense, and the slightly edgy relationship on which they embarked when Jim began as part of the team has not dissipated. The problem of who gets the 'big' interview of the day is compounded if they are paired together on the programme. Each in his own way is a superb interviewer of politicians, though their styles are very different. Jim has an impressively long memory for the detail of the political process and, I think, an admiration for and understanding of the people who practise it. John operates at a more visceral and instinctive level. The impression he gives of someone with a certain natural contempt for politicians undoubtedly reflects the views of significant numbers of his listeners; they enjoy the discomfiture of a cabinet minister caught on the hop.

Sitting next to either John or Jim in the studio is never dull, usually instructive, and often a highly convivial experience, especially if the gossip is good. It is not, though, a job for the faint-hearted: there are enough interviews which over-run their allotted time, plus technical slip-ups and last-minute breaking stories, constantly to test the presenters' relationships.

If women are to reach the top in the broadcasting world, they must, as in any other competitive field, display a certain dedication and single-mindedness. They should also be able to withstand the daily pressures and the setbacks. If they have the additional responsibility of a family at home, then 'having it all' naturally becomes more difficult. That has not changed since the heady days of the sixties and seventies and all the new freedoms they brought. Some extraordinary women do manage it successfully, and I know and admire a number of them. I didn't especially choose not to have children, but I often wonder if I could have spared the energy for a long broadcasting career if I had had a more conventional family life.

And yet the argument is heard widely now that women have gone too far, and have competed too successfully; that men are now the underdogs, and boys the discouraged underlings. In August 2001 I chaired a discussion between the eminent novelist Doris Lessing, feminist icon for many, and Mary-Anne Stephenson of the Fawcett Society, on the effect of feminism on modern men.

Interview with Doris Lessing and Mary-Anne Stephenson, broadcast 15.8.01

DL: You know, when I was a girl I was always being upset or angry because of the way men put you down, and they

often didn't even know they were doing it. If you protested, they didn't know what you were talking about. What has happened is that everything has gone into reverse, and women put men down all the time. I think men ought to protest, the way we did. We protested, and we won . . .
I was in a class room [with] nine- and ten-year-olds being taught history by a young woman who was telling them that the reason that there had been wars throughout history was because men were naturally belligerent. Now, can you imagine the scene – the little fatly complacent girls giving looks to the boys and the boys cowering at their desks. If boys are being put down all the time by unthinking teachers I think it's time we addressed that one too.

SM: Mary-Anne Stephenson, have things swung too far the wrong way? Are men the new victims?

MAS: There is this myth that feminism has gone too far, that we've got too much equality, that men are the new victims, but I think that if you look at the facts you will see that it's just not the case. Women continue to earn less than men. An average woman earns about a quarter of a million pounds less over her lifetime than a man.

SM: We're talking nearly thirty years after the Equal Pay legislation . . .

MAS: Absolutely. And that's before she has children . . . that's not including any time she might take off to have a child. Women are much more likely to be poor in old age and one in four women still suffer domestic violence at some point in their lives. I think the problem we've got is not too much equality but not enough. The problem we've got in schools is a culture that teaches boys that it's not male to learn, and real boys don't work. That's not a problem created by feminism, it's a problem created by a culture of masculinity.

DL: I wasn't talking about that. I quite agree with equal pay and so on. I was talking about the use of language and the rubbishing of men verbally that goes on.

SM: Are you talking about the 'ladette' culture?

DL: Yes. What is happening is that women are now behaving as men used to do.

MAS: I think if we're looking at a culture that undermines and belittles both men and women it's not a culture that's been created by feminists.

DL: Of course it has. Why don't you spend a day, which I've recently been doing, just listening to radio programmes, television advertisements and [reading] newspapers and see just how often men are put down and rubbished. It is quite unpleasant and quite frightening really. What is it doing to the boys? This is what we have to be concerned about.

The start of 2002 marks for me forty years of working on daily live radio programmes, and I have no regrets about having stayed in the radio world. Radio has always been my first love. The physical act of broadcasting, sitting in a studio, headphones clamped on, talking to people, is still a huge and fulfilling pleasure, though I have often asked myself whether I'm at heart a dyed-in-the-wool journalist or just a broadcaster who happens to have stepped into journalism. A true journalist, I sometimes think, has a better developed killer instinct than I do, and does not hesitate to twist the knife. But after four decades of daily deadlines, I have decided that it's time to do less in the studio, and more in the outside world. Eighteen years of early alarm calls are probably enough for me, for my biorhythms and for my listeners, though nothing will diminish my devotion to radio as a means of connecting with people.

The endearing thing about radio is that despite the promises of a digital future and multiple channels, in essence it is relatively unchanging. It is technically simple and easily transportable; it is direct and yet it is intimate. It makes a good companion, and perhaps it shouldn't be surprising that a recent survey showed that radio in Britain is now more popular than television. Generally BBC radio seems to be in encouragingly good health. Radio Four – at its best a uniquely precious asset – seems in safe hands, having ended its flirtation with the Birtian world of focus groups and pie charts. The *Today* programme has recovered from the setbacks of the late nineties and enjoys the support of the bosses as well as the listeners: over six million people a week tune in. The early morning audience for current affairs has not yet found a reliable substitute on either radio or television to draw it away in any great numbers. There are unquestionably events that are utterly defined for us by pictures, the terrible kamikaze attacks on New York and Washington in September 2001 among them – television prints the grim event indelibly into our memory – but for analysis and assessment, radio still works best.

And what of the wider BBC? Thirty-five years ago it was probably the most respected broadcasting organization in the world.

Domestically there was only ITV to challenge it. The BBC attracted clever and dedicated people who produced brilliant programmes, but it was run like the civil service. Many of its staff were comfortably ensconced for life, and there were too few areas into which the harsh light of accountability shone. Today's BBC is almost unrecognizably different: an enormous multifaceted corporation with huge ambitions in the marketplace. It recruits many of its bosses from outside and pays attractive bonuses to members of the top team. The majority of its employees are now on contracts of variable lengths; few of the newer recruits imagine they'll one day be drawing a BBC pension.

As director-general, Greg Dyke has continued John Birt's determination to expand the digital channels and the online services, including the highly regarded BBC News Online. But the number of people watching the BBC's terrestrial television services continues to drop: the audience can now if it wishes zap its way through hundreds of rival channels. The BBC cannot possibly compete with everyone, offering a multitude of services funded by the licence fee alone. Perhaps in future it should concentrate on what it has always done best – being creative, and setting the highest standards – and not try to spread itself too widely. It might then attract back into the fold some of the talented people who left to start up their own production houses, making programmes which they sell back to the BBC.

The unique asset of the licence fee – a poll tax funding only the BBC – will be increasingly hard to defend if large chunks of peak-time television aim so dismally low. I confess that these days I watch television very little, apart from news bulletins and documentaries. I am certain there is a much greater appetite for programmes that excite and stretch the imagination – programmes of real quality and worth – than some of the BBC bosses would have us believe. How wonderful it would be if the BBC dared more often to be what Melvyn Bragg once called 'successfully different'.

Working on *Today* has been boundlessly interesting and very often highly rewarding. It has also been maddening, scary and sometimes a little unforgiving. Mistakes we make are heard by critical millions, but I have learned something new about the adventure of broadcasting on each one of the almost three thousand editions I have presented. Except for the awful early morning hours it is the best job in daily radio. I will miss the buzz of the office, the sudden release of laughter, and the unequalled flutter of excitement as the studio red light says 'go'.

But that was Then, and also Today; now it's time for Tomorrow.

Index